THE WORKS OF JOSEPH DE

THE WORKS OF
Joseph de Maistre

Selected, translated and introduced

by *JACK LIVELY*

New Foreword by Robert Nisbet

SCHOCKEN BOOKS · NEW YORK

CONTENTS

Study on Sovereignty, 93

The Pope, 131

Essay on the Generative Principle of Political Constitutions, 147

The Saint Petersburg Dialogues, 183

Enlightenment on Sacrifices, 291

Index, 299

FOREWORD

A Note on Conservatism

I think it would be hard to find a book that illustrates better than this one the relation ideas have to events and crises in history. Ideas, as Sir Isaiah Berlin has said—and as his own scholarship superbly makes clear—do not beget ideas as butterflies beget butterflies. Ideas, the greater ones at least, are human responses to time, place, and circumstance: above all to historical crises. Even the seminal ideas of the physical sciences have, as Thomas Kuhn has shown us in his *The Structure of Scientific Revolutions,* a relation to event and crisis that has been too often overlooked by those who have allowed themselves to become immured within the metaphor of slow, cumulative growth. How very much more evident is this relation in the history of moral and social thought. It is one of the misfortunes of historiography in the study of ideas that so many intellectual histories resemble the strings of "begats" found in the Old Testament.

One would be justified in concluding from this splendid book that Joseph de Maistre had little other reason for living in the time he did apart from responding to the crisis formed by the values and ideologies of the Enlightenment in their fateful conjunction with the French Revolution at the very end of the eighteenth century. This is as it should be. For, in the sense that we know him, there would have been no Joseph de Maistre had this crisis not existed in the minds of a great many people at that time. The crisis was not the first of its kind in history—the crisis formed by conflict between traditionalism and what we today like to call modernity—but it was one of the most spectacular. And the consequences of the crisis have been with us ever since.

Precisely as Plato responded at the end of the fifth century B.C. to the crisis of the Greek city state posed by Spartan defeat of Athens, and precisely as Thomas Hobbes responded to the events in England that produced the fateful Civil War, so we may properly see Joseph

de Maistre responding to the French Revolution and the Enlighten-
ment-sprung values that activated the Revolution's laws, decrees, and
armies. Neither I nor the editor of this volume would offer Maistre
as of the same stature as Plato and Hobbes. But no one can read far
into this book without acquiring appreciation of a mind of great
power. The essay, "The Generative Principle of Constitutions," and,
perhaps even more, *The Saint Petersburg Dialogues* clearly reveal
an educated mind, but one fully capable of assaulting brilliantly the
conventional wisdom among secular liberals and radicals in his day.

I shall not try to add in this Foreword to what Mr. Lively has
so well written about Joseph de Maistre in his Introduction to the
book. Rather, I shall take my departure from the relationship Mr.
Lively notes (page 31) between Maistre and and the other Conservatives whose writings flourished during the thirty years following
Edmund Burke's momentous *Reflections on the Revolution in France*.
That remarkable volume, published in 1790, is the true fount of
modern Conservatism in the West, and there is no question but that
it served also as the immediate source of what can only be called the
Anti-Enlightenment.

I use that term here, as I have used it elsewhere,° in no pejorative
fashion. Least of all do I imply that the principals were consecrated
to any scuttling of reason and enlightenment or that rational intellect
of highest order may not be found in the pages of the Conservative
philosophers of the early nineteenth century. The learning and brilliance of Burke's own book on the Revolution should be sufficient
evidence of that point.

By Anti-Enlightenment I mean no more than the fact that in
the works of the Conservatives, Joseph de Maistre included, there
was a massive, and calculated, attack upon the fundamental values
and intellectual perspectives of those philosophers who formed the
spectacular Enlightenment of eighteenth-century Western Europe.
Differences among the Conservatives there assuredly were. But so
were there striking differences of perspective among the philosophers
of the Enlightenment. Periods in history and general movements of
ideas take their character not from uniformity or even unison of the
voices to be found in each, but rather from the subtler kinds of orchestration that one finds in, say, a great symphony. It was not neces-

---

°See *The Sociological Tradition* (New York, 1966) and also several of the essays
in *Tradition and Revolt* (New York, 1970).

sary for Rousseau to be in point by point agreement with a Diderot, a Voltaire, or a Condorcet. It suffices that, reading the works of these men and of the others forming the Enlightenment, we find unmistakable themes held in common, harmonies, even rhythms of thought. Whether it is Rousseau on the General Will, Voltaire on the history of modern Europe, Diderot on the psychological faculties in man, or Condorcet on the evolution of mankind, there is no mistaking the fact that the ideas of these men, *the major ideas*, form, for all the distinctiveness each possesses, an orchestration, that is, a true cultural period in history.

So do the ideas of those Conservatives who formed what I call the Anti-Enlightenment. Like the Enlightenment this orchestration of ideas spread across the map of Western Europe—eventually indeed, quite like the Enlightenment, to other continents. If Burke cannot be dislodged from the position of historical primacy, it has to be emphasized that similar ideas came forth so quickly afterward in England, in France, in Germany, in Switzerland, Spain, even in the United States, as to suggest strongly that the ideas would have manifested themselves even had Burke never written his *Reflections*. I say this with no intent of derogating from Burke, who was surely the most powerful of all the Conservative minds, but, rather, to emphasize once again the relation of ideas to crisis; more particularly, the capacity of crisis for eliciting deeply held ideas; and also the congruence and the periodicity of ideas.

Who were the Conservatives? Burke, of course, preeminently: Maistre, as this volume attests eloquently; also Louis de Bonald, François de Chateaubriand, and Félicité Robert de Lamennais—all, like Joseph de Maistre, French. In England there were Robert Southey and Samuel Taylor Coleridge. In Germany Adam Müller, Friedrich Savigny, and, of course, the lustrous Hegel. In Switzerland there was Karl von Haller—whose *The Restoration of the Social Sciences* is probably the greatest of all Conservative works assessed from the point of view of systematic social science. In Spain we have Jaime Balmes and, somewhat later, Donoso y Cortes.

These are, I think, the primary figures. One of them—in some respects the most brilliant of them, Lamennais—broke with Conservatism and became the founder of what is known as liberal Catholicism. There are certainly important differences of emphasis to be noted as one moves from the Anglican Burke to the Ultramontane Catholic

Bonald and Maistre, or from the passionate young Lamennais to the grave and scholarly Haller, or from Coleridge to Hegel. Such differences are admitted readily. There are nevertheless profound likenesses, and from these likenesses flowed a body of thought in nineteenth-century Europe that was not merely important in itself for the ideas on man and society it contained but was to prove even more important in the impressive effect it had upon such later thinkers as Tocqueville, Le Play, Burckhardt, Riehl, Sir Henry Maine, and others whose works may be seen as among the greatest of the century. I shall come back briefly to the influence of Conservatism on historical and social writing at the end of this foreword. First, though, it will be useful to say something about the tenets, the common principles, of the movement I have called the Anti-Enlightenment.

These tenets and principles sprang directly from assault upon those of the Enlightenment. Where the philosophers of the Enlightenment had begun with the assumed priority of the natural order, of the individual, of pure reason, of a natural morality springing directly from man's being, and of certainty of human progress once artificial institutional barriers were removed, the philosophers of the Anti-Enlightenment, the Conservatives, began with a diametrically opposed set of principles. These principles were all abundantly in existence by 1820, just thirty years after the publication of Burke's *Reflections*, and are the sinews of Philosophical Conservatism. I shall list these principles very briefly. One and all they may be found in Maistre's writings as Mr. Lively has brought these together and translated them for this book.

First, God and the divine order, not the natural order, must be the starting point of any understanding of society and history. What the Enlightenment and Revolution had scorned, the Conservatives sought to reestablish: the ineradicably *sacred* character of human history.

Second, society, not the individual, is the subject of the true science of man—or, for that matter, the true philosophy or theology of man. The individual is but an abstraction, a chimera, declared the Conservatives. Society, created by God, is alone real. Man is to be found only in the roles in which he is cast by society.

Third, tradition, not pure reason, is the only possible approach to reform of government and society. Reason, yes, but reason in-

separable from the wisdom of the race that lies about us in our institutions, customs, and laws. The idea of emancipated, secularized
reason proceeding directly from impulse and intuition is a heresy. So
thought the Conservatives.

Fourth, organism, not social contract, is the true image of social
reality. All parts of the social order exist in an interdependence that
is organic, that can no more be idly reassembled through arbitrary
action than can the parts of the human body.

Fifth, the groups and associations of society, not the abstracted
individual, are the true seats of human morality—and also of human
identity. The individual celebrated by the Enlightenment cannot be
other than helpless, alienated, at war with himself. For, separated
from the social sources of morality, which lie in community, not the
state of nature, he must live in a moral void.

Sixth, true authority springs directly from God and is distributed
normally among a plurality of institutions—church, guild, social class,
and family, as well as political state. The greatest crime of the Revolutionaries, thought several of the Conservatives, was the effort, through
a Rousseauian General Will, to make political authority alone sufficient
—and total. In the democracy of the Revolution lies not freedom but
the possibility of a power greater than any known since the late Roman
Empire.

Seventh, a tragic view of man and history is required, one that
sees the recurrence of evil and disaster in human affairs, not the kind
of linear progress most members of the Enlightenment took as being
not merely normal but, in the long run, inexorable. The consequence
of the progressive view of history is *hubris.* Only through recognition
of the ineradicability of evil in man, the result of Original Sin, and
of the absolute necessity of strong institutions and authorities to control this abiding evil is there much hope, thought the Conservatives,
for mankind's security and tranquillity.

These are, I think, the most vital of Conservative principles. They
may be seen, for better or worse to Western thought, as the responses
of some rather extraordinary minds to a scene that they, one and all,
regarded as one of social disintegration and moral desolation—the
work of the Enlightenment and the Revolution. Where liberals and
radicals of their day saw the *new order* rising like phoenix from the
ashes of the old regime, the conservatives saw not the new order but

the *new disorder*—one that they declared would be the permanent condition of man so long as the values of individualism, secularism, progress, and mass democracy prevailed.

No one reading the Conservatives will fail to see a kind of romantic adulation of the Middle Ages in their works. I think this strain is perhaps less in Maistre and Burke, less noticeable at any rate, than it is in the others. But there is little doubt that the Conservatives are the true authors of that recrudescence of fascination with the Middle Ages and all its works, real or imaginary, that forms so notable a part of the nineteenth century in all spheres, scholarly, imaginative, and artistic. The Enlightenment had hated the Middle Ages above all periods of the past. It is fitting, from the point of view of ideas-as-responses that the Conservatives should therefore have venerated medieval society and its values.

It is this profound medievalism in their works that makes us think of the Conservatives as prophets of the past. And, more than anything else, I would imagine, it is this same medievalism that for so long a time prevented more accurate appreciation of what the Conservatives were actually about in their thought and writing.

What they were about, of course, was nothing less than challenge to the whole of what in current writing we call modernity. There are critics of modernity and its values—values of industrialism, technology, mass democracy, secularism, and so forth—all around us today. Even within the New Left, a movement we may safely assume Maistre, Burke, and Bonald would have loathed, a strong tinge of antimodernity, indeed of Anti-Enlightenment, exists. One does not today have to feel lonely when he attacks the political, economic, and cultural trappings of modernity. It was not so easy in the nineteenth and first half of the twentieth centuries, for this was, for most of us, the period of Great Hope: hope to be realized through the very forces the Conservatives had, in the first instance, thrown down the gauntlet to.

Even so it would be a serious error to suppose that the Conservatives were without influence on certain tendencies of thought in the period I refer to. Some of this influence may be properly regarded as baneful, as in the case of that morally crippled genius Maurras and the whole French Action that reached culmination, and then defeat, in the Dreyfus case. Most of the intellectual sustenance of this ugly movement came directly from writers like Maistre and Bonald, and if this included Maurrassian antipathy to technology and industrialism, it included also hatred of individual liberty, parliamentary government, and popular education. We must not blink this consequence of the philosophical conservatives at the beginning of the century.

But they should not have their influence left at this. For every La Tour du Pin and Maurras there was, it has to be conceded, a Comte, a Tocqueville, a Ruskin, and a Burckhardt. No one could properly accuse any of these four, or of many others whose names could be added, of lacking in respect for liberty and civilized values generally. No greater vision of the basis of cultural freedom has ever existed than that to be found in Tocqueville's *Democracy in America,* or greater respect for human equality and for the spread of education and culture in the masses. It would simply be impossible to understand this work apart from the immense impact that had been registered on Tocqueville's mind by philosophical conservatism.

Nor is this all. Comte, in both his great works, *The Positive Philosophy* and *The Positive Polity* (the latter being the first work ever written to use the word "sociology" in its full title) was lavish in his praise of what he called "the retrograde school," giving particular laudation to Maistre and Bonald. From the Conservatives, wrote Comte, has come proper appreciation of the mechanisms of order and stability in society. Comte even credits them with being the true founders of Social Statics—one of the two great divisions (the other being Social Dynamics) of Comte's new science, Sociology. So too did Le Play render specific thanks to the Conservatives, particularly Bonald, whose long essay early in the century on the comparison of rural and urban types of family and community may be seen as clear precursor to Le Play's own monumental study of the European rural and urban working classes.

Others in the social sciences were perhaps not as articulate in their appreciation of the Conservatives, but we do not lack evidences of the effect that was left by Conservative thought on such sterling minds as Tonnies, Simmel, Weber, and Durkheim. None of these men was himself a political conservative; each identified with very liberal and humane political movements. But, as I have shown clearly enough, I think, in *The Sociological Tradition,* we should be hard put to account fully and properly for either the minds or the works of these men apart from the conflict between traditionalism and liberalism that lights up and gives distinction to them. No serious scholar would wish to take away from the influence of the radical Marx or of the utilitarian-liberal Spencer on the intellectual structure of contemporary sociology. But there is also a conservative vein—conservative in the sense of themes and patterns of interest—that goes directly back to the period that Joseph de Maistre helped form.

Leaving the social sciences out of consideration altogether, it is clear enough, reading, say, *The Saint Petersburg Dialogues* which Maistre wrote, among other works, during voluntary exile from his beloved but revolution-torn France, that the essential dialogue begun by the Conservatives continues right down to the present moment. It is to be found nowhere more articulately today than on the university and college campus. In a sense we are witnessing yet another assault on an *ancien régime* in the attacks that have been made on the university, itself a creation of the Middle Ages. Few reading the writings of Joseph de Maistre could possibly miss their relevance to the conflict between traditionalism and modernity today in the whole academic sector of society. But, like and agree with Joseph de Maistre or not, the relevance of his ideas to this conflict goes far beyond the university. It extends to the whole of contemporary culture and pre-eminently to the mind of the contemporary intellectual.

ROBERT NISBET

University of California
at Riverside
August 1970

PREFACE

In this edition, the attempt has been made to present the central arguments of Maistre's most important works. Inevitably this has meant cutting much of interest from them. It has involved leaving out many of the digressions which form a characteristic feature of his style, and pruning drastically his many and lengthy footnotes. I hope that what remains, most of it translated into English for the first time, will allow a wider insight into a much-quoted but little-read thinker.

I should like to thank Professor Sir Isaiah Berlin, Mr. Beynon John, Dr. Hugh Kearney, and Professor John Rees who, at one time or another, have given me most valuable help and advice.

J. L.

University of Sussex
January, 1964

THE WORKS OF JOSEPH DE MAISTRE

Introduction

Joseph de Maistre was born on April 1, 1753, in Savoy. He was the son of François-Xavier de Maistre, a high court judge who had been ennobled by the Sardinian king for his work in legal reform. From school in his home town of Chambéry he went on the faculty of Law in Turin. As soon as he gained his degree, he returned to Chambéry, where he was appointed to a post as a public prosecutor in the Senate of Savoy, a judicial body of which his father was President.

This was in 1774. Until 1789 his life was peaceful, undisturbed by the political convulsions which were to rend his later years or by the intellectual ferment which political strife produced. Nevertheless, there were slight tensions. Brought up by a profoundly pious mother in an equally pious Savoy, he was a deeply committed Catholic. Yet, soon after his return to Chambéry, he joined a Masonic lodge, and was greatly influenced by the mystical notions of Saint-Martin, although Freemasonry had already been condemned by the Pope. The inner conflict was deep enough to reveal itself much later in the argument between the Count and the Senator on mysticism and Martinism in the *Saint Petersburg Dialogues*. The Freemasonry to which Maistre was drawn was mystical rather than "enlightened," conservative rather than reforming and democratic, yet he too was affected by the liberal opinions in the air in the decades before the Revolution. At any rate, he was criticized for an address to the Senate in 1775 in which he had defended freedom of thought, and his first reaction to the Revolution was enthusiastic.

This initial impulse soon subsided, and even before the invasion of Savoy by the new French Republic in 1792, he had taken up fixed positions against revolutionary aspirations and opinions. In November, the month after the French armies entered, he left his country. He returned briefly at the beginning of 1793, but fled again, leaving his children and his wife, whom he was not to see again for twenty years.

He established himself at Lausanne, where he was made the representative of the Sardinian king, and took up an active counter-revolutionary role. More importantly, he began his long career as a political writer. Much of what he wrote when he was in Lausanne was not to be published until 1884 when the complete works appeared, including his *Study on Sovereignty*. But one work, the *Considerations on France*, was published in 1796. This book played a large part in formulating the inchoate reactions of the émigrés to the Revolution. It also laid down lines of thought which Maistre was to pursue later.

In 1798 he returned to Italy and settled in Venice, moving to Piedmont in 1799. This restless and rootless life ended when he was sent to represent the Sardinian Crown at Saint Petersburg in 1802. His period in Russia was to be the most intellectually productive. In the *Saint Petersburg Dialogues*, *The Pope*, the *Essay on the Generative Principle of Political Constitutions*, and the *Examen de la philosophie de Bacon*, he filled in the picture which had been sketched in Lausanne. He remained in Russia until 1817, watching and encouraging the European struggle against Napoleon. Only then was he returned to the family life of which the Revolution had robbed him. Yet in recompense the Revolution gave him European fame, for the writings of his long years of exile caught the imagination first of the émigrés and then of a Europe disillusioned with the revolutionary message. In the fierce and mordant irony of his books, he embodied all the hatred of the lonely and dispossessed for the authors of their sufferings. If in the end he transcended this hatred, his thought always remained a protest against the revolutionary present. He was strictly a reactionary in the sense that this protest was the reason for his writing, but, like all reactionaries, his protest against the present tended to raise up an image of the past no less radical in its implications than the revolutionary dream of the future.

II. MAISTRE AND HIS INTERPRETERS

Maistre had no doubt that the root causes of the Revolution were intellectual and ideological. The degeneration of its first immense hopes into the bloody Terror was not merely the fortuitous result of a ruthless competition for power or of a war situation. He echoed with no less conviction, but much less enthusiasm, Voltaire's boast that "books did it all." The philosophers of the Enlightenment were the true architects of the new regimes, and the shadow between the revolutionary idea and the revolutionary reality could be traced directly to a fatal flaw in their thought.

D'Alembert had with pride characterized his own age as "a century of philosophy," a century in which principles of every kind had been subjected to systematic doubt and analysis. In his efforts to define and expose the flaw in Enlightenment thought, Maistre was willing, like most of his contemporaries, to accept the Age of Reason at d'Alembert's valuation, and to attack an inquisitive and skeptical rationalism as both the prime tenet of the Enlightenment and the fatal principle of the Revolution. But the "revolt against reason," of which Maistre was so striking an exemplar, attacked a wide variety of targets. For some, "reason" was the enemy of all authority—but for others it was the enemy of the romantic ideal of the emotionally mature and socially independent individual: it was attacked by the faithful because it undermined all belief—and by the skeptical because it enthroned apocalyptic political faiths: some hated it because it presumed to make a science out of political morality—and others because it ignored and frustrated the only true scientific method, the empirical.

Among critics of revolutionary thinking, these methods of attack were not clearly distinguished, and nowhere less than in Maistre's writings. Sometimes he flays the Enlightenment because its arid reliance on the intellect dried up the deepest springs of human action and understanding; at other times because it lacked the ability to see politics in its real and concrete complexity, resorting to political formulae as a substitute for political wisdom; and at others because its arrogant individualism had destroyed the basis of all social cohesion.

These crosscurrents in Maistre's thought have led to differences in interpretation. Some commentators see him as the expounder of a realistic social science in face of the a priori reasoning of the Enlightenment, others as the champion of authority in Church and state, and others again as an originator of the modern Fascist tradition. All can draw on Maistre's writings, and all express at least a partial truth.

His empirical and pragmatic strain is strong enough to allow some interpreters to see him as the disciple of Montesquieu and the precursor of Comte and the positivist school.[1] Lord Morley painted him as the French Burke, echoing the belief that "what in the result is likely to produce evil is politically false; that which is productive of good

[1] Cf. F. Bayle, *Les idées politiques de Joseph de Maistre* (1945), pp. 149, 154.

politically true."[2] There is considerable evidence for this view of
Maistre as the protestant against a priori reasoning. He certainly
quoted Burke often and with approval, and Comte leant heavily on his
writings. He complained persistently of the *philosophes* that they
based their political ideas on psychological or contractual or natural-
rights theories which they believed could be discovered independently
of any study of society as it existed, and which indeed they used to
criticize existing societies. In their emphasis on man's capacity for
rational thought and action, they had ignored the fortuitous, uncon-
trollable element in human development, the restrictions and compul-
sions imposed by circumstances upon action, the variety of historical,
geographical, and national situations, the emotional and instinctive
traits of human nature. They had thus created a political science
which, precisely because it spurned social analysis in favor of the construction of ideal models, was totally irrelevant to actual life. False
theory bred destructive practice. The French Revolution, just such an
attempt to realize the Enlightenment's political science, had achieved
only the disruption of European society because its architects had no
conception of the real nature of men or politics.

In place of this destructive a priori reasoning, Maistre wished to
substitute a science of politics firmly rooted in history and experience.
Time and again he referred to history as "la politique expérimentale,"
as the first and indeed the only teacher in politics.[3] His most bitter
venom was reserved for the constitution builders spawned by the
Revolution. No constitution can be created a priori, he argued, for no
one can comprehend or to any great degree affect the multitude of circumstances which fit a nation to a particular constitution. For the
same reason, it is impossible to judge governments by any absolute
standard. "No one should ask what is the best form of government in
general, since none is suitable for every nation. Each nation has its
own, as it has its own language and character, and this government is
the best for it." And, quoting Rousseau with approval, he added that
"there are as many good governments as there are possible combinations in the relative and absolute positions of nations." Institutions
should change with history, customs, climate, and political situation,
and those are best which best fit these varied and shifting factors.[4] By

---

[2] Lord Morley, *Critical Miscellanies* (London, 1871), pp. 113–192.

[3] See, for example, *Essay on the Generative Principle*, p. 162. *Study on Sovereignty*
p. 114. Unless otherwise stated, the references are to this volume.

[4] *Study on Sovereignty*, pp. 100–101, 126.

the side of this empirical attitude and in his eyes as a complement to it, he insisted that political ideas should be judged according to pragmatic standards. In politics, the terms "truth" and "falsehood" mean little; the only meaningful terms are "beneficial" and "harmful." Institutions should be judged not on their origins but on their constant and permanent effects. What might appear in the abstract to be abuses could be necessary and beneficial to a political system as a whole.[5] Like institutions, ideas and beliefs are true so far as they are useful. This is the only sure test, for, in all questions of morality, certainty is impossible and we are reduced to conjecture; and "if our conjectures are plausible, if we can find an analogy for them, if they rest on universally accepted ideas, above all if they console us and make us better men, what do they lack? If they are not true, they are good; or more accurately, since they are good, are they not true?"[6] The best advice he could give to ordinary men was to abide by the rule "Never deny what is useful, never uphold what can be harmful."

Yet this protest is only part of Maistre's criticisms of the Age of Reason. Other interpreters have seized on his defense of authority as the core of his thought.[7] Certainly, what he found most objectionable in this most objectionable of ages was the excessive individualism lying behind its claims for the omniscience and universality of reason. If, as the *philosophes* thought, reason could discern those simple rules on which moral and political obligation were based, and if every human being was possessed of this attribute of reason, society, like religion, became an artifact of the individual. This belief was reflected in eighteenth century political theory, dominated by the ideas of a social contract, making society and government subservient to the freely given and freely revokable consent of the individual, and of natural rights held by the individual independently of government and society. Everything, it seemed to Maistre, had in consequence become the subject of doubt and discussion, no authority being safe from the challenge of the sovereign individual. It seemed equally clear to him that Europe would remain plunged in chaos and anarchy until the authority of spiritual and secular rulers had been restored and the absolute and unquestioning obedience of subjects in both Church and state

---

[5] *Essay on the Generative Principle*, p. 168.

[6] *Considerations on France*, pp. 64–65.

[7] Cf. H. J. Laski, *Studies in the Problem of Sovereignty* (New Haven, 1917), pp. 214-220. R. Soltau, *French Political Thought in the Nineteenth Century* (London, 1931), pp. 17–18.

had been reestablished. Reason and its offspring, the individualist theories of contract and natural rights, could never form the foundation of social or political unity. Without the leading hand of authority, men soon strayed from the path of truth and security. "The human reason is manifestly incapable of guiding men; for few can reason well, and no one can reason well on every subject."[8] Maistre echoes the classic authoritarian cry—let everyone stick to his own last, and particularly let rulers rule and priests interpret the will of God. If men were blind and lost without guidance, nothing remained of the Enlightenment's picture of the self-sufficient individual deciding rationally the advantages of union and fixing rationally the limits of power. And nothing remained of the notion that men moved of their own volition from a natural into a social state.

The truth was, he asserted, that society was the product, not of men's conscious decision, but of their instinctive makeup. Both history and primitive societies illustrated men's gravitation toward some form of communal life, if only in the family. Since government was in this sense natural, the product of a god-given order, it could not legitimately be denied, revoked, or even disobeyed by the people. There could, that is, be no *right* of resistance to any sovereign—or at least, said Maistre, bowing to papal supremacy, no right except when sanctioned by a power outside the people themselves, the Papacy. In sum, sovereignty was not the product of the deliberation or the will of the people; it was a divinely bestowed authority fitted not to man's wishes but to his needs.[9]

Both of these interpretations express a side of Maistre's thought, but both are insufficient as they stand. No one who has read the frightening benedictions Maistre bestows on wars, executions, bloodletting, mass prejudices, and myths can doubt that he was something more (or less) than the realist in a world of unpractical utopians or the simple defender of traditional authority. For, starting from a conventional defense of faith against reason, he ends with a thorough and radical defense of irrationalism. In his eyes, the only cure for present ills was the disavowal of rationalism and the return to the Catholic fold. This stark opposition of faith and reason was not only an argument against the deistic idea that men were rationally led to suppose the existence of God as the Prime Mover of an ordered natural world,

---

[8] *Saint Petersburg Dialogues*, p. 207.
[9] *Study of Sovereignty*, pp. 95–97.

but also, in spite of his own claim to be a faithful disciple of Aquinas, a rejection of the Thomist view that the conclusions of reason were in harmony with revelation and Church dogma. For Aquinas, *"gratia naturam non tollit, sed perfecit"*; but Maistre saw reason as the deadliest enemy of faith, not as its buttress and support, and slipped very easily into the position of defending the irrational elements of man's nature as the sole means of understanding God's purposes. In this, he was not arguing just that the *philosophes* had ignored those emotions vital to an understanding of human motivation; rather he was insisting that full play should be given to instinctive and irrational impulses as the only path by which the moral truths holding society together could be reached. By direct route, this led him to the demand for the denial of those powers of free inquiry which bred moral error. This irrationalist strain plays a large part in his writings, especially in the *Saint Petersburg Dialogues.* Here the spilling of blood emerges as a sacred rite, a means of expiation for men's wickedness; war is glorified as the most terrible and thus most noble embodiment of this holy bloodshed; the executioner is elevated to the rank of high priest of society, the most exact and powerful symbol of its unity. Authority becomes a mystery as holy as any of the religious mysteries and equally beyond both explanation and criticism. The free exercise of reason, as the natural parent of subversion, should be extirpated. The individual should not trust those myths which "in all nations, even in modern nations, clothe many truths." He should accept the unreasoned prejudices handed down to him, and not try to shape traditional morality on the anvil of his personal reason. He should prostrate himself before the religion of the state, sinking his personality in communal life. [10]

There is sufficient here to justify another interpretation of Maistre as one of the first in the modern Fascist tradition.[11] But again this emphasizes one of his many modes of attack upon Enlightenment thought. In truth, he was willing to take up any weapon in his fight with the *philosophes.* Sometimes he attacks the Enlightenment (with which he bracketed the Reformation) for subverting the faith and prejudices which were the only means of perceiving religious and moral truths; at other times, because it had checked the growth of an accurate and fruitful political science; at others, because it had destroyed the bases of social unity. At first sight, these complaints

---

[10] *Ibid.,* pp. 108–111.
[11] Cf., for example, Isaiah Berlin, *The Hedgehog and the Fox* (London, 1953), p. 49.

seem quite separate, if not contradictory. The only common element in his thought seems to be the passionate intensity, the religious fervor, with which he invests the disputes of his age. Yet this emotional fire is the pointer toward certain religious or quasi-religious assumptions that inform the whole of his writings and that bind together the apparently disparate elements of his attack upon eighteenth century rationalism.

III. MAISTRE AND THE ENLIGHTENMENT

There is no mistaking the personal virulence and contempt Maistre levels against the philosophers. Bacon's ideas sprang, not from intellectual error, but from a perverted morality. A contempt for Locke was the beginning for all knowledge. Hume, of all the philosophers of the eighteenth century, had combined the most talent with the most talent for harm. To admire Voltaire was the sign of a corrupt soul. Rousseau had been inspired, not by a love of truth, but by a perverse hatred of all grandeur. The catalogue of calumny is endless, and can be excused only because it was the concrete expression of a very real feeling that the *philosophes* were not merely mistaken but were depraved, even satanic, in their persistent and conscious advocacy of atheism and subversion.

This moral revulsion appears even more strongly when he talks of Enlightenment philosophy as a whole. Time and again Maistre accuses it of being riddled with pride, a ferocious and rebellious pride intent on disturbing every accepted idea and established power. These philosophers, he says, "detest without exception every distinction they do not enjoy; they find fault in every authority; they hate anything above them."[12] Inevitably their thought was destructive and negative. All the philosophers could agree on one thing—"the fury of destruction," but, obsessed by their own personal nostrums, they had no common plans for reclaiming the scorched earth.[13] Equally inevitably, hatred for authority mounted to an assault upon Christianity. This Antichrist "no longer speaks in the cold tone of indifference, still less with the biting irony of skepticism; there is a deadly hatred, a tone of anger and often of fury." These writers did not treat Christianity as a human error, but as a scourge of mankind, a bitter enemy to be fought to the death. They had even raised their hatred for Christianity into a

---

[12] *Saint Petersburg Dialogues*, p. 269.
[13] *Study on Sovereignty*, p. 128.

hatred of its divine author.[14] Yet, on his part, Maistre was no more willing to be tolerant; he would not accept the atheism of the *philosophes* (or what he saw as their atheism) simply as an intellectual error. It was an illness of the soul. "[Atheism] does not reside or start in the intelligence. No man has ceased to believe in God, before having decided that he should not exist; no book would produce atheism, and no book can restore faith."[15] Thus the fatal flaw in Enlightenment thought, as he saw it, lay in the soul, not the mind; it sprang from a moral enormity, "an insurrection against God," whose instigators were as "guilty as the rebel angels."[16]

The French Revolution to his mind was the political manifestation of this satanic revolt. And, like the thought on which it was founded, it was a moral offense clothed in attractive idealist garb.[17] It was nothing more than the expansion, the proselytization, of the pride and consequent moral corruption of the philosophers.[18] It differed in essence from all previous political revolutions, finding a parallel only in the biblical revolt against heaven.[19]

These are obviously not simply the tones of a man disturbed at the intellectual and philosophic errors of his age, nor even of one trying desperately to combat the growing political and social dislocation of his time. They are the passionate and even awe-inspired tones of one who sees the political struggles of his time on a huge and cosmic scale, judges events *sub specie aeternitatis,* and looks on revolution and counter-revolution as a battle for the soul of humanity. These accents echo throughout his work, giving it the force which captured the imagination of men in his own day, and giving it, too, its essential unity; and particularly they sound in his views of human nature, of the position of man in society and of human history.

IV. HUMAN NATURE

It is clear that Maistre's approach to politics would prevent him from basing his system on explicit psychological postulates, as, for instance, Hobbes, Helvétius, and Bentham had done. There are in fact

[14] *Essay on the Generative Principle,* p. 179.
[15] *Examen de la philosophie de Bacon* in *Oeuvres,* t. vi, p. 414.
[16] *Essay on the Generative Principle,* p. 178.
[17] Letter to Vallaise (July 27, 1815) in *Oeuvres,* t. xiii, p. 112.
[18] *Discours à Mme. la Marquise de Costa . . . ,* in *Oeuvres,* t. vii, p. 249.
[19] *Considerations on France,* p. 71.

few open statements in his works on men's psychological makeup. Nevertheless, he does incidentally point to two characteristics which he seems to consider natural to men—their lust for power and their tendency to move into society.

At some points the picture he paints is as devoid of gentle colors as that of Hobbes. Man's lust for power, and especially for the power beyond his possession, is insatiable. "He is infinite in his desires and, always discontented with what he has, he loves only what he has not." Moreover, there is no man who will not abuse the power he wields, who will not use other men so far as he is able for his own ends, finding pleasure in the very act of tyranny. Every human being is a potential despot from the most absolute Asian monarch to the child smothering a bird in his hand to enjoy the pleasure of realizing the existence of a weaker creature.[20]

At other points, he leans toward a more amiable Aristotelianism in his belief that man's most important characteristic is his social nature as willed and created by God. In his eyes, it was ridiculous to envisage the "natural man" as a solitary, isolated individual, for this was a phenomenon never met with in the world. The single man was the embryo, the microcosm, of the whole community. Consequently, to talk of the "state of nature" in contrast to "the state of society" was strictly nonsense: "the nature of any being is only the sum of the qualities attributed to it by the Creator," and in particular, "the nature of man is to be a cognitive, religious, and social animal." The true man of nature was thus the fully mature social being with all his social affections, all his knowledge, all his skills: "Art is man's nature," said Maistre echoing Burke.[21]

As far as he tries, therefore, to draw a picture of man's psychological features, it is an apparently contradictory one. On the one hand, it shows man as devoted to power, not only as the means to the satisfaction of other desires, but also as an end in itself. On the other, it shows man as naturally sociable. This contradiction is, however, one which he consciously accepts and develops; for his whole view of society is built on the notion of the moral schizophrenia of humanity.

Man, Maistre was convinced, has both a good and an evil nature, a theomorphic and a theomachic nature, a dualism which was the inevitable consequence of his creation in the image of God and his fall from

[20] *Study on Sovereignty*, p. 118.
[21] *Ibid.*, pp. 95, 98.

grace.[22] The two psychological traits he describes are simply parts or consequences of this moral antinomy. Lust for power is the child of pride, the overweening satanic pride endemic in the human soul. It was the same pride exhibited so flagrantly in eighteenth century thought, the obsessive quest for independence and self-government which leads finally to a revolt against God. On the other side, the social instincts of man are evidence of his good nature, which, in its widest sense, is the submission to and forwarding of those conditions and laws God has set for men. Without this social nature, without this alleviation of man's corruption by his morality, no society would be possible.[23]

Inevitably, in the shadow of the events of his own time, Maistre dwelt mainly on the evil side of this nature. The idea of original sin, "which explains everything, and without which nothing can be explained,"[24] returns constantly in his work as an explanation of social evil. God is good, and we hold of him all the benefits we enjoy—this could not be doubted. But God is also just, and men are sinful and worthy of punishment.[25] Men are so because they have freedom of will, freedom from any direct command of God or of any mechanical necessity. Why then has God created them with this capacity for moral choice? In part, answers Maistre, because he has created them in his own image, endowing them, unlike the lower animals, with the godlike attribute of conscious decision on the courses they will pursue. In part, too, the condition of the moral order and the existence of man as a moral being presuppose his freedom of will. If God interposed directly in human action, if he prevented every crime of his own will or imposed a personal and immediate punishment on every criminal, the moral order would disappear. For no act could be either moral or immoral if it was necessary and inevitable. Moral action assumes the existence of evil and of man's free choice between good and evil.

Freedom of will constitutes both the grandeur and the corruption of man, the grandeur in that it allows a self-conscious striving after the good, the corruption in that it allows him the possibility of acting against God's wishes, of trying to challenge or change the divine ordination of this world. "The will of man in the sphere of evil can contradict God. . . . God wishes things to happen which do not happen

<hr>

[22] *Enlightenment on Sacrifices*, pp. 291–294.
[23] *The Pope*, p. 134.
[24] *Saint Petersburg Dialogues*, p. 196.
[25] *Ibid.*, pp. 236–237.

because man does not wish them."[26] This is how Maistre could explain
the occurrence of the French Revolution in a divinely ordained world,
for it was the product of man's wickedness, the immediate work of
human, not divine, will. In spite of his hatred of the Revolution, he
could not help being dazzled at times, like Milton before him, by the
audaciousness of the satanic revolt and the immensity of its destructive urges: he preferred the Jacobins, plunged openly into the work of
destruction, and Napoleon, with his naked displays of strength, to the
Constituents with their vain and stupid pretensions of constructing in
the name of reason.

If the Revolution was an exercise of man's independent will, it was
no less a striking illustration of pride's futility. At times, Maistre insists
merely that in political affairs men can modify but never create; they
can plant and tend a tree but never give it life.[27] Often, however, he
goes much further in his fury at attempts to impose human conceptions
on God's work: "Man in harmony with his Creator is sublime, and his
action is creative; equally, once he separates himself from God and acts
alone, he does not cease to be powerful, since this is the privilege of his
nature, but his acts are negative and lead only to destruction."[28] Once
men cease to draw their inspiration from God, they and their works are
condemned to error, decay and sterility.[29]

This, then, is his picture of man's nature: "an incredible combination of two different and incompatible powers, a monstrous centaur."[30]
He sees man as a moral paradox, divine in his origin and in some of his
impulses, evil in the possession of a free will that can quickly lead him
to unbounded pride and to a destructive revolt against God.

V. THE HUMAN CONDITION

If Maistre saw man as being essentially a creature of free will, this
nevertheless did not mean that God did not control man and society
at their every stage and in their every part. He did not sing of Nature
and of "Nature's God," who had created the world and men with their
full complement of natural and psychological laws and forever after
left them to their mechanical progress. On the contrary, he believed

---

[26] *Ibid.*, p. 233.
[27] *Considerations on France*, p. 77.
[28] *Essay on the Generative Principle*, p. 170.
[29] *Studies on Sovereignty*, pp. 110–111.
[30] *Saint Petersburg Dialogues*, p. 199.

firmly that God intervened at every point in human history. The progress of states can, he claimed, be ascribed only to such a continual
intervention by a supernatural power; this alone can explain how a
host of accidental circumstances work toward a coherent yet humanly
unforeseen and unintended end.[31]

Educated in a Jesuit school, he would know the answer of Catholic
theologians to this paradox of free man living in a universe fulfilling
God's intentions. This lay in their distinction between the antecedent
and the consequent divine will. God wishes to save men, and wills
the means of their salvation. This is his antecedent will. But its success depends upon men's own acceptance of God's grace. If this condition is not satisfied, God wishes that men shall not be saved, and
shall refuse the means of salvation. This is God's consequent will.
And, in this sense, even the Revolution was willed by God, although
immediately it was the product of man's sinful nature.

Yet Maistre seldom puts forward this circuitous argument, simply
asserting the truth of the apparent paradox. "Without doubt, God is
the universal moving force, but each being is moved according to the
nature that God has given it. . . . God directs angels, men, animals,
brute matter, in sum all created things, but each *according to its
nature*: and man having been created free, he is led freely."[32] The fact
that there is an ultimate harmony between the fortuitous and often
corrupt wills of men and God's intentions can be inferred from the
order and method inherent in history, but the mode of divine control
is in itself unknowable.

If this is an irrational and mystical assertion, it was at any rate the
sort of assumption made by many liberal thinkers of the time. The
laissez-faire political economists, for instance, assumed that some
benign Providence arranged a harmony between men's self-interested
motives and the general interest; and the same assumption of a "naturally" or "Providentially" arranged harmony lay behind the liberal
idea of progress.

The difference lies mainly in Maistre's willingness openly to
acknowledge, even to vaunt, the mystical, unknowable nature of this
connection. "Without doubt, man is free; he can make mistakes, but
not sufficiently to derange general plans. We are all bound to the
throne of God by a pliant chain which reconciles the self-propulsion

[31] *Ibid.*, p. 212.
[32] *Ibid.*, p. 231.

(*l'automatie*) of free agents with divine supremacy." There is some
secret force which bears every individual into his place in the scheme
of things. This is particularly true of political life, whose organic development is determined by God regardless and even in spite of human
designs. "We recognize in a plant some unknown power, a single, form-
giving force, which creates and conserves, which moves unwaveringly
toward its end, which appropriates what is useful to it and rejects that
which would harm it. . . . How can we deny that the body politic has
also its law, its soul, its form-giving force, and believe that everything
is dependent on the whims of human ignorance?"[33] There is in every
society a "directing spirit" (*esprit recteur*) which animates it, as the
soul animates the body.[34]

Never had there been a clearer example of the divine ordination of
the political and moral world than the French Revolution, and never
had the futility of human ambitions been shown more strikingly. It
carried men along in its flow willy-nilly, and its leaders were leaders
only in name. Mirabeau retained power as long as he served circumstances, but once he tried to turn against the flow of events, he was
thrust aside by men such as Robespierre, who were willing to swim
with the tide. All the revolutionaries had lived in that unreal world
where aspiration equals achievement, in the child's world where wishes
are kings; but in the result, they could be seen as the unconscious and
unwitting instruments of the divine chastisement of themselves and of
France.[35]

As Maistre sees man, therefore, he is doomed to perpetual frustration so long as he worships his own self-will. Born a rebel, he is yet an
impotent rebel. He can revolt against the divinely ordained order of
things; he can freely and voluntarily bring down destruction upon his
own head; but in the end even this serves only to further the purposes
of God.

VI. THE DIVINE VOICE IN HISTORY

If Maistre followed many eighteenth century writers in regarding
history as the sorry record of man's pride and folly, he did not believe
that this condition was an unbreakable impasse. Or, more particu-

---

[33] *Study on Sovereignty*, pp. 124–125.
[34] *Saint Petersburg Dialogues*, p. 212.
[35] *Considerations on France*, pp. 48–50.

larly, he did not see the Revolution as an absolutely inevitable event. It had been inevitable only within a context which men could themselves have shaped. For if God had given men freedom of will, he had also given them some indications on how that freedom should be used, on what choices they ought to make in order to reach a settled harmony between their actions and divine purposes. Men could always ignore these signs, but they were always there to be recognized. Through revelation, punishment, and authority, God made known his wishes, and it was through the acceptance of revelation and submission to punishment and authority that men could reach social and political concord.

Curiously enough, he seldom mentions biblical revelation. More curiously still, he does not insist in his political writings on the power of the Church or the Pope to define dogmatically the political intentions of God. In his work *The Pope*, he does try to reassert the Papacy's spiritual authority, and does attribute to the Pope the power of releasing peoples from their duty of obedience to secular rulers, but even here he does not claim an ecclesiastic monopoly of revelation. Generally, throughout his works, he puts the emphasis rather on traditional beliefs, the inner sentiments of the heart, and the pronouncements of great men of genius as God's means of revealing his will to men.

Bonald and Lamennais (in his early writings) put forward boldly the idea that national traditions embody the primitive revelations of God. While Maistre was never so explicit, he was just as sure that widely held traditional beliefs were in some sense the voice of God. The idea was not novel; Hooker, Bossuet, Burke are just the most well known in a long line of writers who expounded it. And in England, France, and Germany at this time there were many who were defending old institutions and beliefs against the attacks of the Benthamites, the republicans, the writers of the *Aufklärung* on the grounds that any idea or political form which had survived for long must be presumed to perform some practical function in the community. Maistre, however, is not putting forward simply a pragmatic defense of prescriptive forms. He is insisting that traditional beliefs and systems are sacrosanct, not just because they are useful, but because they do in a very literal sense embody the revealed wishes of God. "Man, in spite of his fatal degradation, bears always the evident marks of his divine origin, in that every universal belief is always more or less true. Man may well

have covered over and, so to speak, encrusted the truth with the errors
he has loaded onto it, but these errors are local, and universal truth
will always show itself."[36] In consequence, ideas such as the divine
origin of sovereignty or the necessity of sacrifice, which have formed
part of the communal credo of many different societies at many different stages of development, must be accepted as being true.[37] They are
the outcrops of that submerged collective mind which, rather than the
individual reason, is the true voice of God.

In his defense of prejudice, he argues along the same lines. In part,
he repeats the pragmatic formula of Hume, that prejudices or communal sentiments are the cement necessary to social stability. Good
citizens, he insisted, need beliefs not problems. The word "prejudice"
has been misused: "It does not necessarily signify false ideas, but only
. . . any opinions adopted without examination."[38] Rather than indulg-
ing in systematic doubt, it would be better for men to accept the
codes of morality and the established ideas handed down to them by
their fathers, and to act on this "collection of dogmas or useful prejudices adopted by the national mind."[39]

Yet he goes again beyond this pragmatic defense. As a justification
of his faith in traditional beliefs and prejudices, he draws a picture of
human history which is a strange amalgam of the Christian idea of the
Fall and the Golden Age tradition. Traditional beliefs were the ves-
tiges in human consciousness of an original primitive state of man, in
which he enjoyed perfect virtue and knowledge. Maistre felt able to
pinpoint this desirable age as the time before the Deluge. We know
little of these times, he conceded, but there are unmistakable signs
that it was an age of perfection. The Deluge, being such a heavy punishment, must have been prompted by a great crime; and since guilt
is always proportionate to the knowledge of the guilty, there must have
been a great science before the Deluge. Besides this, the idea of a past
Golden Age of humanity must have some foundation in reality, since
it had entered into the whole of the world's thinking and literature
(including even the works of the hated Voltaire). Maistre could not
find superlatives large enough to describe the men of this primitive
age, these "wonderful men." They had no need for laborious studies,
for their knowledge was intuitive, a direct revelation from God; and

[36] *Saint Petersburg Dialogues*, p. 214.
[37] *Enlightenment on Sacrifices*, p. 294.
[38] *Study on Sovereignty*, p. 108.
[39] *Ibid.*, p. 109.

the truths they felt were of a purer and more profound kind than could be reached by moderns.[40] An original world of harmony and unity, catastrophe, and the subsequent odyssey of mankind in its attempt to reassemble the fragments of its unitary understanding—the pattern is repeated throughout human thought, and was commonplace in the eighteenth century.

Behind these theosophist ideas lay a deep distrust of the empirical scientific tradition. Any complete science, he argued, would involve a study of ultimate causes, but Bacon had taught the modern world to regard physical phenomena as the only material of "science," or rather had tried to explain physical effects solely in terms of physical causes. This was inevitably a hopeless task, since each physical cause became in its turn another effect to be explained in terms of yet another cause. Always the inquirer must come back to the ultimate question of what outside physical phenomena produce them; the principle of movement can never be found in matter. Thus the extensive claims made by Bacon for natural science, and the attempts of the Enlightenment to model moral and metaphysical inquiry on natural science, were built on sand. Since all nature is an effect, the natural science nurtured on Baconian ideas was not really concerned with the discovery of causes, only with the uncovering of facts previously ignored, as in the work on the circulation of the blood, or in relating and connecting previously known facts, as in Newton's theory of gravity.[41] In this, Maistre was more tender of Newton's own cautious distinction between "explanations of nature" and "descriptions of nature" than were Newton's eighteenth century idolaters. Yet, while he admired Newton for this caution, he saw the natural science of his own time as being wholly inferior to the knowledge of ultimate causes enjoyed by primitive men, and inferior by this fact to the wisdom embodied in national traditions and prejudices.

This same fixed view of knowledge as revelation dominated his view of language. Like other romantic writers, he built a mystique of language, which subserved nationalist ends; and, like other romantic writers, he reserved a special scorn for those eighteenth century thinkers, such as Condillac, who had been concerned with the philosophic improvement of language. In his view, language could not be created a priori or perfected by the wit of man or philosopher. Far from phi-

[40] *Saint Petersburg Dialogues*, pp. 201–202.
[41] *Ibid.*, pp. 224–225.

losophy being the instrument by which language could be refined and improved, it had a dead and stultifying influence. In the formation of languages, the primitive were the creative ages, and the civilized and scientific the most sterile. This again was because the primitives had been given language, like the knowledge of which it was the sinews, directly by God. Particular languages might have been born in recorded history, but they were simply modifications and reformations of older tongues. The archetypal language itself emerged, like Minerva, fully formed from the mind of God.[42]

Knowledge and language were then for Maistre the revelations of God, felt most perfectly by man before his corruption, but still glimpsed in the traditions and prejudices of modern man. Yet, despite this nostalgia for a Golden Age, he was willing to talk at times as though men, or rather *righteous* men, had not lost entirely the primitive instinct for truth. Or, to put this another way, he opposed to reason not only prejudices but the inner sentiments of the heart.

In the *Saint Petersburg Dialogues*, Maistre puts the view "that the upright man is very commonly informed, by an inner sentiment, of the truth or falsity of certain propositions before any examination, often even without having made studies necessary to be in a position to examine them with a full knowledge of the case." This secret instinct, won by "rectitude of heart and constant purity of intention," this "intellectual conscience," can even show the righteous the folly of some theories of natural science in the teeth of all demonstration; in matters of morals or metaphysics, it is infallible.[43]

While he had this much faith in the all-seeing eye of the righteous, he did not reserve righteousness to a limited group. It was not the Elect who could hear this inner voice of conscience, but the unsophisticated, all those unstained by excessive rationalism—and this was a state within all men's capacities. This attitude is shown in the way he adapts the notion of innate ideas. Every living creature is endowed, independently of all experience, with those ideas relevant to its place in the universe. If this were not so, and experience was the teacher, all creatures would be capable of the same knowledge. The dog with the same experience as its master would be capable of the same morality. Man has, therefore, instinct within him, all the ideas pertaining to his nature.[44] Here Maistre is opposing Descartes as well as Locke. He is

---

[42] *Ibid.*, pp. 205–206.
[43] *Ibid.*, pp. 185–186.
[44] *Ibid.*, pp. 222–223.

rejecting not only Locke's idea that the mind is a *tabula rasa* on which men's sensory perceptions trace ideas, but also Descartes's claim that what was innate in the mind was the faculty of acquiring knowledge through the perception of qualities such as being, form, or extension. The simple notions alone, granted by God, are innate; and, although they could soon be "sicklied o'er with the pale cast of thought," they are innate in every man.

In all this, he seems to approach much nearer to the "ethical theology" of Rousseau and Kant than to orthodox Catholic ideas;[45] and, just as Rousseau tended to associate the true feelings of the heart with the individual's appreciation of his oneness with the community, and as the Kantian ideal of ethical freedom was being interpreted in Germany by Fichte and Hegel as obedience to the state, so Maistre identified these intuitive glimpses into truth with the general will or sentiments or traditions of the community. There is in every social group—family, town, or people—a mysterious attraction forming the moral unity of that group.[46] This is particularly true of the nation: "nations have a general soul, a true moral unity, which makes them what they are." In pressing this conviction, he expressed as mystical and rabid a nationalism as could ever have come from a Robespierre, a Saint-Just, or a Fichte. Every nation, he urged, has its own particular traditions, its own character, its own mission. To buttress this tradition and character, there should be built "a religion of the state," dedicated to worship of the "national reason" and repression of the individual reason. He sums up his view in a passage that is a classic statement of modern nationalism: "Government is a true religion: it has its dogmas, its mysteries, its priests. To submit it to the individual discussion is to destroy it; it is given life only through the national mind, that is to say, by political faith, which is a creed. Man's primary need is that his nascent reason should be put under a double yoke; it should be frustrated, and it should lose itself in the national mind, so that it changes its individual existence for another communal existence." Patriotism consists in this abnegation of self and this acceptance of political faith; it rises on the two rocks of "submission and belief." This political faith, this national soul, like the inner sentiments and the traditions from which it springs, cannot be created or shaped by man, but is the work of God.[47]

[45] See E. Cassirer, *Rousseau; Kant; Goethe.*
[46] *Saint Petersburg Dialogues,* p. 274.
[47] *Study on Sovereignty,* pp. 108–109.

By this assertion that God reveals himself in traditions, prejudices, and the sentiments of the simple, uncorrupted heart, Maistre,
like other nationalist and racist writers of the nineteenth century, was
trying to construct a popular base to an authoritarian creed. Yet,
again like other nationalist writers, he superimposed on this picture of
popular intuition that of the great individual, the hero of history. For
if in his notion of universal innate ideas he was near enough to eighteenth century egalitarianism, he was in other respects nearer to Fichte
or Hegel or Nietzsche in seeing the historical process as being moved
by great men of genius, hypersensitive both to the demands and possi-
bilities of the moment and to the ultimate ends of history. The link
between the two ideas was that he saw both the inner conscience
prompting ordinary men to right action and the abilities of genius as
gifts of God: "Genius is a grace. The true man of genius acts by movement or by impulsion." The great men of thought, art, and action are
struck by a divine illumination, the only master they acknowledge
being Providence. In this inspirational view of discovery, he found yet
another stick with which to beat Bacon. Bacon had never explored
new fields of knowledge, but had only written about how such explora-
tion should be undertaken. Even in an age relatively unburdened by it,
Maistre could conclude that such methodological discussion was
futile, showing only that the writer was himself incapable of creative
work. It was not Bacon but God who had forwarded natural science.
Galileo saw the church lamp swing, Newton saw the apple fall, and
they had conceived ideas which were to revolutionize science.[48] Every
man of genius was, like Newton, a

> ". . . pure intelligence, whom God
> To mortals lent, to trace his boundless works
> From laws sublimely simple."[49]

In language, too, it was not the theorists who molded words and idi-
oms, but the great writers acting on instinct.[50] What was true of science and art was true of political development. The man who shaped
the childhood of a nation or led it in its maturity was divinely inspired,
gifted with "an extraordinary penetration," and "infallible instinct."
He could discern and nurture national qualities, not through abstract
thought, but through an unconscious grasp of circumstances. Above

---

[48] *Examen de la philosophie de Bacon* in *Oeuvres*, t. vi, 54–61. *De l'église gallicane*
in *Oeuvres*, t. iii, p. 34.
[49] *Saint Petersburg Dialogues*, p. 230.
[50] *Ibid.*, p. 206.

all, he was not a philosopher. "He is never to be seen writing or debating; his mode of action derives from inspiration; and if sometimes he takes up a pen, it is not to argue but to command."[51]

It was by these means, through national traditions, conscience, and the work of great men, that the masses could dimly divine the intentions and ways of God: and Maistre was sufficiently a man of his age to think that what the masses believed was important in itself as well as being effective in political action. The people, the nation, was not just a beast to be subdued. It was the voice of God—but only when it disavowed revolutionary ends and followed without thought and without reserve the mission implicit in its own traditions, its own deepest feelings, and its own God-given leaders. Here he plunged into the intellectual whirlpool in which revolutionary theorists have floundered since 1789, the justification of irresponsible authority by an appeal to the "real" (as distinct from the overt) wishes of the masses. Yet while he was willing to appeal to popular beliefs and prejudices, political facts forced him back to his view of man's schizophrenic nature. If the French people had been true to their traditions and prejudices, they would have avoided the sufferings that revolution had brought in its train, but an innate spirit of revolt had led them to ignore these revelations. Both to reprove and to remedy that sin of pride, they and the world must be punished.

VII. THE PROBLEM OF EVIL

Do pain and suffering exist because God wishes them to exist? Then God is malevolent. Does evil exist despite God's wishes? Then God is not all-powerful. The paradox as stated by Hume was central to the attitudes of the Enlightenment. For it was from the refusal to accept the full implications of the paradox that there arose the revolutionary contrast between nature and reality. Man's true nature, his natural history, his natural morality were widely different from his actual social behavior, his actual history, his actual codes of morality. Pain and suffering abounded in the corrupt world of the present, but once change the environment, the institutions debasing men, once wipe away the stains which that environment had left on man's nature, once write finis to all previous patterns of history, and pain would be finally stilled.

[51] *Study on Sovereignty*, p. 102.

Maistre was stretched on the rack of this same paradox. God controlled the universe, but the Revolution had occurred and had brought untold suffering, especially to the innocent such as Maistre himself. If God did control the world, why had these horrors taken place? His answer reversed all the hopes and all the revolutionary implications of Enlightenment thought. Men suffer with a just inevitability as a punishment for their sins. "All pain is a punishment, and every punishment . . . is inflicted by love as much as by justice."[52] It is useless for men to rail against God, for they are the authors as well as the sufferers; it is not the judge but the criminal who causes punishment.

Why, then, should the innocent and those of the true faith suffer, while the guilty prosper? Maistre tried to soften this question, so real to émigrés convinced equally of their own virtue and of the viciousness of the revolutionaries. The bulk of good fortune does go to the virtuous as a whole. Equally, some suffering is brought directly upon individuals by their own sins. Government was designed to implement such retributive justice. Many illnesses, too, resulted from moral lapses—there were maladies of pride, anger, gluttony, and incontinence. Yet, in spite of these qualifications, he does not adopt any position of theological utilitarianism, advocating virtue, like Paley, as the best means of ensuring both temporal and eternal happiness. On the contrary, the main burden of his theme is that men's sufferings are quite fortuitous and accidental, unrelated to their virtues or vices. God's wrath falls on saints and sinners as indiscriminately as bullets on a battlefield. If good men suffered because they are good, and the wicked prospered because they are wicked, Providence could rightly be attacked; but in truth "every man, as a man, is subject to all the misfortunes of humanity."[53] This undifferentiated suffering is needed, not only because men must bear the burden of the sin inherent in their nature, but also because, if every act was rewarded or punished directly and immediately, the moral order would become meaningless and moral action impossible. Virtue which sprang from fear of punishment would cease to be virtue. Divine justice could not be encompassed by the human justice of giving every man his deserts: it lay in the fact that the total sum of the penalties paid was equal to the sum of crimes committed.

All this builds up into a terrible picture. Men "live under the hand

---

[52] *Saint Petersburg Dialogues*, p. 236.
[53] *Ibid.*, pp. 187–188, 190.

of an angry power, and . . . this power can be appeased only by sacrifices."[54] They have always believed (and it is therefore a truth) that this angry God could be satisfied only by the shedding of blood, the symbol of life in the flesh, and by the expiation of the guilty by the innocent.[55] After the Lisbon earthquake of 1755 which had so seared the European mind, Voltaire had cried out, "Can you say after seeing all these victims that God is revenged, that their death is the price of their crimes? These children, crushed and bloody on their mothers' breasts, what crime or sin had they committed?" With terrible consistency, Maistre replied that these children, like all victims of natural disasters and scourges, were the objects of divine wrath, that their apparently cruel and meaningless deaths were the necessary means of expiation for human fallibility.[56] In the same way, he welcomed the inevitability of social distress. Generally no friend of political economists, he thought highly of Malthus and his gloomy law of population, which condemned the majority of men at best to mere subsistence and at worst to starvation.

Of all the instruments of divine wrath, war, he believed, is the most crushing and effective. He rejected completely the charge that wars spring from the evil designs of rulers: they originate rather in some blind instinct that grips men and pushes them into conflict. Violence and violent death are laws of the whole universe. All animals have their beasts of prey, and man, to satisfy his needs and instincts, must kill, must subdue the animal world. It is in the grip of this same law that man, seized by "a divine fury," seeks to kills his fellows: "He undertakes with enthusiasm what he holds in horror." The divinity of its origins justifies, even sanctifies, this instinct: in the act of slaughter, the soldier, like the executioner, is only "an innocent murderer, a passive instrument in a formidable hand." As mysterious as the causes of war are its results. Success or failure in battle does not depend upon the big battalions or the schemes of generals, but on a host of circumstances and attitudes as much beyond the control of men as they are beyond their comprehension. As a penalty for its sins, mankind is condemned to flounder in this welter of bloodshed and terror, mysterious in its causes and unforeseeable in its results. "The whole earth, continually steeped in blood, is nothing but an immense altar on which

[54] *Enlightenment on Sacrifices*, p. 291.
[55] *Ibid.*, pp. 292–294.
[56] *Saint Petersburg Dialogues*, pp. 217–219.

every living thing must be sacrificed, without end, without restraint, without respite, until the consummation of the world, the extinction of evil, the death of death."[57]

In passages such as this, he seems to see men as inexorably trapped in the tragic dilemma of inevitable crime and necessary punishment, of certain pride and its certain consequences. The crime springs from human corruption, the punishment from God's justice. This is a vision of an ordered world and a meaningful history, but a vision which abjures all tenderness, all compassion, all humanity. Yet, if the logical message of this view is that men should accept, should bare their backs to the strokes of misfortune and the horrors of history, the emotional content of his writings is as often one of protest as of acquiescence. The Revolution was a judgment and a punishment, but the Revolution was a crime as well as a punishment, and if the attendant suffering had to be accepted, the originating act of rebellion had to be condemned. Suffering was a lesson as well as a retribution. In leading men toward humility and submission, it taught them also how to break out of their dilemma and reach some sort of moral and political peace.

VIII. THE POLITICAL SYSTEM

For Maistre there is no sense in which society is the product of men's free association, and equally there is no sense in which sovereignty originates in or is a manifestation of a free act of the popular will. There is a purely logical sense in which sovereignty is founded on popular consent, in that, without some degree of popular loyalty to it, government would be impossible, but from any realistic viewpoint sovereignty derives from God as the creator of man's social nature.

Far from some entity "the people" constituting government, it is impossible to imagine "a people" without a sovereign; "the idea of a people involves that of an aggregation around a common center, and without sovereignty there can be no political unity or cohesion."[58] Here he echoes Burke's view that "the people" has an organic unity, not through any conscious decision on its own part, but through the consolidating work of a "habitual social discipline."[59]

Burke, however, was looking at an England which threw most of the

[57] *Ibid.*, p. 253.
[58] *Study on Sovereignty*, p. 99.
[59] *Appeal from the New to the Old Whigs* in *Works* (2 vols., London, 1854), I, 524-525.

work of government onto the shoulders of aristocrats and squires, the social and economic leaders of society. It is understandable that he should see the unity of the "people" as being the product, not of political organization, but of a hierarchy of social ranks headed by the "natural aristocracy"; and equally understandable that he should consequently think in terms of the limitation of sovereignty by this "natural" social order. Maistre's model, on the other hand, was French absolute monarchy in which there had been a deliberate attempt to strip the aristocracy of political powers and in which social stability seemed to fluctuate with the strength or weakness of central government. In consequence, it was natural for him not only to divorce sovereignty from popular control but to refuse any theoretical limitations of sovereignty. In part, of course, he argued the omnipotence of the sovereign power from its divine origin, but in part his arguments parallel those that had been embodied in the Jacobin constitution of 1793 and that Austin and the Benthamites were to make commonplace in England. It was useless, he claimed, to say that the sovereign power could be restrained by some fundamental law, for this was simply to transfer sovereignty to the individual or body which drew up those rules or decided on their application. Equally, it was useless to suppose that government could be limited by dividing authority between separate institutions, because inevitably in the case of conflict one of them must hold the ultimate power of decision. He disposed of the usual illustrations of the "separation of powers" argument by claiming that in England, King, Lords, and Commons were not independent sovereign powers, but that the king in Parliament was the single and absolute sovereign. Finally, he swept aside the idea that government could be limited through a right of popular resistance by arguing that whatever body or group could decide what was tyranny, and what therefore could legitimately be opposed, would by that fact become sovereign. The only intrusion on the absolutism of the sovereign power that he allowed was that the Pope, "whose sublime prerogatives form part of revelation," can exempt men from the divine law which prescribes obedience to rulers.[60]

This view of sovereignty formed the springboard for his attacks upon the written constitutions which had proliferated in France since 1791. He insisted that these constitutions, like all written constitutions, rested on the mistaken notion that sovereignty and political

[60] *The Pope*, pp. 139–140; *Study on Sovereignty*, pp. 112–113.

obligation derived from the agreement of individuals. In truth, this was to destroy obligation, since the agreement of the individual could always be revoked and certainly could not bind succeeding generations. This criticism pointed to a weakness in contract theory which even its most capable advocates, such as Hobbes or Locke, had not been able to overcome. The weakness had been discerned before Maistre wrote. Hume had pointed it out, and Burke and Paine, despite the fierce controversy between them, had been as one in recognizing this flaw. Paine, however, accepted the virtual dissolution of obligation in order to maintain the ultrademocratic doctrine that the people always had the power to revoke or remodel the contract of government, whereas Burke restated the contract in conservative terms by basing it on the agreement tacit in men's participation in society and in the historical process. Maistre carried the logic of Burke's argument to its extreme by declaring that no permanent obligations can be dependent on the conscious will of those who are to perform them. The very concept of obligation entails that those obliged have no discretionary right to accept or refuse duties. This hardly answers the case, for the contractual writers were concerned with the assumption rather than with the nature of obligation; marriage may carry inescapable responsibilities, but men are not obliged to marry. Nevertheless, Maistre assumed that to argue that political obligations exist is to accept that they proceed from some superior will—in his eyes, the will of God. It followed that no constitution can be imposed upon the body politic. Constitutions, to be effective, have to be the work of God, acting through great leaders or through time. These *"natural constitutions"* are never the result of deliberation, and exist prior to any written laws. In particular, rights cannot be created by written constitutions, for they must exist and be mutually recognized before they can be embodied in constitutional law. "No nation can give itself liberty if it has not it already." On the contrary, written laws are the mark of a weak and not a strong constitution. Rights are made explicit only when they are liable to be attacked, and the more public-spirited a nation is, the less need it will feel for these artificial defenses.[61]

While he made these direct criticisms of the ideas of popular sovereignty and the social contract, it is not easy to see him as a straightforward apologist for monarchic or aristocratic government. Reaching

[61] *Considerations on France*, pp. 77–79; *Essay on the Generative Principle*, pp. 151, 161.

back to an older tradition than the divine right of kings, he contended rather that all authority, no matter what its particular form, is divinely instituted. This leads him into a relativist attitude toward political systems striking back to Montesquieu and Bodin. In his eyes, the power which has created social authority and sovereignty has also ordained different modifications of sovereignty in different circumstances and nations. Institutions must fit myriad historical, climatic, and geographic factors, and thus there can be no firm answer to the question, "What is the best form of government?" The only rule he recommends as an institutional criterion is a modified historical utilitarianism. "The best government for each nation is that which, in the territory occupied by that nation, is capable of producing the greatest possible amount of happiness and strength, for the greatest possible number of men, during the longest possible time."[62] And this criterion was the only feasible one in a writer defending, not the divine right of monarchy or nobility, but the divine right of circumstances.

Maistre maintains this uncommitted attitude fairly consistently throughout his discussions of political institutions. Nevertheless, in his own life he remained painstakingly loyal to the Sardinian king, and this predilection for monarchy shows through at times in his writings. Certainly, he sets out many practical advantages for hereditary monarchy. Because of the hereditary principle, it avoids the instability of power struggles and does not offend *amour-propre*, the main ingredient of ambition. All men can feel equal before a king to whose position they cannot aspire, whereas in a republic, where the field is open to all, rulers are inevitably hated and envied by those shut out of the green pastures of power. Monarchy has also the vigor and unity of will necessary to strong government, and doubly necessary in a great and extensive state or in any great community, such as a Church. Finally, impartiality is best secured where power is entrusted to one man, for the perversity of will and partiality of judgment natural to men is most evident when their own interests are involved, and where there is a single sovereign those personal interests are cut down to a minimum. Although with these advantages in mind he could speak of hereditary monarchy being the most "natural" form of government and the best suited to European conditions, he did not claim it to be the best for all times and in all places. Or, if he thought it abstractly the ideal form of government, he did not believe that all nations can attain this abstract

[62] *Study on Sovereignty*, p. 126.

perfection. Of Poland, for instance, he commented that "certain nations are destined, perhaps *condemned,* to elective monarchy."[63]

He is even less firm an advocate of aristocratic government. An aristocracy, in the sense of a restricted governing class, is an inevitable part of every political system. In a monarchy, it is the prolongation, the executive arm, of royal sovereignty; it was as such that he defended the old French aristocracy and especially the *noblesse de robe,* the legal and administrative aristocracy. All other governments were aristocracies, either hereditary or elective, and all lacked some of the virtues of monarchy.[64]

It was from this point of view that he approached the question of democracy. His definition of a pure democracy was "an association of men without sovereignty," an impossible paradox since for him society originated in sovereignty. He acknowledged that there are many voluntary associations in which men submit themselves to rules as long as they desire the objects of the association; they may even submit themselves voluntarily to punishment. In such an association, these rules and this submission have no sanction other than the will of its members. A true democracy would be an extension of such a system, in which ordinances would be rules imposed by the people on themselves, and not laws. This was a fair description of Rousseau's theory of democracy, but Maistre objected that in reality such a voluntary political association can never exist. Voluntary submission to society would make the notion of political authority meaningless, for the concept of authority must necessarily involve coercion, or involuntary submission. The very fact that there are explicit laws presumes that they do not emanate from the "general will," since if they did they would *ipso facto* not need to be stated. Just as logically an individual cannot have coercive powers over himself, so a people cannot be both subject and sovereign at the same time.

A democracy is, therefore, an unreal political concept, and the republics that the world has known have not been democracies but some type of elective aristocracy. Yet, since the democratic principle is upheld as their basis, they are less able to govern firmly, and make greater demands on public spirit and virtue. If these demands could be satisfied, he conceded that republics would eclipse all other forms of

---

[63] *Ibid.,* pp. 113–119.
[64] *Ibid.,* p. 119.

government, but in practice republican government is suited only to small and externally weak states. Its disadvantages are the converse of the advantages of monarchy. Conflicts of ambitions lead to the leadership of demagogues and a restless spirit of change. More importantly, the administration of justice is bound to be weak; the powerful and illustrious are often sacrificed unjustly to the envy of the majority, while, where the criminal is obscure and has not hurt the pride or interests of the majority, public feeling resents and resists the action of law.[65]

Here he is not condemning republicanism outright. Still less does he condemn representative institutions outright. Nevertheless, he makes a very clear distinction between the revolutionary concept of a representative assembly as the embodiment of the general will and representative institutions as Europe had previously known them. In spite of the warning of Rousseau himself that sovereignty could not be delegated, the French constitution of 1793 had tried to make the assembly representative of national sovereignty. The inevitable consequence was that this constitution had remained a scrap of paper, and the country had been ruled by a clique no less tyrannical for their boasts that they governed in the name of the people. In the same way, the constitution of 1795, while it paid lip service to the slogan of national sovereignty, had abandoned the idea in practice. The people as a whole in the primary assemblies only nominated electors; representatives were not to be tied by the mandates of their constituents; and they were to safeguard the interests of the whole country, not just those of the locality electing them.[66] Yet, if he attacked the French national assemblies, he appealed also to a long tradition of representative institutions, which as parliaments, estates, diets, senates, or cortes had long formed part of the polity of every European state. Echoing Rousseau, he argued that these bodies had emerged out of the feudal monarchies.[67] They had been created by royal authority, they mirrored the medieval hierarchy of estates, and their functions had been to explain to the Crown the needs, grievances, and resources of the people. This limited, historical type of assembly he defended, not during the years of the *Chambre introuvable* when many ultraroyalist

[65] *Considerations on France*, pp. 67–69. *Study on Sovereignty*, pp. 119–126.
[66] *Considerations on France*, p. 67. See L. Duguit, H. Monnier, R. Bonnard, *Les constitutions et les principles lois politiques de la France* . . . (7th ed., Paris, 1952), pp. 77–81.
[67] See *Social Contract*, Book iii, Chap. xv.

writers spread liberal wings, but during the dark days of the 1790's. At this time, he urged that the follies of the French should not turn men away completely from representative institutions, for the people had a right "to instruct the king of their needs, and to denounce abuses to him."[68] Always, however, he believed that the powers of assemblies should remain limited; they should give government the information it needed to govern well, and accept or reject outright proposals made to them, but they should have no power to decide policies, to initiate or draw up legislation, or even to amend to any extent the legislation set before them.[69]

Thus, Maistre's own tastes seem to have favored monarchy, aided and informed but not limited by an assembly of estates. However, these were not recommendations for the social engineer. Where limited assemblies existed, he urged their retention, but he certainly was not advocating the creation of such bodies. In 1816 he declared himself ready to swallow the bitter pill of the 1814 Charter, only because it was a grant by Louis XVIII, a grace of royal authority; but by 1819 he was condemning the Charter outright, and was willing, like the other ultraroyalists, to add "quand même" to the cry "vive le roi."

At bottom, he was not concerned with institutional recommendations. His real interest was not in the machinery of government, but in the individual's relations with the state, and his ultimate purpose was to destroy all individual independence by equating the state with God, and transforming a necessarily qualified political into an imperative and unlimited religious obligation. Power itself, even when symbolized most nakedly by the executioner, was holy. He heard in all governments, not just one particular form of them, the stern commandments of God. Political authority was yet another means by which the divine tactic, the providential plan, could be glimpsed and furthered, and whatever shape authority took, however varied its manifestations, submission to it was a necessary step toward that humility, that sacrifice of pride, that abnegation of self, which was for him the major part of wisdom.

IX. REVOLUTIONARY AND REACTIONARY THOUGHT

Maistre was therefore strictly a reactionary; his whole thought centered on his abhorrence of the Revolution and the philosophy he

---

[68] *Study on Sovereignty,* pp. 118–119.
[69] *Lettres d'un royaliste savoisien,* in *Oeuvres,* t. vii, pp. 196–197.

thought had been its guiding light. He did not attack them simply because they were based on intellectual or political errors. They were for him moral and religious aberrations, Faustian challenges to God, nurtured by that overweening pride which was the basic flaw in human nature. Such pride was futile and disastrous in a world whose flow was governed by divine purposes. The best that men could do was to follow, not their reason, but God as he revealed himself in the inner sentiments of the unsophisticated heart, in traditional beliefs, and in the work of genius, to submit themselves to the divine punishments of war and natural disaster, and to obey those established authorities whose powers derived from God alone.

These central assumptions inform all his particular modes of attack upon Enlightenment thought. He extolled myth and prejudice because he believed them to be part of divine revelation. His insistence on the importance of studying the minutiae of political life and history was not derived simply from the factual taste of the political scientist, but drew life from a reverence for and acceptance of the variegated and complex universal flux, which at every moment God controlled and through which he realized his will. Finally, his attitude toward political authority was not just utilitarian. He believed that authority needed to be strong and harsh, not only to prevent the individualism of the time from breaking the frail bonds of society, but also to act as a bridle on men's inherent sinfulness, as an instrument of the just wrath of God.

The charges against the Enlightenment were those made by many other romantic writers—shallowness of interest and judgment, a dogmatic certainty within these narrow boundaries, a dull and arid blindness to the deeper, more impulsive (and nobler) springs of behavior, a complete failure to grasp the complexity of moral and political problems, and consequently a facile optimism about the degree or possibility of human improvement; in sum, confidence of judgment combined with sterility of imagination. Burke, Coleridge, and Carlyle in England, Novalis, Müller, Fichte, and Hegel in Germany, Chateaubriand and Bonald with Maistre in France, all loosed their fire on the "presumption and pert loquacity" of the *philosophes*.

In all this, they were seeking to criticize the dominant revolutionary and radical tendencies of their own time through an interpretation of the age they thought had given birth to them. This picture of the Enlightenment was simplified and distorted. Yet misinterpretations of the past, because they are simplifications, are usually influential. The conflict between past and present is exaggerated, and sons, wiser than their fathers, forget the links of kinship. The Romantics' view of their immediate past was just such a misinterpretation. Colored at every point by their experience of the Revolution, it was a striking demonstration of the fallacy of *post hoc, ergo propter hoc,* and was no less a misinterpretation because its advocates objected so often and so bitterly to "unhistorical" or "abstract" notions of man and society. Many of the charges they brought are unreal, and many of the characteristics of their own thought find parallels and roots in that eighteenth century thinking which nurtured revolutionary attitudes and the revolutionary temperament.

The early Enlightenment was in fact little more dogmatically confident about man's rationality or the power of reason than was Maistre himself. It insisted on the central position of reason because it thought with Hobbes that reason was the final barrier against the antisocial tendencies of the passions. But, when subordinated to wilfulness, reason could easily step beyond the narrow bounds within which it was effective. "In pride, in reas'ning pride, our error lies." The anti-Christian and skeptical trends in the Enlightenment, which Maistre hated so vehemently, were not originally the products of intellectual arrogance. It is difficult to see Hume or Voltaire as dogmatic atheists consumed with the pride of reason. They were rather insisting on the frailty and limitations of the human mind. As Locke had taught, men's knowledge came only from experience, and the origin of knowledge defined its boundaries, for men could know nothing with certainty of any of the ultimate causes and mysteries of life. "Let us become thoroughly sensible of the weakness, blindness, and narrow limits of human reason," urged Hume.[70] "Our intellects," sighed Voltaire, "are very confined as well as the strength of our bodies."[71] What Hume and Voltaire were protesting against was the use by organized religions of their presumed knowledge of the unknowable to justify and perpetuate intolerance and persecution. They were urging men only to look more fully at the areas of knowledge where their intelligence did throw light; it was better to look in these places of light for clues as to the nature of the darkness beyond than to stumble in the darkness for the meaning of the known world.

[70] *Dialogues* (ed. N. Kemp Smith, 2nd ed., 1947), p. 131.
[71] *Le Philosophe ignorant,* Chap. ix.

While Hume carried his skepticism as far as questioning the argument from design as a proof of the existence of God,[72] this was not a common attitude of his time. In England and France, most men were willing to accept the evidence of an ordered universe as proof of an ordering mind or will. In his deism, Voltaire was much more typical than Hume of that desire of the eighteenth century to discover or apply some order in the world and in the universe, some principle of interrelationship and interdependence which had been instituted by the "first Almighty Cause," and which worked through general laws as so brilliantly revealed in the natural world by Newton. While Maistre tried to find this divinely instituted order in history rather than in nature, while for him as for most nineteenth century thinkers the divine plan was dynamic rather than static, he never abandoned the Enlightenment quest. The world might be cruel and harsh, but this was because it was attuned to God's wishes; it was perhaps a place of affliction, but it was not purposeless.

Yet, if the Newtonian spectacle of the cosmic interrelationship of events and phenomena could nourish an awed acceptance of God's work, it could lead also to a desire to find or create some equivalent principle of order in the sphere of morals and politics. The same Voltaire who accepted the divine ordering of the universe could inveigh against the pain and suffering of mankind, and especially the inhumanity of man to man. To Helvétius, d'Holbach, Beccaria, and Bentham, the example of Newton pointed the way to the elimination of moral and social evils. If it was possible to discover in gravity a universal and fundamental law of the natural world, it should be equally possible to find some constant law of human behavior which would form the foundation of a social science. The sensationalism of Locke and Condillac had taught that the individual was an empty receptacle of external impressions, and thus placed the emphasis in character formation on environment. The psychological principle by which this environment could be controlled and ordered was men's attraction to pleasure and their revulsion from pain. What fascinated them in Newton, that is, was the idea of a single unifying principle, not the empirical method. In spite of their lip service to the scientific master, therefore, they did not end with a description of the actual relationships between social phenomena, but with pictures of an ideal community or system of laws, securing the logical end of society, its greatest

[72] *Dialogues*, pp. 144–192.

happiness, through a knowledge of the springs of human behavior. Nature was contrasted with reality, the ideal with the actual, and political "science" geared to the future, not the present. In the hopes of finally resolving the problem of political evil that these contrasts generated lay their revolutionary potentiality.

It was in the atheist circle that emerged in France after the mid-century—the circle of Helvétius and Baron d'Holbach, the "personal enemy of God"—that Maistre's charges against the Enlightenment are most real. Systematic dogmatism, narrow rationalism, and shallow optimism could hardly be taken to greater lengths than in Helvétius's book *De l'esprit*. Yet Helvétius represented only one element in Enlightenment thought, and his theories were to some extent a reaction against its dominant temper. Moreover, not all of the charges apply. Helvétius, d'Holbach, and Bentham (at least in his early days) were no opponents of authority. They did not believe that the principles of social order were inherent in the individual, that men had some faculty or instinct which would lead them to appreciate and pursue the common good. In this respect, the individual was morally neutral and could serve as the tool of either a proper or a perverted social system. These writers were "rationalist" not because they believed in some universal *lumen naturale*, but because they were confident that the philosopher was capable of constructing a social and legal code which would fulfill the self-evident purpose of the community, while at the same time being compatible with the equally self-evident traits of human nature. There is little in this belief that is individualistic or democratic, and much that is authoritarian. The shadowy figure of "the Legislator" returns again and again in eighteenth century political writing, and, if he was not greeted so hysterically as was the "hero" of Carlyle or Nietzsche, he was nevertheless supposed to act the same Messianic role. Rousseau, anticipating once again the nineteenth century, looked for "a superior intelligence beholding all the passions of men without experiencing any of them," a god, understanding men yet not participating in their nature, whose reward lay in service and the expected approval of the future.[73] Even the prosaic Bentham could imply the need for the superior legislator who, above the normal egotism of men, would institute the reign of utility. Normally this authoritarian trend was transformed into a faith in enlightened despotism. The *philosophes* generally accepted the monarchy as the vehicle for

[73] *Social Contract*, Book ii, Chap. vii.

the reforms which explicitly or implicitly the Encyclopedia had demanded; Voltaire with his admiration for Louis XIV and Catherine exemplified this faith. In the German *Aufklärung*, the authoritarian tradition of the Cameralists and Seckendorf was carried on by Justi, and given its most complete practical embodiment in the government of Frederick the Great: even the most advanced German thinkers such as Möser and Schlözer asked only for a redirection of the policies of princes, a more enlightened absolutism. In England, Bentham pinned his hopes for legal reform on an enlightened aristocracy modeled on his patron, Shelburne.

The revolutionary "revolt against authority," which horrified Maistre so much, was in a sense accidental, for democratic aims were more the product of circumstance than a logical development of this strand of Enlightenment thought. In France the failure of the Physiocrats and the increasing distrust after 1789 of Louis XVI himself killed hopes that the ideal of "order" would be realized through the monarchy, and Bentham turned democrat only late in his career, when he became convinced that no legal reforms could be achieved within the existing constitutional system. Political democracy remained the means to an end: its ultimate purpose was the enthronement of "revolutionary virtue" or "the greatest happiness of the greatest number." Enlightened democracy, like enlightened monarchy, was single-minded and, of its nature, authoritarian.

While the Newtonian example led some thinkers to search for the ideal and ordered government and society, others were more solicitous of the empirical method. "I have drawn my principles, not from my prejudices, but from the nature of things," claimed Montesquieu of his *De l'esprit des lois*.[74] He wished to find the general laws hidden behind the variety and diversity of political and constitutional phenomena, but believed these laws could be discovered only by studying the observed facts of political life; they were only "the necessary relations deriving from the nature of things."[75] This determination to draw the unifying principles of social life solely from the investigation of the workings of society is seen at its clearest in Hume. He saw his task in the *Treatise of Human Nature* as "the application of experimental philosophy to moral subjects"; and this he believed could be achieved only by building the science of man on the solid foundation of "experi-

[74] *Spirit of the Laws*, Preface.
[75] *Ibid.*, Book i, Chap. i.

ence and observation."[76] This application of the Newtonian example formed a second and contrary, although by no means clearly defined, trend in Enlightenment thought. Its effect was to weaken rationalist thought in both its natural law and its utilitarian forms. For Hume, reason can concern itself only with the discovery of the relationship between ideas or with the verification from experience of the probable relationship of cause and effect; it cannot control either the will or the passions which direct the will. In moral terms, reason is neutral. "Moral distinctions . . . are not the offspring of reason. Reason is wholly inactive, and can never be the source of so active a principle as conscience, or a sense of morals."[77] In place of reason, Hume substituted convention as the defining factor in any moral code, and sentiment as the cause or occasion of moral judgment. The content of any particular social code is defined by the habitual and conventional standards of the society, not by its conformity to some objective and rational criteria of good and bad. The motives for men's adherence to a social code are emotional; vice and virtue are not objective facts in themselves but descriptions of feelings of approval or disapproval. For Hume, therefore, morality belonged to the world of action, not to that of philosophy and meditation. But this skepticism was not intended to overturn social morality or provide the fuel for a revolutionary fire; having refuted Christianity, he locked the refutation in a drawer. Morality, freed of its subjection to an objective rational order, became no less subject to the authority of social custom and convention. Hume's dual insistence on the relativity of social codes and the importance of convention and custom found many parallels in French thought and was to be re-embodied in Burke's attack upon the Revolution. Nevertheless his questioning of reason as the determinant of morality was symptomatic of a trend in eighteenth century thought which was to prove much more effective in laying the ideological foundations of the Revolution than the ultrarationalism of Helvétius, d'Holbach, or Bentham. If his insistence on the importance of custom as the main source of the moral order buttressed conservative conclusions, his stressing of the subjective and sentimental, as against the rational, basis of morality paved the way for Rousseau and the naturalistic ideas of the later part of the century. Although on occasions Hume depicted moral action as the product of the attraction to pleas-

[76] *Op. cit.*, Introduction.
[77] *Ibid.*, Book iii, Part i, Sec. i.

ure and aversion from pain, at least sufficiently for later English Utilitarians to regard him as one of their masters, there emerges generally in his work the idea of a moral sense, distinct both from reason and from self-interest, by which men regulate their moral action or judgment. This notion, which was sustained in English moral thought by the writings of Hutcheson, Ferguson, and Adam Smith, and was dominant in English aesthetics, found its first expression in Shaftesbury. For Shaftesbury, the appreciation of moral truths, like the appreciation of beauty, was neither a product of nor subject to rational analysis; it followed on an effort of the intuitive understanding, some sixth sense which caught the lights and shades of virtue and vice just as it unthinkingly distinguished the beautiful and the false in the act of artistic creation. Thus, Rousseau's apostrophes to conscience did not fall on unprepared ground. What shocked the Encyclopedists, Burke, and Dr. Johnson in Rousseau's early writings was not the dissociation of reason and morality, but the divorce of progress and civilization. Burke, who could satirize the idea of the man of nature,[78] could at the same time follow Shaftesbury's aesthetics in his essay *On the Sublime and Beautiful.*

This tendency toward subjectivism and antirationalism becomes dominant toward the end of the century. It was particularly strong in Germany, where the Pietist movement, with its emphasis on the inner life and the personal link between God and man, aroused the same faith in the individual conscience as the Genevan ethos had done in Rousseau. Taken to one extreme, this tendency manifested itself in primitivism, the taste for the unsophisticated or even the magical and occult, which was so fashionable in the years preceding the Revolution. Taken to another extreme, it led to the moral anarchism of the writers of the *Sturm und Drang,* of Byron and of Shelley, and to the search for the political embodiment of the Promethean man "equal, unclassed, tribeless and nationless, exempt from awe, worship, degree, the king over himself." Yet Rousseau and Kant, the greatest writers within this later eighteenth century movement, tried to avoid the mysticism and the anarchism of these two extremes, and to overcome the indiscipline of their basic assumptions, by assuming or arguing that the individual conscience either was, or should be treated as being, capable of realizing an objective moral order. Rousseau's faith that the general will embodied and enunciated such an objective order was so strong that

[78] Cf. *Vindication of Natural Society.*

he could dismiss the actual wills of men as being unreal and invalid so long as they conflicted with this order; and Kant's moral reason, although its source was the individual's capacity for making moral decisions and accepting self-imposed values independently of circumstance or environment, was at the same time firmly tied to an objective and universal right and wrong by the categorical imperative. In other words, the increasing subjectivism of moral thinking did not undermine, but fortified, the old natural-law and natural-rights ideas. Natural law was saved from the relativist tendencies of the age by transferring from the reason to the moral sentiments, from the mind to the heart, from culture to instinct, the power of discerning an immutable social morality.

In content, therefore, there is little breach between Rousseau and the natural-law thinkers; and of course the theory of natural rights gained its most signal victories in the American and French Declarations. What changed was not what sort of reforms were demanded, and what sort of claims were made on the community; these were dictated both by the concrete political and social circumstances of the time and by the long dictation of intellectual life by the Encyclopedists. The change lay rather in a swing of emphasis from the belief that progress could be achieved only through the diffusion of knowledge from the philosophers outward, toward the faith in the uncivilized, uncorrupted, instinctive, and even irrational judgments of "the natural man," the man outside society, interpreted as the man outside Society, the peasant[79]; and this faith was extended to the communal *élan* of the masses in which these judgments were expressed most ardently. By the end of the century, it is not the philosophers but the people, and those who claim to represent them, who are the vanguard of virtue.

If Maistre's picture of eighteenth century thought is partially justified by the writings of Helvétius and d'Holbach, it ignores this other development. Against this tradition, many of his own ideas, far from seeming novel, appear as emerging out of the age he was attacking.

The root demand of Enlightenment thought was for some principle of order in the moral as in the natural world, a demand which was not stifled in the later part of the century by the undermining of its rationalist basis. In spite of all the attacks upon reason and civilization in his early writings, Rousseau is still, in the *Social Contract*, searching for

---

[79] Cf. Rousseau: *Projet pour la Corse* in *The Political Writings* (ed. C. E. Vaughan, Oxford, 1962), Vol. ii, pp. 310–311.

the source of the moral unity of society. This demand sounds also in Maistre's work, but he looks for the principle of order in history, not philosophy. In history, men studied the concrete and the factual, the real stuff of life in all its contradictions, its variety, its individuality, its unpredictability, in all the complexity of human behavior and the mystery surrounding human ends: in philosophy, men sought for order and design, treated the particular and unique only as means to the general, relied exclusively on formal logic and rational analysis to explore the realms of truth and beauty, and, in doing all this, they lost touch with life itself and dried up that aesthetic and even religious sense which alone could find a meaning not beyond but in the flux of things. Yet, in practice, Maistre, like other romantic writers, took the panoramic rather than the particular view of history, seeking, not to describe and relate the unique event, but to find behind the sweep of history some logic, some divine pattern, that would satisfy the selfsame urge for design and order felt so strongly by Enlightenment thinkers. History was substituted for nature, but the object remained the same.

Whether it took shape in a faith in philosophic reason or in popular virtue, this late eighteenth century belief in a realizable principle of moral order raised high hopes of some static and perfect political order in the future. In much early nineteenth century thinking, these hopes were maintained, even when paradoxically combined with some form of historical determinism. On the one side there emerged the concentration on history as the key to political and social analysis, and on the other the objective of escaping from history by appreciating and dominating history's laws. If Hegel ends with an interpretation of freedom as the individual's self-conscious acceptance and mastery of the dialectical process, and Marx with humanity's leap from historical necessity to freedom, Maistre's work, too, is shot through with the longing, not for the peace of another world, but for the final resolution of conflict, doubt, and movement in this. Although he sees God's hand in both history and human suffering, his work is not finally fatalistic; if men would forswear pride, if they would recognize the signs that were granted to them, they could achieve the peace of a final order. Admittedly, this was not a world of perfection that could be hoped for, only perhaps "the best of all possible worlds" in which men would have the least possible scope to indulge their savage satanism, but at least it would be a world in which the flux and flow of things would be finally stilled, in which the harsh lessons of history would no longer be needed since they would have been learned.

In neither his historicism nor his hopes of escape from the historical process was Maistre the champion of Christian principles against atheism that he claimed to be. His thought is not strictly theological, nor, in spite of his deference to the Papacy, theocratic. He was not just trying to apply Christian or Catholic principles to a specific and limited field of human activity, politics, and to define Christian rights and duties within that field; and in only one work did he make anything like an approach to demanding control of secular government by the Church. He was translating, as the revolutionaries had done before him, theological and religious terms into political and historical discussion. If he did not, like the revolutionary philosophers, interpret the Heavenly City in secular terms, he used the ideas of the fall from grace and man's dualistic nature for political ends. He did not, for instance, follow Aquinas in seeing human laws as ideally declarations of divine justice, and in defending authority so far as it fulfilled this ideal (or so far as it obeyed the best interpreter of divine justice, the Church). Aquinas may not have been the first Whig, but these ideas left too many restrictions on authority, they were too concerned with the ends rather than the origin of power, for Maistre's taste. For him, authority was the hand of God, and was not to be called to account for the uses to which it was put or the laws which it enforced. This appeal to the divine origin of power was not, as was the Thomist theory, an assertion of the existence of a divine law over sovereigns, but an assertion of the freedom and irresponsibility of authority. Only revolutionary authority was excluded from this absolute defense, and this because it originated in a revolt against authority.

Maistre, like many late eighteenth century writers, secularized not only theological terminology but also religious emotion. What he and Rousseau had in common, in fact what characterized romantic political thinking generally, was not so much particular political attitudes as the general emotional intensity with which they invested the relationship between the individual and the state. For neither man was the question of political obligation a matter of convenience, nor was it, even for Maistre, part of a larger theological issue in which secular obligations were dictated by men's relations with God, the Church, or a particular religious creed. For both, political obligation was an end in itself, independent of both utility and wider moral duties; and both ended by advocating a political religion, an intensified and deepened attachment to and absorption in the state, which laid the foundation for nineteenth century nationalism.

Patriotism or "love of country" was a favorite phrase of eighteenth century writers, but was more closely associated with republican than with nationalist feeling. The ideal is set out clearly by Montesquieu. Among the principles which distinguish different forms of government, virtue is that which must necessarily be found in popular republics. The loose political framework of a republic would break beneath the weight of conflicting interests and ambitions unless it was protected by a universal love of the republic or love of *la patrie* (terms which Montesquieu regarded as synonymous).[80] This classical ideal of patriotism was an attachment, therefore, to certain political standards rather than to "the nation." As such, it was one of the guiding principles of the framers of the American Constitution, and survived until the French Revolution. Rousseau at times accepted this connection between patriotism and republican virtue, and in 1789 Price in his *Discourse on the Love of Our Country* maintained the same argument, that political loyalties were inspired by and should be proportionate to the constitutional virtue of the state. Even in Maistre himself there are survivals of Montesquieu's attitude when he admits that the perfect republic, if it could exist, would be the perfect state, since its existence would presuppose the complete diffusion of public spirit among its citizens.

This notion of patriotism was nevertheless undergoing a transformation in the late eighteenth century through its association, mainly under Rousseau's influence, with the idea of popular sovereignty. The usual eighteenth century view of sovereignty was that it consisted in common obedience to a ruler; and this was really the only feasible definition in a Europe whose state boundaries were fixed largely by dynastic considerations. This view was accepted by Maistre but had already been challenged by Rousseau. For Rousseau, sovereignty resided in the last resort in the general will of a society, the communal soul of a people, which distinguished it from other peoples and provided the moving impulse in its development. So "love of country" changed from attachment to a universal political ideal to the citizen's personal involvement in the moral and corporate consciousness of his own particular homeland, defined in national or racial terms.

[80] *Spirit of the Laws*, Book iii, Chap. iii; Book v, Chap. ii.

Despite their apparently complete disagreement on the definition of sovereignty, the differences between Rousseau and Maistre are in practice slight. Rousseau throws very little light on the question of how the sovereignty of the people is actually to be established, and the concrete conclusions that he comes to—that a representative chamber cannot embody or enunciate the general will, that popular sovereignty is suited only to small states and not to the great monarchies of his time, and that the best hopes for a perfect system of laws lay in the advent of a superhuman legislator—were not denied by Maistre. At bottom, Rousseau was as little concerned as Maistre with constitutional problems as such. Both were more anxious about the moral quality of communal life than about the source of sovereignty, and both judged that moral quality by the degree of emotional, unreasoned involvement in the community felt by the individual. For both, intensity and community of belief were more important than its objects. This emphasis on faith rather than on dogma was reflected in romantic religious writing. In *Le Génie du christianisme* Chateaubriand proved the "truth" of Christianity by pointing to its satisfaction of men's emotional and imaginative needs, and the German theologian Schleiermacher defended the unity of religions by stressing the common religious feelings which lay behind and overshadowed the varying and conflicting creeds. In Maistre, as in Rousseau, the same emphasis on emotional unity and disdain of the content of faith served nationalist rather than ecumenical ends, stressing the common faith of the nation rather than mankind. Rousseau would give to the state the power of defining the dogmas of the "civil religion" whose ends were the furtherance of political loyalty and unity of belief.[81] Government was, for Maistre, a religion, whose articles of faith were defined by the "national reason," and against which the individual should have no power of opposition; even his Catholicism is made subservient to this nationalist and *étatist* end, for as often as he treats Catholicism as a body of religious truths, he regards it as a peculiarly French faith pertaining to the French national soul and defining the French national mission. The terms have changed, but the language is that of Robespierre. Both revolutionary and counter-revolutionary rejected that separation of political and intellectual authority, which was, as Guizot and Comte were rightly to observe, the salient feature of Western European civilization.

Maistre also shared with Rousseau the conviction that this power of

<hr/>

[81] *Social Contract*, Book iv, Chap. viii.

perceiving and participating in the emotional unity of the nation lay in some inner light or divine instinct. As much as Rousseau or Robespierre, he wanted the reign of that eternal justice, the laws of which were "engraved not on marble or brass, but in the hearts of citizens." This change, so strikingly demonstrated by Rousseau and Maistre, prepared the ground for the anti-intellectualism of both right and left extremes during the nineteenth century, the *trahison des clercs* implicit in the exaltation of the earthy, taproots wisdom either of the peasant or of the proletarian masses.

As has been seen, Maistre reconciled this trust in the human potentiality for good with his view of history as the record of man's hubristic and unsuccessful attempts to rule his own destiny, by postulating a duality in human nature, but, like so many thinkers of the eighteenth century, he was not willing to accept this as a permanent schism. In asserting that the sorry world of the revolutionary present was impermanent and eradicable, he was driven to envisaging both the possibility of escape from the grip of history and also a previous state of mankind when it had been free of the fateful combination of ignorance and pride. Rousseau had been caught in the same ambivalent attitude toward past and future. Appealing in the *Social Contract* to a future when social bonds would be intensified and purified, he had yet yearned in his early works toward a past when man was still uncorrupted by his entry into social relations. Maistre's Golden Age was even less related to any historical reality than the romantic medievalism so attractive to many reactionary writers. Like Rousseau's state of nature, it was little more than a device by which to criticize present degeneracy. It was a strange reversal of the biblical story. Man's fall was marked not by the eating of the fruit from the tree of knowledge but by his loss of knowledge; ignorance, not knowledge, was the basis of sin. Here Maistre is much closer to eighteenth century ideas of the state of nature than to the Christian idea of the Fall. That he himself felt this parallel is suggested by his desperate and ultimately unsuccessful attempts to dissociate his own view of the primitive state of man from that of eighteenth century writers, especially Rousseau. Primitive man, he argued, was the noble creature of pre-Deluge times, but the men whom Rousseau and his followers admired were not the primitives but the savages, the backward peoples of the contemporary world, who were in truth plunged in an even deeper slough of moral sickness than civilized man. Just as there were two kinds of physical sickness, illness and infirmity, so there were two kinds of moral sickness, the ordinary state of human imperfection and an absolute state of degradation occasioned by some absolute sin in the past; this last was the state of the savage whom Rousseau had labeled "noble."[82] If this sophistical argument has some relevance to Chateaubriand's idealization of the North American Indian, it patently falsifies Rousseau's intentions. Rousseau spoke as a moralist, not as an anthropologist, and his description of an ideal past was meant to criticize existing society much more than to describe an actual historical state. In this, there is very little difference between the two writers.

Maistre saw Rousseau as one of the archvillains of his century of villains. Although he quotes him several times with approval, he does this with surprise that so much good sense should have come from the man who, more than any other, symbolized the self-will and pride of his age. Rousseau was the democrat who, appealing to the illusory right of self-government and to the state of nature in which that independence had been complete, had shaped the revolutionary challenge to all established authorities. Yet it can be seen that Maistre shared many basic assumptions and emotional attitudes with Rousseau, and with the eighteenth century tradition of thought of which Rousseau was the most positive and influential spokesman. His ultimate object, like Rousseau's, was to resolve the conflict between man's self-will and his social nature, to release the capacity for virtue frustrated by existing civilization, to reestablish a state of harmony lost through the persistent exercise of self-will. For both, this vision involved sacrifices by the individual rather than restrictions on the state. Freedom from the domination of the passions or self-interest or pride it might be called, but in reality it required the willing subordination of men to authorities whose moral justification consisted, in the last resort, not in what they aimed at, but in the unity they enforced, the stifling of doubt they demanded, and the certainty and freedom from responsibility they promised. In both, personal insecurity led to the fruitless quest for the politics of absolute security.

There is therefore a strong link of kinship between Maistre and the tradition of thought he attacked so violently. He was not the simple defender of established beliefs and authorities, nor merely the advocate of an empirical social science. His ideas were as novel as those of the revolutionaries, and novel in many of the same ways. If it is born

[82] *Saint Petersburg Dialogues,* pp. 196–197, 202–204.

of the recognition of differences, hatred is often nurtured by the reali-
zation of similarities, and Maistre's ferocious contempt for the Enlightenment hides similarities as much as it reveals differences. One of the
first, the most influential and the most original of reactionary thinkers,
he illustrates also the closeness of the right and left political extremes
in modern political thinking.

Considerations on France

We are all bound to the throne of the Supreme Being by a flexible chain which restrains without enslaving us. The most wonderful aspect of the universal scheme of things is the action of free beings under divine guidance. Freely slaves, they act at once of their own will and under necessity: they actually do what they wish without being able to disrupt general plans. Each of them stands at the center of a sphere of activity whose diameter varies according to the decision of the *eternal geometry*, which can extend, restrict, check, or direct the will without altering its nature.

In the works of man, everything is as poor as its author; vision is confined, means are limited, scope is restricted, movements are labored, and results are humdrum. In divine works, boundless riches reveal themselves even in the smallest component; its power operates effortlessly: in its hands everything is pliant, nothing can resist it; everything is a means, nothing an obstacle: and the irregularities produced by the work of free agents come to fall into place in the general order.

If one imagines a watch all of whose springs continually vary in power, weight, dimension, form, and position, and which nevertheless invariably shows the right time, one can get some idea of the action of free beings in relation to the plans of the Creator.

In the political and moral world, as in the physical, there is a usual order and there are exceptions to this order. Normally, we see a series of effects following the same causes; but in certain ages we see usual effects suspended, causes paralyzed and new consequences emerging.

A *miracle* is an effect produced by a divine or superhuman cause which suspends or is inconsistent with an ordinary cause. If in the middle of winter a man, before a thousand witnesses, orders a tree to cover itself suddenly with leaves and fruit, and if the tree obeys, everyone will proclaim a miracle and prostrate themselves before the thaumaturge. But the French Revolution, as well as everything that is happening in Europe at this time, is just as miraculous in its way as the instant fructification of a tree in January; yet men ignore it or talk nonsense about it, instead of admiring. In the physical order, into which man does not intrude as a cause, he is quite ready to admire what he does not understand; but in the sphere of his own activity, where he feels he acts freely as a cause, his pride easily leads him to see *disorder* wherever his own power is suspended or upset.

Certain actions within the power of man regularly produce certain effects in the ordinary course of events; if he misses his mark, he knows, or thinks he knows, why; he recognizes the difficulties, he appreciates them, and nothing astonishes him. But in revolutionary times, the chain that binds man is shortened abruptly, his field of action is cut down, and his means deceive him. Carried along by an unknown force, he rails against it, and instead of kissing the hand that clasps him, he ignores or insults it.

I don't understand anything is the popular catchphrase. The phrase is very sensible if it leads us to the root cause of the great sight now presented to men; it is stupid if it expresses only spleen or sterile despondency. The cry is raised on all sides, "How then can the guiltiest men in the world triumph over the world? A hideous regicide has all the success for which its perpetrators could have hoped. Monarchy is dormant all over Europe. Its enemies find allies even on thrones themselves. The wicked are successful in everything. They carry through the most immense projects without difficulty, while the righteous are unfortunate and ridiculous in everything they undertake. Opinion runs against faith throughout Europe. The foremost statesmen continually fall into error. The greatest generals are humiliated. And so on."

Doubtless, because its primary condition lays it down, there are no means of preventing a revolution, and no success can attend those who wish to impede it. But never is purpose more apparent, never is Providence more palpable, than when divine replaces human action and works alone. That is what we see at this moment.

The most striking aspect of the French Revolution is this overwhelming force which turns aside all obstacles. Its current carries away like a straw everything human power has opposed to it. No one has run counter to it unpunished. Purity of motive has been able to make resistance honorable, but that is all; and this jealous force, moving inexorably to its objective, rejects equally Charette, Dumouriez, and Drouet.

It has been said with good reason that the French Revolution leads men more than men lead it. This observation is completely justified; and, although it can be applied more or less to all great revolutions, yet it has never been more strikingly illustrated than at the present time. The very villains who appear to guide the Revolution take part in it only as simple instruments; and as soon as they aspire to dominate it, they fall ingloriously. Those who established the Republic did so without wishing it and without realizing what they were creating; they have been led by events: no plan has achieved its intended end.

Never did Robespierre, Collot, or Barère think of establishing the revolutionary government or the Reign of Terror; they were led imperceptibly by circumstances, and such a sight will never be seen again. Extremely mediocre men are exercising over a culpable nation the most heavy despotism history has seen, and, of everyone in the kingdom, they are certainly the most astonished at their power.

But at the very moment when these tyrants have committed every crime necessary to this phase of the Revolution, a breath of wind topples them. This gigantic power, before which France and Europe trembled, could not stand before the first gust; and because there could be no possible trace of greatness or dignity in such an entirely criminal revolution, Providence decreed that the first blow should be struck by the Septembrists, so that justice itself might be degraded.

It is often astonishing that the most mediocre men have judged the French Revolution better than the most talented, that they have believed in it strongly while skilled men of affairs were still unbelievers. This conviction was one of the foremost elements of the Revolution, which could succeed only because of the extent and vigor of the revolutionary spirit or, if one can so express it, because of the revolutionary *faith*. So untalented and ignorant men have ably driven what they call *the revolutionary chariot*; they have all ventured without fear of counter-revolution; they have always driven on without looking behind them; and everything has fallen into their lap because they were only the instruments of a force more farsighted than themselves. They have taken no false steps in their revolutionary career, for the same reason that the flutist of Vaucanson never played a false note.

The revolutionary current has taken successively different courses; and the most prominent revolutionary leaders have acquired the kind of power and renown appropriate to them only by following the demands of the moment. Once they attempted to oppose it or even to turn it from its predestined course, by isolating themselves and following their own bent, they disappeared from the scene. . . .

In short, the more one examines the apparently more active personalities of the Revolution, the more one finds something passive and mechanical about them. It cannot be too often repeated that men do not at all guide the Revolution; it is the Revolution that uses men. It is well said that it has its own impetus. This phrase shows that never has the Divinity revealed itself so clearly in any human event. If it employs the most vile instruments, it is to regenerate by punishment.

CHAPTER II. THOUGHTS ON THE WAYS OF PROVIDENCE
IN THE FRENCH REVOLUTION

Every nation, like every individual, has a mission which it must fulfill. It would be futile to deny that France exercises a dominant influence over Europe, an influence she has abused most culpably. Above all, she was at the head of the religious system, and it was not without reason that her king was called *most Christian*: Bossuet has not overstressed this point. However, as she has used her influence to pervert her vocation and to demoralize Europe, it is not surprising that terrible means must be used to set her on her true course again.

It is long since such an appalling punishment has been seen, visited on so many sinners. No doubt there are innocent people among the unfortunates, but they are far fewer than is commonly imagined.

All those who have worked to separate the people from their religious beliefs; all those who have opposed metaphysical sophistries to the laws of property; all those who have said, "Attack anything, so long as we gain by it"; all those who have meddled with the fundamental laws of the state; all those who have recommended, approved, favored the violent methods used against the king; even our restricted vision can perceive that all these have willed the Revolution, and all who willed it have most appropriately been its victims.

It is frightening to see distinguished intellectuals fall under Robespierre's ax. From a humane standpoint they can never be too much mourned, but divine justice is no respecter of mathematicians or scientists. Too many French intellectuals were instrumental in bringing about the Revolution; too many approved and encouraged it so long as, like Tarquin's wand, it cut off only the ruling heads. Like so many others, they said, *A great revolution cannot come about without some distress.* But when a thinker justifies such means by the end in view; when he says in his heart, *A hundred thousand murders are as nothing, provided we are free;* then, if Providence replies, *I accept your recommendation, but you shall be one of the victims,* where is the injustice? Would we judge otherwise in our own courts?

The details would be odious; but, among those who are called innocent victims of the Revolution, it is not much of a Frenchman whose conscience would not remind him:

> *Now you see the sad fruits that your faults have produced,*
> *You can feel the blows that you yourselves have induced.*

Our ideas on good and evil, on innocence and guilt, are too often affected by our prejudices. We frown on men who fight with daggers, but a duel with swords is considered honorable. We brand a man who steals a halfpenny from a friend, but think it nothing if he steals his wife. We pardon even if we do not make a virtue of all those flashy offenses involving great or likable qualities, above all those rewarded by success: whereas, the brilliant qualities which surround the guilty man blacken him in the eyes of true justice, for whom his greatest crime is the abuse of his gifts.

Every man has certain duties to perform, and the extent of these duties depends on his position in society and the extent of his means. The same action is by no means equally culpable when committed by two different men. Not to stray from our subject, the same act which results only from a mistake or a foolish characteristic in an obscure person, thrust suddenly into unlimited power, could be a foul crime in a bishop or a duke or a peer.

Indeed, some actions, which are excusable and even praiseworthy from an ordinary point of view, are fundamentally infinitely criminal. For example, if someone says, *I have espoused the cause of the French Revolution in good faith, through a pure love of liberty and my country; I have believed in my soul and conscience that it would lead to the reform of abuses and to the general good,* we have nothing to say in reply. But the eye of him who sees into every heart discerns the stain of sin; he discovers in a ridiculous misunderstanding, in a small puncturing of pride, in a base or criminal passion, the prime moving force behind those ambitions we wish to present to the world as noble: and for him the crime is compounded by grafting the falsehood of hypocrisy onto treason. But let us look at the nation in general.

One of the greatest possible crimes is undoubtedly an attack upon sovereignty, no other having such terrible consequences. If sovereignty resides in one man and this man falls victim to an outrage, the crime of lese-majesty augments the atrocity. But if this sovereign has not deserved his fate through any fault of his own, if his very virtues have strengthened the guilty against him, the crime is beyond description. This is the case in the death of Louis XVI; but what is important to note is that *never has such a great crime had more accomplices.* The death of Charles I had far fewer, even though it was possible to bring charges against him that Louis XVI did not merit. Yet many proofs were given of the most tender and courageous concern for him; even the executioner, who was obliged to obey, did not dare to make himself known. But in France, Louis XVI marched to his death in the middle of 60,000 armed men who did not have a single shot for their king, not a voice was raised for the unfortunate monarch, and the provinces were as silent as the capital. *We would expose ourselves,* it was said. Frenchmen—if you find this a good reason, talk no more of your courage or admit that you misuse it!

The indifference of the army was no less remarkable. It served the executioners of the king much better than it had served the king himself since it had betrayed him. It never showed the slightest sign of discontent. In sum, never have so many taken part in such a great crime (although no doubt in varying degrees).

It is necessary to add one important remark: it is that every offense committed against sovereignty, *in the name of the nation,* is always to a greater or lesser degree a national crime, since it is always to some degree the fault of the nation if any faction whatever is put in a position to commit the crime in its name. Thus, although no doubt not all Frenchmen have willed the death of Louis XVI, the immense majority of the people have for more than two years willed all the follies, injustices and offenses leading up to the catastrophe of January 21st.

Now, every national crime against sovereignty is punished swiftly and terribly; that is a law without exception. Not many days after the death of Louis XVI, someone wrote in the *Mercure universel*, "Perhaps it was not necessary go to so far; but since our legislators have taken this act on their shoulders, let us rally round them: let us smother all hatreds and question it no longer." Good—it was not perhaps necessary to assassinate the king, but since the deed is done, let us talk of it no more and let us all be good friends. What madness! Shakespeare showed more understanding when he said:

> "The single and peculiar life is bound,
> With all the strength and armour of the mind,
> To keep itself from noyance; but much more
> That spirit upon whose weal depend and rest
> The lives of many. The cease of majesty
> Dies not alone; but, like a gulf, doth draw
> What's near it with it."[1]

Each drop of Louis XVI's blood will cost France torrents; perhaps four million Frenchmen will pay with their lives for the great national crime of an antireligious and antisocial insurrection, crowned by a regicide.

Where are the first national guards, the first soldiers, the first generals who swore an oath to the nation? Where are the leaders, the idols of that first guilty Assembly, for whom the epithet *constituent* will stand as a perpetual epigraph? Where is Mirabeau, where is Bailly with his "beautiful day"? Where is Thouret who invented the term "to expropriate"? Where is Osselin who reported to the Assembly on the first law proscribing the émigrés? The names of revolutionary activists who have died a violent death would be numbered in the thousands.

Yet it is here that we can appreciate order in disorder; because it is evident, however little one reflects on it, that the great criminals of the Revolution can fall only under the blows of their accomplices. If force alone were to bring about what is called the *counter-revolution* and replace the king on the throne, there would be no means of doing justice. For a sensitive man, the greatest misfortune would be to judge the murderer of his father, relatives, and friends or even the usurper of his property. However, this is precisely what would happen in the case of a counter-revolution, as the word is understood, because the higher judges, by the very nature of things, would belong to the injured class, and justice, even when it was aimed only at punishment, would have the air of vengeance. Moreover, legitimate authority always retains some moderation in the punishment of crimes in which large numbers have been involved. When it executes five or six crimi-

[1] *Hamlet,* Act III, Scene iii.

nals for the same crime, this becomes a massacre; if it goes beyond certain limits, it becomes detestable. In short, great crimes unfortunately demand great punishments; and in this way it is easy to pass the limits when it is a question of crimes of lese-majesty and flattery becomes the executioner. Would the sacred sword of justice have fallen as relentlessly as Robespierre's guillotine? Would all the executioners of the kingdom and every artillery horse have been summoned to Paris in order to quarter men? Would lead and tar have been melted in vast boilers to sprinkle on limbs torn by red-hot tongs? Moreover, how could different crimes be characterized? How could punishments be graduated? And above all how could punishments be imposed without laws? It might be said that *some of the most guilty would have to be chosen and all the rest would have to be pardoned.* This is precisely what Providence would not wish. Since it is omnipotent, it is ignorant of pardons produced by inability to punish. The great purification must be accomplished and eyes must be opened; the French metal, cleared of its sour and impure dross, must become cleaner and more malleable to a future king. Doubtless in times past Providence had no need to punish in order to justify its courses; but in this age, it puts itself within our range of understanding and punishes like a human tribunal.

There have been nations literally condemned to death like guilty individuals, and we can understand the reasons for this. If it was part of God's designs to reveal to us his intentions with regard to the French Revolution, we should read the chastisement of the French as if it were a legal decree. But what should we understand beyond this? Is not this chastisement apparent? Have we not seen France dishonored by a hundred thousand murders? The whole territory of this fair kingdom covered with scaffolds? And this unhappy land drenched with the blood of its children through judicial massacres, while inhuman tyrants squandered it abroad in a cruel war, sustained in their own private interests? Never has the bloodiest despot gambled with men's lives with so much insolence, and never has an apathetic people presented itself for butchering more willingly. Sword and fire, frost and famine, privations and sufferings of every kind, none of these disgust it with its punishment: everything that is laid down must accomplish its destiny: there will be no disobedience until the judgment is fulfilled.

Yet, in this cruel and disastrous war, there are points of interest, and admiration follows grief turn by turn. Let us take the most terrible epoch of the Revolution; let us suppose that, under the government of the diabolical Committee of Public Safety, the army by a startling change became suddenly royalist; let us suppose that it rallied the primary assemblies to its side and freely named the worthiest and most enlightened men to guide it in this difficult position; let us suppose, finally, that one of these representatives of the army rose and said:

"Brave and loyal soldiers, there are occasions when all human wisdom is reduced to choosing between different evils. It is no doubt hard to fight for the Committee of Public Safety, but it would be yet more disastrous to turn our arms against it. The moment the army meddles in politics, the state will be dissolved and the enemies of France, profiting from this period of disorder, will invade and divide it. We must act, not for the moment, but for the future: above all, the integrity of France must be maintained, and this we can do only by fighting for the government, whatever it may be; because by these means France, in spite of her internal dissensions, will preserve her military power and international influence. To press the point home, it is not for the government that we fight, but for France and for the future king, who will be indebted to us for an empire much greater perhaps than that found by the Revolution. It is therefore our duty to overcome the repugnance which makes us hesitate. Perhaps our contemporaries will calumniate our conduct, but posterity will do us justice."

This man would have spoken very wisely. In fact, the army has appreciated this hypothetical argument without knowing it; and the terror on the one hand and immorality and extravagance on the other, have done precisely what a consummate and almost prophetic wisdom would have dictated to the army. Fundamentally, it can be seen that, the revolutionary movement once having taken root, France and the monarchy could be saved only by Jacobinism.

The king has never had an ally; although he was never imprudent enough to state the fact, it is quite evident that the coalition had no love for French territorial integrity. However, how was the coalition to be resisted? By what supernatural means could the European conspiracy be broken? Only the evil genius of Robespierre could achieve this miracle. The revolutionary government hardened the French spirit, by drenching it in blood: it heightened soldiers' morale and doubled their power by a ferocious despair and contempt for life which derived from fury. The horror of the gallows, pushing the citizen to the frontiers, built up military strength in proportion as it destroyed the least internal resistance. Every life, all wealth, every power was in the hands of the revolutionary government; and this Leviathan, drunk with blood and success, the most appalling phenomenon ever seen and doubtless that ever will be seen, was both a frightful punishment of the French and the only means of saving France.

What were the royalists asking for when they demanded a counter-revolution such as they envisaged, that is to say, brought about suddenly and by force? They were asking for the conquest of France, and therefore for its division, the destruction of its influence and the abasement of its king, that is to say, perhaps three centuries of massacre, the inevitable result of such a breakdown of equilibrium. But our descendants, who will not bother themselves much with our sufferings and will dance on our graves, will laugh at our present ignorance; they will easily console themselves for the excesses that we have seen, and which have conserved the integrity "of the most beautiful kingdom after that of Heaven."[2]

It seems that all the monsters spawned by the Revolution have worked only for the monarchy. Through them, the luster of victories has won the world's admiration and has surrounded the name of France with a glory not entirely dimmed by the crimes of the Revolution; through them, the king will return to the throne with all his brilliance and power, perhaps even with an increase in power. And who knows if, instead of miserably sacrificing some of his provinces to obtain the right of ruling over the others, he will not be restored with the pride of power which gives what it can withhold? Certainly, less probable things have been seen to happen.

This same idea that everything works for the advantage of the French monarchy leads me to believe that any royalist revolution is impossible before the war ends; for the restoration of the Crown would weaken suddenly the whole machinery of the state. The black magic operating at this moment would vanish like a mist before the sun. Kindness, clemency, justice, all the gentle and peaceful virtues would suddenly reappear and bring back with them a certain general gentleness of character, a certain cheerfulness entirely opposed to the somber rigor of the revolutionary regime. No more requisitions, no more legal thefts, no more violence. Would the generals, preceded by the white

[2] Grotius, *Rights of War and Peace*, Dedication to Louis XIII.

flag, call *revolutionary* the inhabitants of the invaded areas who legitimately defended themselves? And would they enjoin them not to
move on pain of being shot as rebels? These horrors, very useful to the
future king, could not, however, be employed by him; he would then
have only human means at his disposal. He would be on a level with
his enemies; and what would happen at that moment of suspension
which necessarily accompanies the transition from one government to
another? I do not know. I am well aware that the great conquests of
the French seem to put the integrity of the kingdom beyond dispute.
(I even intend to touch here on the reason for these conquests.) However it still appears more advantageous to France and the monarchy
that peace, and a glorious peace for the French, should be achieved by
the Republic, and that, when the king returns to the throne, a stable
peace should remove him from every kind of danger.

On the other hand, it is clear that a violent revolution, far from curing the people, would confirm them in their errors and they would
never pardon the power that snatched their dreams from them. Since
it was the *people*, properly speaking, or the masses, that the rebels
needed to overturn France, it is evident that in general they have had
to spare the people and that the heaviest burdens have had to fall first
of all on the wealthy class. Thus the usurping power needs to weigh
for some time on the people in order to disgust them with it. They have
only seen the Revolution; they must feel it and enjoy, so to speak, its
bitter consequences. Perhaps, at the moment when I write, this is not
yet sufficiently the case. . . .

Let us now glance at the outrageous persecution stirred up against
the national religion and its ministers: it is one of the most interesting
facets of the Revolution.

It cannot be denied that the French clergy was in need of reform;
and, though I am very far from taking up the vulgar attacks on the
clergy, nonetheless it appears to me incontestable that wealth, luxury,
and a general tendency toward laxity had lowered this great body of
men; that it was often possible to find under the surplice a man of the
world rather than an apostle; and finally that, in the years immediately
before the Revolution, the clergy had fallen, almost as much as the
army, from the place it had occupied in public esteem.

The first blow aimed at the Church was the appropriation of its
estates; the second was the constitutional oath; and these two tyrannical measures started the reformation. The oath screened the priests,

if it can be so expressed. All who took it, save a few exceptions whom we can ignore, saw themselves led by stages into the abyss of crime and disgrace; opinion has only one view of these apostates.

The faithful priests, recommended to this same opinion by an initial act of firmness, won even more renown by the bravery with which they have been able to bear sufferings and even death in defense of their faith. The massacre of Carmes is comparable in its beauty to anything of this sort that ecclesiastical history can offer.

No more revolting tyranny can be imagined than that which expelled them from their country by thousands, against all justice and decency; but on this point, as in all the others, the crimes of the French tyrants became the weapons of Providence. It was probably necessary for French priests to be shown to foreign nations; they have lived among Protestant peoples, and this closeness has greatly diminished hatreds and prejudices. The considerable migration of the clergy, and particularly of the French bishops, to England especially seems to me a remarkable event. Surely words of peace will have been spoken and schemes of rapprochement formed during this remarkable reunion. Even if only common hopes were created, this would still be a great deal. If ever Christians draw together, as everyone asks them to, it seems that the impulse must come from the Church of England. Presbyterianism was a French, and consequently an exaggerated, creation. We stand too far away from the adherents of this insubstantial religion; there are no means of communication between us. But the Anglican Church, which touches us with one hand, touches with the other those whom we cannot approach; and although, from a certain point of view, it is exposed to attacks from the two sides, and although it presents the slightly ridiculous sight of a rebel who preaches obedience, it is nevertheless very valuable from another standpoint and can be seen as a catalyst, capable of combining elements incompatible of themselves.

The property of the clergy having been dissipated, no despicable motive can for a long time to come attract new members to it: so that everything combines to revive the clergy. There is reason to believe, moreover, that the contemplation of the work with which it is charged will give to it a degree of exaltation which raises men above themselves and makes them capable of great things.

Add to these circumstances the ferment of ideas in certain European countries, the inspiring opinions of several great men, and that kind of disquiet which is affecting religious people, especially in Protestant countries, and is pushing them along unwonted paths.

Notice at the same time the storm rumbling over Italy, Rome menaced as well as Geneva by the power that wants the destruction of all sects, and the national supremacy of religion abolished in Holland by a decree of the National Convention. If Providence *deletes,* it is no doubt in order to *rewrite.*

I notice that when great systems of belief have established themselves in the world, they have been favored by great conquests in the formation of great sovereignties, and the reason can clearly be seen.

How indeed have these remarkable schemes which have baffled all human foresight come about in one day? In truth, there is a temptation to believe that political revolution is only a secondary object of the great plan which is developing before our eyes with such terrible majesty.

I talked, at the beginning, of the leadership that France exercises over the rest of Europe. Providence, which always fits means to ends and gives to nations, as to individuals, the instruments necessary to accomplish their destiny, has in this way given to the French nation two weapons and, so to speak, two hands with which to mold the world, its language and the spirit of proselytism that forms the core of its character; so that it has always the ability and the wish to influence other men.

The power, I almost said the *royalty,* of the French language is apparent; this cannot be seriously disputed. As for the spirit of proselytism, it is as obvious as the sun; from the dress designer to the philosopher, it is the foremost trait of the national character.

This proselytism is commonly ridiculed, and really it often merits it, particularly in the forms it takes, but fundamentally it has a *function.*

It is a constant law of the moral world that every *function* produces a duty. The Gallican Church was the cornerstone of the Catholic system or, more properly, since there is in truth only one system, the Christian system. Although perhaps they doubt it, the Churches opposing the universal Church exist only by virtue of it, being like those parasitic plants, those sterile mistletoes which draw their nurture from and weaken the tree that supports them.

From the fact that the action and reaction of opposing powers is always equal, the greatest efforts of the goddess of Reason against Christianity were made in France; the enemy attacked the citadel.

The French clergy should not therefore fall asleep; it has a thousand reasons for believing that it is called to a high destiny; and the same arguments that show it why it is suffering allow it also to believe itself fated for a crucial task.

In a word, if a moral revolution does not occur in Europe, if religious feeling is not strengthened in this part of the world, the social bond will be destroyed. Nothing can be predicted, and anything may be expected. But if any change for the better does come, either analogies, induction, and conjectural skills are useless or else it is France that is called to produce the change.

This is above all what leads me to believe that the French Revolution is a watershed in history and that its consequences of every kind will be felt far beyond the time of its outburst and the limits of its birthplace.

Political considerations confirm this view. How many European powers have deceived themselves over France! How many have dreamed up vain endeavors! You who think yourselves free because you have no judges on this earth, never say: *This suits me;* DISCITE JUSTITIAM MONITI! What hand, at once severe and paternal, scourged France with every imaginable plague, and held sway with supernatural means by turning every effort of its enemies against themselves? Let no one come to speak to us of assignats and the power of numbers, for the possibility of assignats and of the power of numbers is itself the work of the supernatural. Moreover it is neither through paper money nor through numerical advantage that the winds guided the French ships and thrust back those of their enemies; that winter gave the French bridges of ice just when they needed them; that kings who impede them die conveniently; that they invade Italy without artillery, and that the most reputedly brave armies of the world, although equal in number, throw down their arms and allow themselves to be taken captives. . . .

In fact, the punishment of the French breaks all the ordinary rules, as does also the protection accorded to France: but these two miracles combined serve to reinforce one another, and present one of the most astonishing sights of human history.

As events unfold, other and more wonderful reasons and relationships will show themselves. Moreover, I see only a fraction of those which a more perceptive insight could have discovered at this time.

The horrible effusion of human blood caused by this great upheaval is a terrible means, yet it is a means as much as a punishment, and can give rise to some interesting reflections.

CHAPTER III. OF THE VIOLENT DESTRUCTION OF HUMANITY

Unhappily, that king of Dahomey, in the interior of Africa, was not so very wrong when he said a short time ago to an Englishman; *God made the world for war; all kingdoms, both great and small, have indulged in it at all times, although on different principles.*[3]

History proves unfortunately that war is in a sense the habitual condition of mankind, that is to say that human blood must constantly flow somewhere or other on earth; and that for every nation peace is no more than a respite.

The closing of the temple of Janus under Augustus can be cited, as also can the one year in the stormy reign of Charlemagne (the year 790) when there was no war. There can be quoted a short period after the Peace of Ryswick in 1697, and another equally short after the Peace of Carlowitz in 1699, in which there was peace, not only throughout Europe but even in the whole of the known world. But these periods are only isolated exceptions. And who can know what is happening over the whole globe at a given time?

The century which is ending started for France with a bloody war which ended only in 1714 with the Treaty of Rastadt. In 1719, France declared war on Spain; the Treaty of Paris put an end to it in 1727. The election to the Polish throne rekindled war in 1733; peace came in 1736. Four years later, the terrible war of the Austrian Succession broke out and lasted without break until 1748. Eight years of peace started to heal the wounds of eight years of war, when English ambition forced France to take up arms. The Seven Years' War is only too well known. After fifteen years' respite, the American Revolution dragged France once more into a war whose consequences no human wisdom could have foreseen. Peace was signed in 1782; seven years later, the Revolution started; it has lasted to this day and has so far cost France three million men.

[3] Archibald Dalzel, "The History of Dahomey," *Bibliothèque Britannique*, May, 1796, Vol. II, No. 1, p. 87.

Thus, looking at France alone, here are forty years of war out of ninety-six. If some nations have been more fortunate, others have been much less so.

But it is not enough to consider one point in time and one place on earth; a quick glance should be thrown on that long sequence of massacres which has soiled every page of history. War has raged ceaselessly like a persistent fever marked by terrifying crises. . . .

If one goes back to the childhood of nations or if one comes down to our own day, if one looks at societies in every possible stage of development from barbarism to the most advanced civilization, war will always be found. Through this primary cause and all the others connected with it, the spilling of human blood has never ceased on earth. At one time it flows thinly over a wide area, at another it flows fast in a restricted area, so that it remains about constant. But occasionally unusual events come about which augment the flow prodigiously, like the Punic Wars, the Triumvirates, the victories of Caesar, the barbarian invasions, the Crusades, the wars of religion, the Spanish Succession, the French Revolution, and so on. If tables of massacre were available like meteorological tables, who knows if some law might not be discovered after centuries of observation? Buffon has very clearly shown that a great number of animals are destined for a violent death. He could apparently have extended this argument to man; but the facts speak for themselves.

There is, moreover, good reason for doubting if this violent destruction is in general as great an evil as is believed; at least, it is one of those evils that play a part in an order of things in which everything is violent and *against nature* and which has its compensations. First, when the human spirit has lost its resilience through indolence, incredulity, and the gangrenous vices that follow an excess of civilization, it can be retempered only in blood. It is far from easy to explain why war produces different effects in different circumstances. What is sufficiently clear is that humanity can be considered as a tree that an invisible hand is continually pruning, often to its benefit. In fact, if its trunk is hacked or if it is pruned badly, a tree can die, but who knows the limits for the human tree? What we do know is that a great deal of bloodshed is often connected with a high population, as has been seen particularly in the ancient Greek republics and in Spain under Arab domination. The platitudes on war mean nothing: no great intelligence is needed to know that the more men killed, the fewer at that moment remain, just as the more branches are cut, the fewer remain on the tree. It is the results of the operation that must be considered. However, to stick to the comparison, the skilled gardener prunes less to ensure growth as such than to ensure the fructification of the tree; he requires fruit, and not wood or leaves from the plant. Now the true fruits of human nature—the arts, sciences, great enterprises, noble ideas, manly virtues—spring above all from the state of war. It is well known that nations reach the apex of the greatness of which they are capable only after long and bloody wars. Thus the most glorious hour of the Greeks was the terrible era of the Peloponnesian War; the Age of Augustus followed immediately the civil war and proscriptions; the French genius was roughhewn by the League and polished by the Fronde; all the great men of the age of Queen Anne were born amidst political upheavals. In a word, it could be said that blood is the manure of that plant we call *genius*.

I am not sure if those who claim that *the arts are the friends of peace* know what they are saying. At the least, this proposition would have to be explained and limited; because I see nothing in the least peaceful in the ages of Alexander and Pericles, of Augustus, of Leo X and Francis I, of Louis XIV and Queen Anne.

Is it possible that the spilling of human blood has not had a great cause and great effects? Let us reflect on it; history and myth, the discoveries of modern psychology and ancient traditions, unite to provide materials for these reflections. We should not be more ashamed to proceed cautiously on this point than on a thousand others less relevant to man. Let us still thunder against war and try to turn sovereigns from it, but let us not share the imaginings of Condorcet, the philosopher so dear to the Revolution, who spent his life preparing the misfortune of the "perfection" we now possess, benignly leaving the future to our ancestors. There is only one way of restraining the scourge of war, and that is by restraining the disorders that lead to this terrible purification. . . .

I know very well that, in all these discussions, we are assailed continually with the wearisome picture of the innocents who perish with the guilty. But, without penetrating far into this extremely profound question, it can be considered solely in its relation to the universally held dogma, as old as the world itself, *that the innocent suffer for the benefit of the guilty.*

It seems to me that it was from this dogma that the ancients derived the custom of sacrifices that they practiced throughout the world and that they judged useful not only to the living but still more to the dead, a typical custom that habit has made us regard without astonishment, but whose roots are nonetheless difficult to trace.

The self-sacrifices, so famous in antiquity, spring again from the same dogma. Decius believed that the sacrifice of his life would be accepted by the Divinity and that he could redress the balance for all the evils that threatened his country.

Christianity consecrated this dogma, which is completely natural to men, although it appears difficult to arrive at by reasoning.

Thus, there could have been in the heart of Louis XVI, in that of the saintly Elizabeth, such an impulse, an acceptance, capable of saving France.

It is sometimes asked what the purpose is of those harsh austerities practiced by certain religious orders, which are also self-sacrifices; it might as well be asked what the purpose of Christianity is, since it is wholly an extension of the same doctrine of innocence paying for crime.

The authority approving these orders chooses certain men and *isolates* them to make them into *guides*.

There is nothing but violence in the world; but we are tainted by modern philosophy which has taught us that *all is good*, whereas evil has polluted everything and in a very real sense *all is evil*, since nothing is in its proper place. The keynote of the system of our creation being lowered, the whole melody is lowered in proportion, following the rules of harmony. *The whole of creation bemoans its fate*[4] and strives, with effort and grief, for a new order of things.

Observers of great human tragedies must be led to these sad conclusions, but let us not lose our courage; there is no punishment which does not purify, no disorder which the ETERNAL LOVE does not turn against the principle of evil. It is refreshing amid general upheaval to get a glimpse of the plans of Divinity. Never shall we see the whole scheme of things in our voyage through life, and we shall often mislead ourselves, but in every possible science, except the exact sciences, are we not reduced to conjecture? And if our conjectures are plausible, if we can find an analogy for them, if they rest on universally accepted ideas, above all if they console us and make us better men,

[4] Romans 8:22.

what do they lack? If they are not true, they are good; or more accurately, since they are good, are they not true?

Having looked at the French Revolution from a purely moral point of view, I shall turn my attention to politics, without, however, forgetting the primary aim of my work.

CHAPTER IV. CAN THE FRENCH REPUBLIC LAST?

It would be better to put a different question: *Can the Republic exist?* This is assumed much too quickly, and the preliminary question seems justified, for nature and history agree that a great and indivisible republic is an impossibility. A small number of republicans contained within the walls of a town can no doubt rule over millions of subjects, as was the case with Rome, but there cannot exist a great free nation under a republican form of government. This is so clear in itself that theory can dispense with experience; but experience, which decides every question in politics as in science, is here in perfect accord with theory.

What arguments have been put to Frenchmen to persuade them that a republic of twenty-four million people is possible? Only two: (1) There is nothing to prevent something being created that has never been known before; (2) the discovery of the representative system allows us to do things which our predecessors could not do. Let us examine the force of these two arguments.

If it was said to us that a dice, thrown a hundred million times, always showed only the five numbers 1, 2, 3, 4, and 5, could we believe that there was a 6 on one of its faces? The answer is undoubtedly no; and it would be as obvious to us as if we had actually seen it that one of the six faces was blank or that one of the numbers had been duplicated.

Very well, if we look at history, we shall see what is called *Fortune* throwing dice endlessly for four thousand years: has it ever brought a GREAT REPUBLIC? No. Therefore this *number* was not on the dice.

If the world had witnessed the successive growth of new forms of government, we would have no right to claim that such and such a form is impossible just because it has never been known; but the contrary is the case. Monarchies have always been known, and republics have sometimes been known. If one wishes to enter into subdivisions, one can call *democracy* the government in which the masses exercise sovereignty and *aristocracy* that in which sovereignty belongs to a more or less restricted number of privileged families.

That is the end of the matter.

The comparison with the dice is therefore perfectly exact: the same numbers having always been thrown from the dice box of fortune, we are allowed by the theory of probabilities to maintain that there are no others.

Let us not confuse the essences of things with their modifications; the first are unalterable and always recur; the second change and alter the picture a little, at least for the multitude; for every practiced eye easily sees through the changing garb in which eternal nature dresses according to time and place. . . .

Thus, there is nothing new, and a great republic is impossible, since there has never been a great republic.

As for the representative system, by which it is believed the problem can be resolved, I feel tempted to digress, if the reader will pardon me.

Let us begin by pointing out that this system is by no means a modern discovery, but a *product*, or more properly a *part*, of feudal government, when it reached that point of maturity and balance which made it, on the whole, the most perfect in the world.

Having formed the local communities, the royal authority called them to the national assemblies; they could appear there only through deputies, and from this arose the representative system. . . .

One would have to have very little insight into what Bacon called *interiora rerum* to believe that men could have achieved such institutions by an anterior process of reasoning and that such institutions could be the product of deliberation.

Moreover, national representation is by no means peculiar to England: it is found in every European monarchy, but it is living in Great Britain, whereas elsewhere it is dead or dying. It is no part of the plan of this small work to consider if its suspension works to the harm of humanity and if it would be advisable to draw nearer to the old forms. It is sufficient to point out from history: (1) that in England, where national representation has gained and retained more power than anywhere else, there is no mention of it before the middle of the thirteenth century; (2) that it was not an invention, or the product of deliberation, or the result of the action of the people making use of its ancient rights; but that in reality an ambitious soldier, to satisfy his own designs, created the balance of the three powers after the Battle of Lewes, without knowing what he was doing, as always happens; (3) that not only was the calling of the commons to the national council a concession of the monarch, but that in the beginning the king named the representatives of the counties, cities, and boroughs; (4) that, even after the local communities had assumed the right of naming their representatives in Parliament during Edward I's journey in Palestine, they had there only a consultative voice; that they presented their grievances, like the Estates-General in France; and that concessions by the Crown following from their petitions were always *Granted by the king and his spiritual and temporal lords, on the humble prayers of the Commons*; (5) finally that the co-legislative power attributed to the House of Commons is still very new since it goes back at the most to the mid-fifteenth century.

If therefore the term "national representation" is taken to mean a *certain* number of representatives sent by *certain* men, taken from *certain* towns or boroughs, by virtue of an old concession by the sovereign, there is no dispute, for such a government exists—it is England.

But if it is intended that *all* the people should be represented, that they can be represented only by virtue of a mandate,[5] and that every citizen is capable of giving or receiving these mandates, with a few physically and morally inevitable exceptions; and if it is still more intended to add to such a system the abolition of all hereditary distinctions and offices, this representation is a thing that has never been seen and that will never be successful.

America is often cited to us: I know nothing so provoking as the praise showered on this babe-in-arms: let it grow.

But to bring as much light as possible into this discussion, it should be pointed out that the supporters of the French Republic are obliged to prove, not only that *perfected* representation (as they put it) is possible and desirable, but also that the people can by these means retain its sovereignty (as they also put it) and form as a whole a republic. This is the crux of the matter, for if the *Republic* is in the capital and the rest of France is *subject* to the Republic, it is not accountable to the *sovereign people*.

[5] Through bad faith or inattention, it is fairly often assumed that a *proxy* alone can be *representative*. This is an error. Every day in the courts, children, the insane, and absentees are represented by men who derive their mandate solely from the law. Now the *people* unite to a high degree the three qualities, for it is always a *child*, always *foolish*, always *absent*. Why then can its *guardians* not dispense with its mandates?

The committee that was last charged with devising a method for revising the third estate put the French population at thirty millions. Let us accept this number and assume that France retains its conquests. By the terms of the constitution, every year two hundred and fifty people leave the legislature and should be replaced by two hundred and fifty others. It follows that, if the fifteen million men (implied by this total population) were immortal, capable of being representatives, and nominated in strict rotation, each Frenchman would come to exercise in time the national sovereignty every sixty thousand years.

Since, however, it must be admitted that men will die from time to time in such a period, that moreover some men will be reelected and that a good number of individuals by nature and good sense will always be incapable of representing the nation, the imagination boggles at the enormous number of sovereigns condemned to die without having reigned.

Rousseau held that *the national will cannot be delegated;* one is free to agree or disagree, and to wrangle for a thousand years on these academic questions. But what is certain is that the representative system is completely incompatible with the exercise of sovereignty, above all under the French system in which popular rights are limited to electing electors, in which not only can the people not impose specific mandates on their representatives but also the law takes care to break any relationship between representatives and their respective constituencies by warning them that *they are by no means representatives of those who have elected them,* but of the *nation,* a splendid and extremely convenient word since one can make of it whatever one wishes. In short, it is impossible to conceive a constitutional code better calculated to destroy the rights of the people. Thus that vile Jacobin conspirator was nevertheless quite right when he asserted roundly during a judicial inquiry: *"I believe the present government to be a usurper of authority, a violator of all the rights of the people, whom it has reduced to the most deplorable slavery. It is a dreadful system aimed at the happiness of a small number and founded on the oppression of the masses. The people are so muzzled, so bound in chains by this aristocratic government, that it is becoming more difficult than ever for them to break them."*[6]

What does this empty benefit of representation mean for the *nation* when it is involved so indirectly and when millions of individuals will

---

[6] See the interrogation of Babeuf, June, 1796.

never participate? Are sovereignty and government any less alien to them?

But, it has been said in reply, what does it matter to the nation that representation is a vain honor, if this system establishes public liberty?

This is irrelevant, for the question is not whether the French people can be *free* under the constitution that has been given to it, but whether it can be *sovereign*. The question is changed to avoid the argument. Let us begin by leaving out the exercise of sovereignty and insist on the fundamental point that the sovereign will always be in Paris, that the whole fuss about representation means nothing, that the *people* remain quite alien to government, that they are subject to government more than in a monarchy, and that a *great republic* is as self-contradictory as a *squared circle*. For both can be demonstrated with mathematical precision.

So the question is reduced to deciding if it is in the interest of the French people to be subject to an executive directory and two councils instituted according to the 1795 constitution rather than to a king ruling according to ancient forms.

It is very much less difficult to resolve a problem than to pose it.

It is necessary to dismiss this word *republic* and to talk only of the government. I shall not discuss whether it is capable of acting for the general happiness; the French can judge this well enough! Let us see only if, such as it is and whatever name is given to it, it can last.

Let us first of all raise ourselves to the height that befits intelligent beings and, from this elevated viewpoint, consider the origin of this government.

Evil has nothing in common with life; it cannot create, since its power is purely negative. *Evil is a fissure in being; it has no reality*.

What distinguishes the French Revolution and what makes it an event unique in history is that it is radically *evil*; no element of good relieves the picture it presents; it reaches the highest point of corruption ever known; it is pure impurity.

In what scene of history can be found so many vices acting at once on the same stage, such an appalling combination of baseness and cruelty, such profound immorality, such a disdain for all decency?

The age in which liberty grows has such striking characteristics that it is impossible to mistake it. In such a period, love of country is a religion and respect for laws a superstition; individuality is outstanding, general habits of life are austere, every virtue flourishes at once, parties work for the good of the country since they fight only for the honor of serving it; everything, even crime, carries the imprint of grandeur.

If this picture is compared to that offered by France, how can one believe in the continuance of a liberty which grows from a canker? Or more exactly, how can one believe that this liberty can be born (for it still does not exist) and that from the heart of the most loathsome corruption can emerge that form of government that requires virtues more than any other. Listening to these so-called republicans talk of liberty and virtue is like seeing a faded courtesan playing the virgin with blushes of rouge. . . .

No doubt the French Revolution has gone through a number of different phases, yet its general character has never varied, and even at birth it showed everything it was destined to become. There was a certain inexplicable delirium, a blind impetuosity, a shameful contempt for all human decency, an immorality of a new kind that jested about its crimes, above all an insolent prostitution of reasoning and of all those words designed to express ideas of justice and virtue. . . .

Can there then emerge from this bloodstained mire a durable government? It is not a valid objection that ferocious and licentious barbarian peoples have nevertheless become civilized, for no doubt ignorant barbarism has been the seedbed for a number of political systems, but clever barbarism, systematic atrocity, calculated corruption, and above all irreligion have never produced anything. Greenness leads to maturity; decay leads to nothing.

Has there ever been seen, moreover, a government, and more particularly a free constitution, started in spite of its members and dispensing with their consent? Yet this is the sight that would be presented to us by this meteor called the *French Republic* if it could last. This government is thought to be strong because it is violent, but strength differs from violence as much as from weakness, and this government's astonishing method of operation at this time furnishes of itself sufficient proof that it cannot endure for long. The French nation does not *want* this government, it *suffers* it, and remains submissive either because it cannot shake it off or because it fears something worse. The Republic rests only on these two unsure foundations; it can be said that it relies entirely on two negatives. It is also very remarkable that the apologists of the Republic are not at all keen to show the benefits this government brings, feeling rightly that this is the weak spot in their armor. They say only, as boldly as they can, that it is possible; and, passing as lightly over this argument as if it were hot coals, they want solely to show the French that they will expose themselves to the gravest dangers if they return to their old government. It is on this topic they become eloquent; they never stop talking of the evils of revolution. If pressed, they are the kind of people to admit that those who created the present government committed a crime provided it is conceded that it is unnecessary to start a new revolution. They throw themselves at the feet of the French nation; they beg it to guard the Republic. Everything they say about the stability of the government seems to be the result not of reasoned convictions but of fanciful hopes.

Let us move to the great anathema that weighs on the Republic.

CHAPTER V. ON THE FRENCH REVOLUTION CONSIDERED IN ITS ANTIRELIGIOUS CHARACTER—DIGRESSION ON CHRISTIANITY

There is a *satanic* element in the French Revolution which distinguishes it from any other revolution known or perhaps that will be known. Remember the great occasions—Robespierre's speech against the priesthood, the solemn apostasy of the priests, the desecration of objects of worship, the inauguration of the goddess of Reason, and the many outrageous acts by which the provinces tried to surpass Paris: these all leave the ordinary sphere of crimes and seem to belong to a different world.

Now that the Revolution has lost its force, the grossest abuses have disappeared, yet the principles still remain. Have not the *legislators* (to make use of their term) made the historically unique claim that *the nation will not pay for any form of worship?* Some men of this age seem to me to raise themselves at certain moments to a hatred for the Divinity, but this frightful act is not needed to make useless the most strenuous creative efforts: the neglect of, let alone scorn for, the great Being brings an irrevocable curse on the human works stained by it. Every conceivable institution either rests on a religious idea or is ephemeral. Institutions are strong and durable to the degree that they partake of the Divinity. Not only is human reason, or what is ignorantly called philosophy, unable to replace those foundations ignorantly called superstitions, but philosophy is, on the contrary, an essentially destructive force.

In short, man can mirror his Creator only by putting himself in harmony with him. How senseless to believe that, to make a mirror reflect the sun, we should turn it toward the earth!

These reflections apply to everyone, to the believer as well as the skeptic, for I am advancing a fact and not an argument. It does not matter whether these ideas are laughed at or respected; true or false, they no less form the only base for every stable institution.

Rousseau, perhaps the most mistaken of men, has nevertheless hit on this truth, without wanting to draw the full consequences from it.

The Judaic law, he says, which is still in existence, and that of the child of Ishmael, which for ten centuries ruled half the world, still proclaim the great men who laid them down. . . . Pride-ridden philosophy or the blind spirit of faction sees in them no more than lucky impostors.[7]

He ought to have drawn the conclusion, instead of talking about *the great and powerful genius which watches over durable institutions,* as if this high-flown language explained anything.

When one reflects on the facts attested by the whole of history, when one grasps that the whole range of human institutions from those that have shaped world history to the smallest social organization, from empires to monasteries, have a divine basis, and that human power, whenever it stands alone, can create only faulty and ephemeral works, what are we to think of the new French system and the power that has produced it? For my own part, I will never believe in the fecundity of a vacuum.

It would be interesting to go thoroughly through our European institutions and to show how they are all *christianized,* how religion, touching on everything, animates and sustains everything. Human passions can well pollute or even pervert primitive institutions, but if the principle is divine, this is enough to ensure them a long life. . . .

This is a divine law as certain and as palpable as the laws of gravitation.

Every time a man puts himself, according to his ability, in harmony with the Creator and produces any institution whatever in the name of God, he participates in some way in the omnipotence of which he has made himself the instrument, however great his individual weakness, his ignorance and poverty, the obscurity of his birth, in a word his

[7] *Social Contract,* Book ii, Chap. vii.

absolute lack of any ordinary means of influence; he produces works whose power and durability confound reason.

I beg every attentive reader to look closely round him, for he will see these great truths demonstrated even in the smallest of objects. It is not necessary to go back to the *son of Ishmael,* to Lycurgus, to Numa, to Moses, whose laws were completely religious; a popular festival, a rustic dance is sufficient for the observant. They will see in some Protestant countries gatherings and popular rejoicings that no longer have any apparent purpose and spring from Catholic usages which have been completely forgotten. There is nothing moral or worthy of respect in these festivals in themselves, but it makes no difference, for they derive, however tenuously, from religious ideas, and this is enough to perpetuate them. Three centuries cannot bury their memory.

But just let the masters of the world—princes, kings, emperors, powerful majesties, invincible conquerors—let them only try to make the people dance on a certain day each year in a set place. This is not much to ask, but I dare swear that they will not succeed, whereas, if the humblest missionary comes to such a spot, he will make himself obeyed two thousand years after his death. Every year the people meet together around a rustic church in the name of St. John, St. Martin, St. Benedict, and so on; they come filled with boisterous yet innocent cheerfulness; religion sanctifies this joy and the joy embellishes religion: they forget their sorrows; at night, they think of the pleasure to come on the same day next year, and this date is stamped on their memory.

By the side of this picture put that of the French leaders who have been vested with every power by a shameful Revolution and yet cannot organize a simple fete. They pour out gold and call all the arts to their aid, yet the citizen remains at home, listening to the appeal only to laugh at the organizers. . . .

How great is human folly and weakness! Legislators, reflect on this example, for it shows you what you are and what you can do. Do you need anything further to enable you to judge the French system? If its sterility is not clear, nothing is certain in the world.

I am so convinced of the truths I am defending that, when I consider the general decline of moral principles, the anarchy of opinions, the weakness of sovereignties lacking any foundations, the immensity of our needs and the poverty of our means, it seems to me that every true philosophy must choose between two assumptions, either that it is going to fashion a new religion or that Christianity will be revived in some miraculous way. One of these suppositions must be chosen, according to the view that is held about the truth of Christianity.

This conjecture will not be rejected disdainfully except by the shortsighted who believe that nothing is possible except what they see before their eyes. Who in the ancient world could have foreseen Christianity? And who outside this religion could, in its beginnings, have foreseen its future success? How do we know that a great moral revolution is not in progress? Pliny showed in his famous letter that he had not the slightest idea how enormous was to grow the infant he saw.

But a host of ideas crowd in on me at this point and push me to the widest of considerations.

The present generation is witnessing one of the most dramatic sights humanity has ever seen; it is the fight to the death between Christianity and the cult of philosophy. The lists are open, the two enemies have come to grips, and the world looks on.

As in Homer, *the father of gods and men* is holding the scales in which these two great forces are being weighed; soon one of the scales must tilt.

To the biased man, whose heart is master of his head, events prove nothing; having chosen sides irrevocably either for or against, observation and reasoning are equally useless. But for all men of goodwill, who deny or doubt perhaps, let the great history of Christianity settle their doubts. For eighteen centuries, it has ruled over a great part of the globe, and particularly the most enlightened part. This religion does not go back just to this age; going back to before its founder came to earth, it links up with another order of things, a prophetic religion that preceded it. The one cannot be true without the other being so: the one prides itself on promising what the other prides itself on having; so that this religion, by a visible sequence, goes back to the origin of the world.

It was born on the day that days were born.

There is no other example of such durability; and, to confine oneself just to Christianity, no institution in the world can be compared to it. Any comparison with other religions can only be misleading, for several striking characteristics exclude it. It is not the place here to detail them; one word only must suffice. Can anyone show me another religion founded on miraculous facts and revealing incomprehensible dogmas, yet believed for eighteen centuries by a good part of humanity and defended in every age by the best men of the time, from Origen to Pascal, in spite of every effort of a rival sect which, from Celsus to Condorcet, has ceaselessly fulminated against it?

It is a wonderful thing that, when one reflects on this great institution, the most natural hypothesis, that which all the probabilities point to, is that of a divine creation. If it were a human artifact, there would no longer be any means of explaining its success; by excluding the idea of a miracle, an explanation can be given.

Every nation, it is said, has mistaken copper for gold. Very well, but has this copper been thrown into the European crucible and tested for eighteen centuries by chemical observation? Or, if submitted to this test, has it emerged from it with honor? Newton believed in the Incarnation, but Plato, I think, had very little belief in the miraculous birth of Bacchus.

Christianity has been preached by the ignorant and believed by the learned, and in this it resembles no other known thing.

Moreover, it passes every test. It is said that persecution is a wind that keeps alive and spreads the flame of fanaticism. Very well: Diocletian favored Christianity, but, on this assumption, Constantine should have stifled it, and this did not happen. It has withstood everything, peace and war, scaffolds and victories, daggers and temptations, pride and humiliation, poverty and affluence, the night of the Middle Ages and the broad daylight of the periods of Leo X and Louis XIV. An all-powerful emperor and master of much of the known world once exhausted every resource of his genius against it; he tried everything to revive ancient beliefs; he cleverly linked them with the Platonic ideas that were then in fashion. Hiding the anger which animated him beneath a mask of purely external tolerance, he used against the rival religion the weapons before which every human work had been powerless; he let loose ridicule on it: he impoverished the priesthood to bring it into contempt; he deprived it of every support that men can bring to the aid of their works: slanders, intrigues, injustice, oppression, ridicule, violence, and cunning, all were useless; *the Galilean* prevailed over Julian the *philosopher*.

Today, finally, the experiment is being repeated in still more favorable circumstances, since they all conspire to make it decisive. All those who have not learned thoroughly the lessons of history pay particular attention. You have said that the Crown propped up the Papacy; well, the Crown no longer plays any part on the world's stage;

it has been smashed and the pieces thrown into the mud. You suspected that the influence of a rich and powerful priest could enforce the dogmas he preached. I do not think that there is any power that can make men believe, but let that pass. There are no longer any priests; they have been exiled, slaughtered, and degraded; they have been deprived of everything, and those who have escaped the guillotine, the stake, daggers, fusillades, drowning, and deportation receive the alms that formerly they themselves gave. You feared the force of custom, the ascendancy of authority, the illusions of imagination: there is no longer any of that, no longer custom and no longer masters; each man's mind is his own. Philosophy having corroded the cement binding man to man, there are no longer any moral ties. The civil authority, promoting with all its resources the overthrow of the old system, gives to the enemies of Christianity all the aid which it formerly gave to Christianity itself: the human mind uses every imaginable means to combat the old national religion. These efforts are applauded and paid for, while anything against them is a crime. You have no longer anything to fear from visual delights, always the most deceiving; displays of pomp and vain ceremonies no longer impress the people before whom everything has been mocked for seven years. The churches are closed, or are opened only for the noisy discussions and drunken revels of a frenzied people. The altars are overthrown; filthy animals have been led through the streets in bishops' vestments; chalices have been used in disgraceful orgies; and around the altar that the old faith surrounded with dazzling cherubims, nude prostitutes have been painted. The cult of philosophy has therefore no longer any room for complaint; fortune is completely in its favor; everything is working for it and against its rival. If it is victorious, it will not say like Caesar, *I came, I saw, and I conquered,* but in the end it will have won: it can applaud and sit proudly on an overturned cross. But if Christianity emerges from this terrible test purer and more virile; if the Christian Hercules, strong in his own vigor, lifts *the son of the earth* and crushes him in his arms *patuit Deus.* — Frenchmen, give place to the Christian King, place him yourselves on his old throne; raise once more his oriflamme, and let his coinage, traveling again from one pole to the other, carry to every part of the world the triumphant device:

CHRIST COMMANDS, HE REIGNS,
HE IS THE VICTOR.

CHAPTER VI. OF THE DIVINE INFLUENCE IN POLITICAL CONSTITUTIONS

Man can modify everything in the sphere of his activity, but he creates nothing: such is the law binding him in the physical as in the moral world.

No doubt a man can plant a seed, raise a tree, perfect it by grafting, and prune it in a hundred ways, but never has he imagined that he can make a tree.

How has he thought that he has the power to make a constitution? Was it through experience? See what it can teach us.

All free constitutions known to the world took form in one of two ways. Sometimes they *germinated*, as it were, in an imperceptible way by the combination of a host of circumstances that we call fortuitous, and sometimes they have a single author who appears like a freak of nature and enforces obedience.

In these two assumptions can be seen the signs by which God warns us of our weakness and of the right he has reserved to himself in the formation of governments.

1. No government results from a deliberation; popular rights are never written, or at least constitutive acts or written fundamental laws are always only declaratory statements of anterior rights, of which nothing can be said other than that they exist because they exist.

2. God, not having judged it proper to employ supernatural means in this field, has limited himself to human means of action, so that in the formation of constitutions circumstances are all and men are only part of the circumstances. Fairly often, even, in pursuing one object they achieve another, as we have seen in the English constitution.

3. The rights of the *people*, properly speaking, start fairly often from a concession by sovereigns, and in this case they can be established historically; but the rights of the sovereign and of the aristocracy, at least their essential rights, those that are constitutive and basic, have neither date nor author.

4. Even the concessions of the sovereign have always been preceded by a state of affairs that made them necessary and that did not depend on him.

5. Although written laws are always only declarations of anterior rights, yet it is very far from true that everything that can be written is written; there is even in every constitution always something that can-

not be written, and that must be left behind a dark and impenetrable cloud on pain of overturning the state.

6. The more that is written, the weaker is the institution, the reason being clear. Laws are only declarations of rights, and rights are not declared except when they are attacked, so that the multiplicity of written constitutional laws shows only the multiplicity of conflicts and the danger of destruction.

This is why the most vigorous political system in the ancient world was that of Sparta, in which nothing was written.

7. No nation can give itself liberty if it has not it already. Its laws are made when it begins to reflect on itself. Human influence does not extend beyond the development of rights already in existence but disregarded or disputed. If imprudent men step beyond these limits by foolhardy reforms, the nation loses what it had without gaining what it hopes for. In consequence, it is necessary to innovate only rarely and always moderately and cautiously.

8. When Providence has decreed the more rapid formation of a political constitution, a man appears invested with indefinable powers: he speaks and exacts obedience: but these heroes belong perhaps only to the ancient world and the youth of nations. However that may be, the distinctive characteristic of these legislators is that they are kings or high nobles; there is and can be no exception to this. . . .

9. Even these legislators with their exceptional powers simply bring together preexisting elements in the customs and character of a people; but this gathering together and rapid formation which seem to be creative are carried out only in the name of the Divinity. Politics and religion start together: it is difficult to separate the legislator from the priest, and his public institutions consist principally *in ceremonies and religious holidays*.

10. In one sense, liberty has always been a gift of kings, since all free nations have been constituted by kings. This is the general rule, under which the apparent exceptions that could be pointed out will fall if they were argued out.

11. No free nation has existed which has not had in its natural constitution germs of liberty as old as itself, and no nation has ever succeeded in developing by written constitutional laws rights other than those present in its natural constitution.

12. No assembly of men whatever can create a nation; all the

Bedlams in the world could not produce anything more absurd or extravagant than such an enterprise.

To prove this proposition in detail, after what I have said, would, it seems to me, be disrespectful to the wise and over-respectful to the foolish.

13. I have spoken of the basic characteristic of true legislators; another very striking feature, on which it would be easy to write a whole book, is that they are never what are called *intellectuals*; they do not write; they act on instinct and impulse more than on reasoning, and they have no means of acting other than a certain moral force that bends men's wills as the wind bends a field of corn.

In showing that this observation is only the corollary of a general truth of the greatest importance, I could say some interesting things, but I am afraid of digressing too much: I want rather to omit the intermediary arguments and simply to state conclusions.

There is the same difference between political theory and constitutional laws as there is between poetics and poetry. The famous Montesquieu is to Lycurgus in the intellectual hierarchy what Batteux is to Homer or Racine.

Moreover, these two talents positively exclude each other, as is shown by the example of Locke, who floundered hopelessly when he took it into his head to give laws to the Americans.

I have heard an ardent supporter of the Republic seriously lamenting that the French had not seen in the works of Hume a piece entitled *Plan for a Perfect Republic—O coecas hominum mentes! You* cannot be sure that an ordinary man of good sense has not the making of a legislator, even if he has never shown in any way any external sign of superiority. There is no reason for a firm opinion either way; but as far as men like Bacon, Locke, and Montesquieu are concerned, you can be perfectly sure without hesitation that they have no such ability, for it is excluded by the talent they do possess.

The application to the French constitution of the principles I have just set out is perfectly clear, but it is useful to look more closely at it from a particular viewpoint.

The greatest enemies of the French Revolution must freely admit that the commission of eleven which produced the last constitution has apparently more intelligence than its work and that perhaps it has done all it could do. It worked on incalcitrant materials, which did not allow it to act on principle; although these "powers" are divided only by a wall, the division of powers is of itself still a splendid victory over the prejudices of the moment.

But it is not only a matter of the intrinsic merits of the constitution. It is no part of my purpose to seek out the particular faults which show us that it cannot last; moreover, everything has been said on this point. I shall point out only the error of the theory on which this constitution is based and which has misled the French from the beginning of their Revolution.

The 1795 constitution, like its predecessors, was made for *man*. But there is no such thing as *man* in the world. During my life, I have seen Frenchmen, Italians, Russians, and so on; thanks to Montesquieu, I even know that one can be *Persian*; but I must say, as for *man*, I have never come across him anywhere; if he exists, he is completely unknown to me.

Is there a single country in the world in which there is a council of five hundred, a council of elders, and five leaders? Such a constitution may be offered to every human association from China to Geneva. But a constitution that is made for all nations is made for none: it is a pure abstraction, an academic exercise of the mind, according to some hypothetical ideal, that should be addressed to *man*, in whatever imaginary realm he inhabits.

Is not a constitution a solution to the following problem: *Given the population, customs, religion, geographical situation, political relations, wealth, good and bad qualities of a particular nation, to find the laws which suit it?*

Yet this problem is not even approached in the 1795 constitution, which was aimed solely at *man*.

Thus every imaginable reason combines to show that this enterprise has not the divine blessing. It is no more than a schoolboy's exercise.

Already at this moment, how many signs of decay does it reveal!

CHAPTER VII. SIGNS OF NULLITY IN THE FRENCH GOVERNMENT

The legislator is like the Creator; he does not always labor, he gives birth and then rests. Every true legislator has his Sabbath, and intermittency is his distinctive characteristic; so that Ovid spoke a truth of the first order when he said:

Quod caret alterna requie durabile non est.

If perfection was an attribute of human nature, each legislator would speak only once: but, although all our works are imperfect and the sovereign is obliged to support political institutions with new laws to the degree that they become tainted, yet human legislation draws closer to its model by that intermittency of which I was just now speaking. Its repose honors it as much as its original action; the more it acts, the more human, that is to say fragile, are its achievements.

What a prodigious number of laws has resulted from the labors of three French National Assemblies!

From July 1st to October, 1791, the National Assembly passed	2,557
The Legislative Assembly passed, in eleven and a half months	1,712
The National Convention, from the first day of the Republic until 4 Brumaire year IV [October 26, 1795], passed in 57 months	11,210
TOTAL	15,479

I doubt if the three houses of the Kings of France have spawned a collection of such magnitude. Reflecting on this infinite number, two very different emotions are felt successively. The first is that of admiration or at least of astonishment; one is amazed, with Mr. Burke, that this nation, whose frivolity is a byword, has produced such obstinate workers. This structure of law is so huge that it takes the breath away. But astonishment must quickly change to pity when the futility of these laws is recalled, and then one sees only children killing each other to raise a house of cards.

Why are there so many laws? Because there is no legislator.

What have these so-called legislators done for six years? Nothing— for to *destroy* is not to *do*.

One cannot tire of the incredible sight of a nation giving itself three constitutions in five years. No legislator has groped his way cautiously: he says *fiat*, as is his method, and the engine starts. In spite of the different efforts made in this field by the three assemblies, everything has gone from bad to worse, since the assent of the nation to the work of the legislators has been increasingly lacking. . . .

Modern philosophy is at one and the same time too materialistic and too presumptuous to see the real springs of action in politics. One of its follies is to believe that an assembly can constitute a nation, that a constitution, that is to say, the totality of fundamental laws which suit a nation and should give it a certain form of government, is an artifact like any other, requiring only intelligence, knowledge, and practice, that the job of constitution-making can be learned, and that, the moment they think about it, men can say to other men, *Make us a government*, as a workman is told, *Make us a fire engine or a loom.*

Yet it is a truth as certain in its way as a mathematical proposition tha * *no great institution results from deliberation* and that human works are fragile in proportion to the number of men concerned in them and the degree to which science and reasoning have been used a priori.

A written constitution such as that which today governs the French is no more than an automaton possessing only the external forms of life. Man, by his own powers, is at the most a *Vaucanson;* to be a *Prometheus* he must climb to heaven; for *the legislator cannot gain obedience either by force or by reasoning.*[8]

It could be said that, at this time, the experiment has been tried; for it would be unobservant to say that the French constitution is *working*, since this would be to mistake the constitution for the government. This last, which is a highly advanced despotism, works only too well, but the constitution does not exist except on paper. It is observed or broken according to the interests of the rulers; the people counts for nothing, and the outrages its masters commit on it under the forms of respect should be quite enough to cure it of its errors.

The life of a government is as real as the life of a man; it can be felt or, rather, it can be seen, and no one can deceive himself on this point. I beg every Frenchman with a conscience to ask himself if he does not do violence to himself to give his representatives the title of *legislators*, if this title of etiquette and *courtesy* does not strain him slightly, a little as he felt when, under the *ancien régime*, he was pleased to call the son of the king's secretary *count* or *marquis*.

Every honor springs from God said Homer of old; he literally speaks the language of St. Paul yet without plagiarizing him. What is certain is that man cannot bestow that indefinable quality that is called *dignity*. To the sovereign alone belongs *honor* above all; from him, as from an inexhaustible fountain, it flows in varying degrees on to classes and individuals.

I noticed that, when a member of the legislature talked of his RANK in print, the newspapers made fun of him, because in fact there is no *rank* in France, but only *power* which depends only on force. The peo-

[8] Rousseau, *Social Contract* Book ii, Chap. vii.

ple see nothing in a deputy except the seven hundred and fiftieth part of a power of doing great harm. The respected deputy is not respected because he is a *deputy*, but because he is worthy of respect. . . .

It may perhaps be an illusion on my part, but this *wage* that a conceited neologism terms *indemnity* seems to me to be a count against French representation. Free by law and independent by fortune, the Englishman who comes to London to represent the nation at his own expense has something impressive about him. But these French *legislators* who extract large salaries from the nation in order to make laws for it; these decree sellers, who exercise the national sovereignty for a sack of wheat a day and live off their legislative power; such men, in truth, are not very impressive; and when it is asked what they are worth, one cannot but value them in wheat.

In England, the two magic letters M.P., bracketed with the least-known name, immediately exalt it and give it the right to a distinguished marriage. In France, anyone who sought a position as a deputy in order to clinch a marriage above his station would probably be making a sad miscalculation.

This is because no representative, no instrument whatever of a false sovereignty, can excite anything other than curiosity or terror. . . .

What merits close attention is the conquests of the French which have given rise to delusions about the durability of their government; the brilliance of their military successes dazzles even the best minds who do not at first perceive to what degree these successes are irrelevant to the stability of the Republic.

Nations have conquered under every possible form of government, and revolutions even lead to victories by exalting morale. The French always succeed in war under a firm government with the ability to despise them while praising them, to throw them like bullets against the enemy while promising them epitaphs in the newspapers.

Even now, it is still Robespierre who wins battles; it is his iron despotism that leads Frenchmen to slaughter and victory. It is by squandering money and blood, by straining every muscle, that the rulers of France have gained the victories we are witnessing. A supremely brave nation, exalted by any fanaticism whatever and led by able generals, will always conquer, but will pay dearly for its conquests. Was the durability of the 1793 constitution assured by its three years of victory? Why should it be otherwise with the 1795 constitution, and why should victory give to it a character which it could not give to the other? . . .

No one feels more strongly than myself that the present circumstances are out of the ordinary and that what has always been the case is now no indication of what is the case, but this question does not touch the main purpose of this book. It is sufficient for me to indicate the logical flaw in the statement: *The Republic is victorious, therefore it will last.* If it were absolutely necessary to prophesy, I would rather want to say: *War is keeping it alive, therefore peace will kill it.*

The author of some scientific theory would doubtless congratulate himself if he found all the facts of nature agreed with it, as I am able to quote in support of my conclusions all the facts of history. Looking scrupulously at the patterns of change which it presents to us, I see nothing that favors this chimerical system of deliberation and political engineering through previous reasoning. In the last resort, America could be quoted, but I answered this in advance by saying that it is not yet the time to quote it. I will, however, add a few remarks.

1. English America had a king, but did not see him; it was a stranger to the splendor of monarchy and to it the sovereign was a kind of supernatural power that did not impinge on the senses.

2. It possessed the democratic element that was present in the constitution of the mother country.

3. It possessed, besides, elements carried to it by many of the first colonists who were born amid political and religious troubles and were almost all republican-minded.

4. With these materials and on the plan of the balance of three powers that they drew from their ancestors, the Americans have built, and not started from a *tabula rasa* as did the French.

But everything that is really novel in their constitution, everything that is the result of common deliberation, is fragile in the extreme; weakness and decay could not be better combined.

Not only do I doubt the stability of American government, but the particular institutions of English America inspire no confidence in me. For example, the towns, inspired by a rather unworthy jealousy, were not able to agree on a place where the Congress should sit; none of them was willing to surrender this honor to another. Consequently, it has been decided to build a new town as the seat of government. The site was chosen on the banks of a great river; it was decided that the town should be called *Washington;* the situation of all the public buildings was marked out; the work has been set in hand and the plan of the capital city is already circulating throughout Europe. In essentials, there is nothing in this beyond human powers; a town can very easily be built: nevertheless, there is too much deliberation, too much of mankind, in all this, and it is a thousand to one that the town will not be built, or that it will not be called *Washington,* or that Congress will not sit there.

CHAPTER VIII. ON THE OLD FRENCH CONSTITUTION—DIGRESSION ON THE KING AND THE DECLARATION TO THE FRENCH OF JULY, 1795

Three different theories have been held on the old French constitution: some have claimed that the nation had no constitution; others held the opposite; and finally others again have taken up a middle position, as happens in every important matter of dispute, holding that the French had in fact a constitution but that it was not observed.

The first view is unsustainable, while the other two do not really contradict each other.

The error of those who claimed that France had no constitution sprang from the great error over the nature of human power, previous deliberation and written laws.

If a man of goodwill, relying only on good sense and rectitude, asks what the old French constitution was, the straightforward reply can be given: "It is what you felt when you were in France: it is the mixture of liberty and authority, law and opinion, that made the foreign traveler in France believe that he was living under a government different from his own."

But to go deeper into the question, in the corpus of French public law will be found features and provisions that raise France above all the known monarchies.

A particular feature of this monarchy is that it has a certain theocratic element peculiar to it that has given it a life of fourteen centuries and that is particularly French in its nature. The bishops, in this respect successors to the Druids, only perfected it.

I do not believe that any other European monarchy has used, for the good of the state, a greater number of pontiffs in civil government. . . .

But, while the priesthood was in France one of the three columns upholding the throne and played in the councils of the nation, in its courts, its great offices of state, its embassies, so outstanding a role, it had no or very little influence in civil administration, and even when a priest was prime minister, there was not in France *a government of priests.*

Every interest was very well balanced and everyone was in his place. From this point of view England most closely resembled France. If ever it banishes the words *Church and state* from its political vocabulary, its government will perish like that of its rival.

It was the fashion in France (for in this country fashion is all) to say that they were slaves; but why then was the word *citoyen* found in the French language (even before the Revolution had taken it up in order to debase it), a word that cannot be translated into other European languages? The younger Racine addressed this beautiful verse to the King of France in the name of his city of Paris:

Under a citizen King, all citizens are Kings.

To praise the patriotism of a Frenchman, it was said, *C'est un grand citoyen.* It is hopeless to try to translate this expression into our other languages; *gross burger* in German, *gran cittadino* in Italian, and so on, do not answer the case. . . .

Everything leads to the conclusion that the French wanted to surpass human power, that these ill-considered attempts are leading them to slavery, that they needed only what they already possessed, and that, if they were made for a greater degree of liberty than they enjoyed seven years ago (which is not at all certain), they have in their own hands, in all their historical and legislative authorities, everything necessary to make them the honor and envy of Europe. . . .

CHAPTER IX. HOW WILL THE COUNTER-REVOLUTION COME ABOUT
IF IT HAPPENS?

When men form theories about counter-revolution, they too often make the mistake of arguing as if this counter-revolution should and could be only the result of some popular deliberation. *The people are afraid,* it is said; *the people want, the people will never consent, it is not agreeable to the people,* and so on. It is a pity, but the people count for nothing in revolutions, or at least they play a part only as a passive instrument. Perhaps four or five people will give France a king. . . . If the monarchy is restored, the people will no more decree its restoration than they decreed its downfall or the establishment of the revolutionary government.

I beg men to dwell on these thoughts, and I recommend them particularly to those who believe revolution to be impossible because there are too many Frenchmen attached to the Republic and because a change would cause suffering to too many men. . . . It can certainly be contested that the Republic has the support of the majority, but, whether or not this is the case, it does not matter in the least. Enthusiasm and fanaticism are not durable states. The human palate soon tires of this heady wine; so that, even supposing that a people, and particularly the French people, can will something continually, it is at least certain that they cannot will it ardently. On the contrary, once the fever has abated, despondency, apathy, and indifference always follow great bursts of enthusiasm. This is the case with France, which no longer desires anything strongly except tranquillity. Therefore even if it is assumed that there is a republican majority in France (which is indubitably false), what does it matter? When the king presents himself, certainly heads will not be counted and no one will object, first, because even those who prefer the Republic to monarchy still prefer tranquillity to the Republic, and then because those opposing royalty will not be able to join forces.

In politics as in mechanics, theory goes astray if it does not take into account the different qualities of the materials that make up *machines*. At first sight, for example, it seems true that *the previous consent of the French is necessary to the restoration of the monarchy*. Yet nothing could be more false. . . .

God has warned us that he has reserved the formation of sovereignties to himself by never entrusting the choice of their masters to the masses. Never do they get what they want; they always accept, they never choose. If the phrase is excused, it could even be called an *affectation* of Providence that the very attempts of a nation to attain its objects are the Providential means of frustrating it. Thus the Roman people gave itself masters whilst thinking it was struggling against the aristocracy following Caesar. This is the epitome of all popular insurrections. In the French Revolution, the people have continually been enslaved, insulted, exploited, mutilated by every faction, and these factions in their turn, playthings all of them, have continually drifted with the stream, in spite of all their efforts, to break up finally against the reefs awaiting them.

But if one wants to predict the probable result of time, it is enough to examine what unites all the factions. All of them have aimed at the degradation, even the destruction, of the universal Church and of monarchy, *from which it follows* that all their efforts will end in the glorification of Christianity and the monarchy.

Everyone who has written on or thought about history has admired the secret force that makes game of human plans. . . . But it is especially in the establishment and the overthrow of sovereignties that the working of Providence shows itself in the most striking manner. Not only do peoples as a whole participate in historical movements only like wood and rope used by a workman, but even their leaders are leaders only to inexperienced eyes: in fact, they are ruled just as they rule the people. These men who, taken together, seem the tyrants of the multitudes are themselves tyrannized by two or three men, who are tyrannized by one. And if this single individual could and would tell his secret, it would be seen that he himself does not know how he has seized power, that his influence is a greater mystery to him than to others, and that circumstances he was unable either to foresee or bring about have done everything for him and without him. . . .

No nation can give itself a government; only, when such and such a right exists in its constitution and this right is unrecognized or suppressed, some men, aided by circumstances, can brush aside obstacles and get the rights of the people recognized. Human power extends no further. . . .

CHAPTER X. OF THE PRETENDED DANGERS OF A COUNTER-REVOLUTION

Part 1 General Considerations

Nowadays it is a very common fallacy to insist on the dangers of a counter-revolution in order to buttress the view that we should not return to a monarchy.

A great number of works intended to persuade Frenchmen to be content with the Republic are only developments of this idea. Their authors rest their argument on the evils inseparable from revolutions; then, pointing out that the monarchy cannot be restored in France without a new revolution, they conclude that it is necessary to maintain the Republic. This gross fallacy, whether it arises from fear or from the desire to mislead, deserves to be carefully discussed. . . .

To carry through the French Revolution it was necessary to overthrow religion, insult morality, violate every propriety, and commit every crime; to do this diabolic work, such a number of vicious men had to be used that perhaps never before had so many vices acted in concert to perform any evil whatever. In contrast, to restore order, the king will call together all the virtues; no doubt, he will wish this, but he will also be forced to it in the very nature of things. His most pressing interest will be to unite justice and mercy; worthy men will come of their own accord to take up positions in the posts where they can be of use; and religion, lending its authority to politics, will give it a power which it can draw only from its august sister.

I have no doubt many men will ask to be shown the basis for these splendid hopes; but can it be believed that the political world progresses haphazardly and that it is not organized, directed, and moved by the same wisdom that reveals itself in the physical world? The guilty hands that overthrow a state necessarily inflict the most grievous wounds; for no free agent can run against the plans of the Creator without bringing down, in the sphere of his activity, evils proportionate to the extent of the crime; and this law springs from the kindness rather than from the justice of the Supreme Being.

But when man works to restore order, he associates himself with the author of order; he is favored by *nature*, that is to say, by the combined working of secondary forces, which are the agents of the Divinity. His action has something divine in it; it is both gentle and authoritative; it forces nothing yet nothing resists it; in carrying out its plans, it restores to health; as it acts, so is calmed that disquiet and painful agitation which are the effect and the symptom of disorder; just as men know that a skillful doctor has put back a dislocated joint by the cessation of pain. . . .

What culpable blindness makes you Frenchmen persist in fighting painfully against the power that renders all your efforts void in order to warn you of its presence? You are powerless only because you have dared to separate yourselves from it and even to work against it. Once you act in harmony with it, you will participate in some manner in its nature, all obstacles will disappear before you, and you will laugh at the private fears which now agitate you. All the parts of the political machine have a natural tendency to move toward the place assigned to them, and this divine tendency will favor all the efforts of the king; and order being the natural element of man, you will find in it the happiness you vainly seek in disorder. The Revolution has caused you suffering because it was the work of all the vices and because the vices are man's tortures. For the opposite reason, the return to monarchy, far from producing the evils you fear for the future, will put a stop to those which are today destroying you. All your efforts will have positive results; you will destroy only destruction.

Rid yourself for once of those distressing doctrines which have dishonored an age and caused the fall of France. You have already learned to know the preachers of these fatal dogmas, but the impression they have made on your mind has not been wiped out. In all your plans of creation and restoration, you forget nothing but God; they have driven a rift between you and Him: it is by no more than an effort of reasoning that you raise your thoughts to the unfailing source of all existence. You want to see only man, his actions so weak, so dependent, so circumscribed, his will so corrupt and irresolute; and the existence of a superior cause is nothing but a theory to you. Yet it presses in on you and surrounds you: it impinges on you, and the whole world tells you of it. When you are told that without it you will be strong only in destruction, this is no vain theory that is retailed to you, but a practical truth founded on the experience of every age and on the knowledge of human nature. Look at history and you will not see one political foundation, indeed any sort of institution of consequence and durability, that is not based on a religious idea, no matter of what kind, for there is no entirely false religious theory. . . .

It can be said without fear of contradiction that, generally speaking, monarchy is the form of government that gives the most distinction to the most people. In this kind of government, the sovereign possesses sufficient luster to share some of it, with the necessary gradations, between a host of agents which it distinguishes to a greater or lesser degree. In a republic, sovereignty is not tangible as in a monarchy, but is a purely moral concept whose greatness is incommunicable. In addition in republics public offices are nothing outside the seat of government, and moreover have consequence only insofar as they are occupied by members of the government; there it is the man who honors the office rather than the office the man, who is distinguished not as *agent* but as a *portion* of sovereignty.

One can see in the provinces subject to republican government that public offices (except those reserved for members of the sovereign body) raise their holders very little in the eyes of their fellowmen and have practically no significance in public opinion, for of its nature a republic is the government that gives the most rights to the very small number of men who are called the *sovereign,* and that takes away the most from the others who are called *subjects.*

The nearer a republic approaches a pure democracy, the more striking this observation will be.

Just recall the innumerable offices (even leaving out of account all the offices that were for sale) that the old government of France opened to universal ambition. . . . It is true that the highest positions were more difficult for the ordinary citizen to reach, but this is perfectly reasonable. There is too much movement in the state and not enough subordination where *all* can aspire to *everything.* Order demands that offices should be graduated like the condition of citizens and that talents, and sometimes even simply patronage, should surmount the barriers dividing different classes. In this way there is emulation without humiliation and mobility without chaos; indeed, the distinction attached to an office is directly proportionate to the greater or lesser difficulty of attaining it.

To object that these distinctions are bad is to change the question, but I would say: "If your offices do not elevate those filling them, do not boast about giving them to everyone, for you are not giving anything. If, however, offices do and must create distinctions, I repeat that no man of good faith can deny that monarchy is the government which, by its offices alone and independently of nobility, *distinguishes* the greatest number of the rest of its citizens."

Moreover, one must not be duped by that egalitarian ideal that is simply a matter of words. The soldier who is free to talk to his officer in a grossly familiar tone is not by that his equal. The hierarchy of office, which disappeared at first in the general confusion, begins to emerge. . . .

Study on Sovereignty

BOOK ONE

ON THE ORIGINS OF SOVEREIGNTY

CHAPTER I. THE SOVEREIGNTY OF THE PEOPLE

It is said that the people are sovereign; but over whom?—over themselves, apparently. The people are thus subject. There is surely something equivocal if not erroneous here, for the people which *command* are not the people which *obey*. It is enough, then, to put the general proposition, *"The people are sovereign,"* to feel that it needs an exegesis.

This exegesis will not be long in coming, at least in the French system. The people, it will be said, exercise their sovereignty by means of their representatives. This begins to make sense. The people are a sovereign which cannot exercise sovereignty. . . .

There has been much heated discussion on whether sovereignty comes from God or from men, but I do not know if anyone has noticed that both propositions can be true.

It is certainly true, in an inferior and crude sense, that sovereignty is based on human consent. For, if any people decided suddenly not to obey, sovereignty would disappear; and it is impossible to imagine the establishment of a sovereignty without imagining a people which consents to obey. If then the opponents of the divine origin of sovereignty want to claim only this, they are right, and it would be quite useless to

dispute it. Since God has not thought it appropriate to use supernatural agents in the establishment of states, it is certain that all developments have come about through human agencies. But saying that
sovereignty does not derive from God because he has made use of men
to establish it is like saying that he is not the creator of man because
we all have a father and a mother.

Every *theist* would no doubt agree that whoever breaks the laws
sets his face against the divine will and renders himself guilty before
God, although he is breaking only human ordinances, for it is God who
has made *man* sociable; and since he has *willed* society, he has *willed*
also the sovereignty and laws without which there would be no society.

Thus laws come from God in the sense that he wills that there
should be laws and that they should be obeyed. Yet these laws come
also from men in that they are made by men.

In the same way, sovereignty comes from God, since he is the
author of all things except evil, and is in particular the author of society, which could not exist without sovereignty.

However, this same sovereignty comes also from men in a certain
sense, that is to say insofar as particular forms of government are established and declared by human consent.

The partisans of divine authority cannot therefore deny that the
human will plays some part in the establishment of governments; and
their opponents cannot in their turn deny that God is preeminently the
author of these same governments.

It appears then that the two propositions, *Sovereignty comes from
God* and *Sovereignty comes from men,* are not absolutely contradictory, any more than the other two, *Laws come from God* and *Laws
come from men.* . . .

CHAPTER II. ORIGINS OF SOCIETY

It is one of man's curious idiosyncrasies to create difficulties for the
pleasure of resolving them. The mysteries that surround him on all
sides are not sufficient for him; he still rejects clear ideas and reduces
everything to a problem by some inexplicable twist of pride, which
makes him regard it as below him to believe what everyone believes. So,
for example, there have long been disputes on the origin of society; and
in place of the quite simple solutions that naturally present themselves

to the mind, all sorts of metaphysical theories have been put forward to support airy hypotheses rejected by common sense and experience.

If the causes of the origins of society are posed as a problem, it is obviously assumed that there was a human era before society; but this is precisely what needs to be proved.

Doubtless it will not be denied that the earth as a whole is intended for man's habitation; now, as the multiplication of man is part of the Creator's intentions, it follows that the nature of man is to be united in great societies over the whole surface of the globe. For the nature of a being is to exist as the Creator has willed it. And this will is made perfectly plain by the facts.

The isolated man is therefore by no means the *man of nature*. When a handful of men were scattered over vast territories, humanity was not what it was to become. At that time, there were only families, and these scattered families, either *individually* or by their subsequent union, were nothing but embryonic peoples.

And so, long after the formation of the great societies, some small desert tribes still show us the spectacle of humanity in its infancy. There are still infant nations that are not yet what they are to become.

What would one think of a naturalist who said that man is an animal thirty to thirty-five inches high, without strength or intelligence, and giving voice only to inarticulate cries? Yet this naturalist, in sketching man's physical and moral nature in terms of an infant's characteristics, would be no more ridiculous than the philosopher who seeks the political nature of this same being in the *rudiments* of society.

Every question about the *nature* of man must be resolved by history. The philosopher who wants to show us by a priori reasoning what man must be does not deserve an audience. He is substituting expediency for experience and his own decisions for the Creator's will.

Let me assume that someone manages to prove that an American savage is happier and less vicious than a civilized man. Could it be concluded from this that the latter is a degraded being or, if you like, further from *nature* than the former? Not at all. This is just like saying that the nature of the individual man is to remain a child because at that age he is free from the vices and misfortunes that will beset him in his maturity. History continually shows us men joined together in more or less numerous societies, ruled by different sovereignties. Once they have multiplied beyond a certain point, they cannot exist in any other fashion.

Thus, properly speaking, there has never been a time previous to society for *man*, because, before the formations of political societies, man was not a complete man, and because it is ridiculous to seek the characteristics of any being whatever in the embryo of that being.

Thus society is not the work of man, but the immediate result of the will of the Creator who has willed that man should be what he has always and everywhere been.

Rousseau and all the thinkers of his stamp imagine or try to imagine a people *in the state of nature* (this is their expression), deliberating formally on the advantages and disadvantages of the social state and finally deciding to pass from one to the other. But there is not a grain of common sense in this idea. What were these men like before the *national convention* in which they finally decided to find themselves a sovereign? Apparently they lived without laws and government; but for how long?

It is a basic mistake to represent the social state as an optional state based on human consent, on deliberation and on an original contract, something which is an impossibility. To talk of a state of *nature* in opposition to the social state is to talk nonsense voluntarily. The word *nature* is one of those general terms which, like all abstract terms, are open to abuse. In its most extensive sense, this word really signifies only the totality of all the laws, power, and springs of action that *make up* the world, and the *particular* nature of such and such a being is the totality of all the qualities which make it what it is and without which it would be some other thing and could no longer fulfill the intentions of its creator. Thus the combination of all the parts which make up a machine intended to tell the time forms the *nature* or the essence of a *watch;* and the *nature* or essence of the *balance wheel* is to have such and such a form, dimensions, and position, otherwise it would no longer be a balance wheel and could not fulfill its functions. The *nature* of a viper is to crawl, to have a scaly skin, hollow and movable fangs which exude poisonous venom; and the *nature* of man is to be a cognitive, religious, and sociable animal. All experience teaches us this; and, to my knowledge, nothing has contradicted this experience. If someone wants to prove that the nature of the viper is to have wings and a sweet voice, and that of a beaver is to live alone at the top of the highest mountains, it is up to him to prove it. In the meantime, we will believe that what is must be and has always been.

"The social order," says Rousseau, "is a sacred right which is the

basis of all others. Yet this right does not come from *nature:* it is therefore founded on convention."[1]

What is *nature?* What is a *right?* And how is an *order* a *right?* But
let us leave these difficulties: such questions are endless with a man
who misuses every term and defines none. One has the right at least to
ask him to prove the big assertion that *the social order does not come
from nature.* "I must," he says himself, "establish what I have just
advanced." This is indeed what should be done, but the way in which
he goes about it is truly curious. He spends three chapters in proving
that the social order does not derive from family society or from force
or from slavery (chapters 2, 3, 4) and concludes (chapter 5) *that we
must always go back to a first convention.* This method of proof is very
useful: it lacked only the majestic formula of the geometers, *"which
was to be proved."*

It is also curious that Rousseau has not even tried to prove the one
thing that it was necessary to prove; for if the social order derives from
nature, there is no social compact.

"Before examining," he says, "the act by which a people chooses a
king, it would be as well to examine the act by which a people is a
people: for this act, being necessarily previous to the other, is the true
foundation of society" (Chapter 5). This same Rousseau says elsewhere, "It is the inveterate habit of philosophers to deny what is and to
explain what is not."[2] Let us on our side add that it is the inveterate
habit of Rousseau to mock the philosopher without suspecting that he
also was a *philosopher* in all the force he gave to the word; so, for
example, the *Social Contract* denies from beginning to end the nature
of man, which *is,* in order to explain the social compact, which *does not
exist.*

This is how one reasons when one separates man from the Divinity.
Rather than tiring oneself out in the search of error, it would take little
effort to turn one's eyes to the source of all creation; but so simple, sure,
and consoling a method of philosophizing is not to the taste of writers
of this unhappy age whose true illness is an aversion to good sense.

Might it not be said that man, this property of the Divinity, was
cast on this earth by a blind cause, that he could be either this or that,
and that it is as a consequence of his choice that he is what he is?
Surely God intended some sort of end in creating man: the question

[1] *Social Contract*, Book i, Chap. i.
[2] *Nouvelle Héloïse*, Part 4.

can thus be reduced to whether man has become *a political animal,* as Aristotle put it, *through* or *against* the divine will. Although this question stated explicitly is a real sign of folly, it is nevertheless put indirectly in a host of writings, and fairly often the authors even decide that the latter is the case. The word *nature* has given rise to a multitude of errors. Let me repeat that the nature of any being is the sum of the qualities attributed to it by the Creator. With immeasurable profundity, Burke said that art is man's nature. This is beyond doubt; man with all his affections, all his knowledge, all his arts is the true *natural man,* and the weaver's cloth is as *natural* as the spider's web.

Man's *natural state* is therefore to be what he is today and what he has always been, that is to say, *sociable.* All human records attest to this truth. . . .

CHAPTER III. SOVEREIGNTY IN GENERAL

If sovereignty is not anterior to the *people,* at least these two ideas are collateral, since a sovereign is necessary to make a *people.* It is as impossible to imagine a human society, a people, without a sovereign as a hive and bees without a queen: for, by virtue of the eternal laws of nature, a swarm of bees exists in this way or it does not exist at all. Society and sovereignty are thus born together; it is impossible to separate these two ideas. Imagine an isolated man: there is no question of laws or government, since he is not a whole man and society does not yet exist. Put this man in contact with his fellowmen: from this moment you suppose a sovereign. The first man was king over his children; each isolated family was governed in the same way. But once these families joined, a sovereign was needed, and this *sovereign* made a *people* of them by giving them laws, since society exists only through the sovereign. Everyone knows the famous line,

The first king was a fortunate soldier.

This is perhaps one of the falsest claims that has ever been made. Quite the opposite could be said, that

The first soldier was paid by a king.

There was a *people,* some sort of civilization, and a sovereign as soon as men came into contact. The word *people* is a relative term that has no meaning divorced from the idea of sovereignty: for the idea of a *people* involves that of an aggregation around a common center, and without sovereignty there can be no political unity or cohesion. . . .

CHAPTER IV. PARTICULAR SOVEREIGNTIES AND NATIONS

The same power that has decreed social order and sovereignty has also decreed different modifications of sovereignty according to the different character of nations.

Nations are born and die like individuals. Nations have *fathers*, in a very literal sense, and *teachers* commonly more famous than their fathers, although the greatest merit of these teachers is to penetrate the character of the infant nation and to create for it circumstances in which it can develop all its capacities.

Nations have a general *soul* and a true moral unity which makes them what they are. This unity is evidenced above all by language.

The Creator has traced on the globe the limits of nations. . . . These boundaries are obvious and each nation can still be seen straining to fill entirely one of the areas within these boundaries. Sometimes invincible circumstances thrust two nations together and force them to mingle. Then their constituent principles penetrate each other and produce a *hybrid* nation which can be either more or less powerful and famous than if it was a *pure* race.

But several national elements thrown together into the same receptacle can be harmful. These seeds squeeze and stifle each other. The men who compose them, condemned to a certain moral and political mediocrity, will never attract the eyes of the world in spite of a large number of individual virtues, until some great shock, starting one of these seeds growing, allows it to engulf the other and to assimilate them into its own substance. *Italiam! Italiam!*

Sometimes a nation lives in the midst of another much more numerous, refuses to integrate because there is not sufficient affinity between them, and preserves its moral unity. . . .

When one talks of the *spirit* of a nation, the expression is not so metaphorical as is believed.

From these different national characteristics are born the different modifications of governments. One can say that each government has its separate character, for even those which belong to the same group and carry the same name reveal subtle differences to the observer.

The same laws cannot suit different provinces which have different customs, live in opposite climates, and cannot accept the same form of government.

The general objects of every good institution must be modified in each country by the relationships which spring as much from the local situation as from the character of the inhabitants. It is on the basis of these relationships that each people should be assigned a particular institutional system, which is the best, not perhaps in itself, but for the state for which it is intended.

There is only one good government for a particular state; yet not only can different governments be suitable for different peoples; they can also be suitable for the same people at different times, since a thousand events can change the inner relationships of a people.

There has always been a great deal of discussion on the best form of government without consideration of the fact that each can be the best in some instances and the worst in others!

Therefore it should not be said that *every form of government is appropriate to every country: for example, liberty, since it will not grow under every climate, is not open to every nation.* The more one thinks about this principle laid down by Montesquieu, the more one feels its force. The more it is contested, the more strongly it is established by new proofs.

Thus the absolute question, What is the best form of government? is as insoluble as it is indefinite; or, to put it another way, it has as many correct solutions as there are possible combinations in the relative and absolute positions of nations.

From these incontestable principles springs a no less incontestable consequence, that the social contract is a chimera. For, if there are as many different governments as there are different peoples, if the forms of these governments are laid down absolutely by the power that has given to each nation its particular moral, physical, geographical, and economic features, it is no longer permissible to talk of a *compact.* Each method of exercising sovereignty is the immediate result of the will of the Creator, like sovereignty in general. For one nation, despotism is as natural and as legitimate as democracy for another. If a man himself worked out these unshakable principles[3] in a book designed to establish that *"it is always necessary to go back to a convention,"*[4] if he

---

[3] *Social Contract*, Book ii, Chap. ix; Book iii, Chaps. i, iii, viii.
[4] *Ibid.*, Book i, Chap. v.

wrote in one chapter that "man was born free"[5] and in another that "liberty, since it will not grow under every climate, is not open to every nation,"[6] his utter folly could not be contested.

As no nation has been able to give itself the character and position that fit it to a particular government, all have been agreed not only in accepting this truth in the abstract but also in believing that the Divinity had intervened directly in the institution of their particular sovereignties. . . .

These are fables, it will be said. In truth, I do not know; but the fables of every nation, even modern nations, cover many realities. . . . It is complete folly to imagine that this universal prejudice is the work of sovereigns. Individual interest might well make bad use of a general belief, but it cannot create it. If that which I am talking about had not been based on the previous consent of nations, not only could a sovereign not have made them accept it; he would have been unable to conceive such a fraud. In general, every universal idea is natural.

CHAPTER V. AN EXAMINATION OF SOME IDEAS OF
ROUSSEAU ON THE LEGISLATOR

Rousseau wrote a chapter on *the legislator* in which all the ideas are confused in an intolerable way. In the first place, this word *legislator* can have two different meanings: usage allows us to apply it to the extraordinary men who promulgate constitutional laws, and also to the less remarkable men who pass civil laws. It seems that Rousseau understood the word in the first sense, since he talks of the man "who dares to undertake to institute a people and who constitutes the Republic." But soon after he says that "*the legislator is in all respects an extraordinary man* IN THE STATE." Then there already is a state; the people is then constituted; it is thus no longer a question of *instituting* a people but, more or less, of reforming it. . . .

Rousseau confuses all these ideas, and states in general that the legislator is neither an official nor a sovereign. "His task," he says, "is a superior function that has nothing in common with human rule."[7] If Rousseau means that a private individual can be consulted by a sovereign and can propose good laws which might be accepted, this is one

[5] *Ibid.*, Book i, Chap. i.
[6] *Ibid.*, Book iii, Chap. viii.
[7] *Ibid.*, Book ii, Chap. vii.

of those truths so trivial and sterile that it is useless to bother with them. If he intends to hold that a sovereign cannot make civil laws, . . . this is a discovery of which he has all the honor, no one ever having suspected it. If he means to prove that a sovereign cannot be a legislator in the strongest sense of the term, and give truly constituent laws to a people, by creating or perfecting their constitutional system, I appeal to the whole history of the world. . . .

CHAPTER VII. THE FOUNDERS AND THE POLITICAL
CONSTITUTION OF NATIONS

Thinking about the moral unity of nations, there can be no doubt that it is the result of a single cause. What the wise Bonnet said about the animal body in answer to a fancy of Buffon can be said about the body politic: every seed is necessarily *one*; and it is always from a single man that each nation takes its dominant trait and its distinctive character.

To know, then, why and how a man literally *engenders* a nation, and how he passes on to them the moral temperament, the character, the general soul which must, over the course of centuries and an infinite number of generations, exist perceptibly and distinguish one nation from all others, this is a mystery like so many others on which it is fruitful to dwell. . . .

The government of a nation is no more its own work than its language. Just as in nature the seeds of an infinite number of plants are destined to perish unless the wind or the hand of man puts them where they can germinate, so also there are in nations certain qualities and powers which are ineffective until they get a stimulus from circumstances either alone or used by a skillful hand.

The founder of a nation is precisely this skillful hand. Gifted with an extraordinary penetration or, what is more probable, with an infallible instinct (for often personal genius does not realize what it is achieving, which is what distinguishes it above all from intelligence), he divines those hidden powers and qualities which shape a nation's character, the means of bringing them to life, putting them into action, and making the greatest possible use of them. He is never to be seen writing or debating; his mode of acting derives from inspiration; and if sometimes he takes up a pen, it is not to argue but to command.

One of the greatest errors of this age is to believe that the political constitution of nations is the work of man alone and that a constitution can be made as a watchmaker makes a watch. This is quite false; but still more false is the belief that this great work can be executed by an assembly of men. The author of all things has only two ways of giving a government to a people. Most often he reserves to himself its formation more directly by making it grow, as it were, imperceptibly like a plant, through the conjunction of a multitude of those circumstances we call fortuitous. But when he wants to lay quickly the foundations of a political structure and to show the world a creation of this kind, he confides his power to rare men, the true Elect. Scattered thinly over the centuries, they rise like obelisks on time's path, and, as humanity grows older, they appear the less. To fit them for these unusual tasks, God invests them with unusual power, often unknown to their contemporaries and perhaps to themselves. Rousseau himself has spoken the truth when he said that the work of the founder of a nation was a MISSION. . . . If the founders of nations, who were all prodigious men, were to come before our eyes and we were to recognize their genius and their power, instead of talking nonsensically of usurpation, fraud, and fanaticism, we would fall on our knees and our sterility would disappear before the sacred sign shining from their brows. . . .

What is certain is that the constitution of a nation is never the product of deliberation.

Almost all the great legislators have been kings, and even those nations destined to be republics have been constituted by kings. They are the men who preside at the political establishment of nations and draw up their first fundamental laws. . . .

Look at every one of the world's constitutions, ancient and modern: you will see that now and again long experience has been able to point out some institutions capable of improving governments on the basis of their original constitution or of preventing abuses capable of altering their nature. It is possible to name the date and authors of these institutions, but you will notice that the real roots of government have remained the same and that it is impossible to show their origin, for the very simple reason that they are as old as the nations and that, not being the result of an agreement, there can be no trace of a convention which never existed.

No important and truly constitutional reform ever establishes anything new; it simply declares and defends previously existing rights. This is why the constitution of a country can never be known from its written constitutional laws, because these laws are made at different periods only to lay down forgotten or contested rights, and because there are always a host of things which are not written. . . .

The different forms and degrees of sovereignty have given rise to the belief that it is the work of nations which have modified it at will. Nothing could be further from the truth. Every nation has the government suited to it, and none has chosen it. The remarkable thing is that, nearly every time a nation tries to give itself a government, or more accurately every time too great a section of the people set out with such an aim, the attempt works to its misfortune; for in this fatal confusion, it is too easy for a nation to mistake its real interests, to chase desperately after what cannot be suitable for it, and at the same time reject what is best for it: and we all know how harmful errors in this field are. This is what made Tacitus say, with his simple profundity, that "it is much better for a people to accept a sovereign than to seek him."[8]

Besides, as every exaggerated proposition is false, I by no means intend to deny the possibility of political improvements brought about by a few wise men. I might as well deny the power of moral and physical education to improve men's morality and physique; but this truth confirms rather than shakes my general argument by proving that human power can create nothing and that everything depends on the original aptitudes of nations and of individuals.

It follows from this that a free constitution is stable only when the different parts of the political system come into being together and side by side, so to speak. Men never respect what they have made. This is why an elective king never possesses the moral force of a hereditary sovereign because he is not sufficiently *noble*, that is to say, he does not possess that kind of grandeur independent of men which is the work of time. . . .

The mass of men play no part in political events. They even respect government only because it is not their work. This feeling is written indelibly on their hearts. They submit to sovereignty because they feel that it is something sacred that they can neither create nor destroy. If, through corruption and treacherous suggestions, they reach the point of effacing in themselves this preserving sentiment, if they have the misfortune to think that they are called as a body to reform the state, everything is lost. This is why, even in free states, it

[8] Tacitus, *History* I, 56.

is extremely important for rulers to be separated from the mass of the people by that personal respect which stems from birth and wealth; for if opinion does not put a barrier between itself and authority, if power is not outside its scope, if the governed many can think themselves the equals of the governing few, government will collapse. Thus the aristocracy is a sovereign or ruling class by nature, and the principle of the French Revolution runs directly contrary to the eternal laws of nature.

CHAPTER VIII. THE WEAKNESS OF HUMAN POWER

In all political or religious works, whatever their aim or importance, it is a general rule that there is never any proportion between cause and effect. The effect is always immense in relation to the cause, so that man may know that he is only an instrument and that alone he can create nothing. . . .

The more human reason trusts in itself and tries to rely on its own resources, the more absurd it is and the more it reveals its lack of power. This is why the world's greatest scourge has always been, in every age, what is called *philosophy*, for philosophy is nothing but the human reason acting alone, and the human reason reduced to its own resources is nothing but a brute whose power is restricted to destroying. . . .

Far from being a theological exaggeration, it was a simple, rigorously expressed truth that one of our prelates (who died happily for his own sake while he was still able to believe in a new turn in affairs) spoke when he said, "In its pride, philosophy has said, *To me belongs wisdom, knowledge and power; to me belongs the conduct of men, since it is I who enlighten.* In order to punish and disgrace it, **God** needs only to condemn it to rule for a moment."

In fact, it has ruled over one of the most powerful nations of the world; it rules and no doubt will rule long enough for it not to be able to complain that it had not sufficient time. There has never been a more disgraceful example of the complete futility of human reason when left to its own resources. What lessons have the French legislators taught us? Aided by the whole of human knowledge, the teachings of all the philosophers both ancient and modern, and the whole of historical experience, masters of opinion, disposing of immense wealth, having allies everywhere, in a word backed by every kind of human power, they have spoken with full authority. The world has seen the result. Never has human pride disposed of so many resources and, forgetting its crimes for a moment, never has it been more ridiculous.

Our contemporaries will believe it as they will, but posterity will have no doubt that the most insane of men were those who gathered around a table and said, "We will separate the French people from their ancient constitution and give them another" (this one or that one, it does not matter). Although this folly is common to all the parties who have desolated France, yet the Jacobins spring first to mind as destroyers rather than as builders, and leave in the imagination a certain impression of grandeur resulting from the immensity of their successes. There is even some doubt whether they have seriously planned to organize France into a Republic, for the Republican Constitution they have fabricated is no more than a kind of comedy put on before the people as a moment's distraction, and I cannot think that even the least enlightened of its authors have been taken in by it for a moment.

But the men who held the stage in the first days of the Constituent Assembly really believed themselves to be legislators. Completely seriously and very obviously, they aimed at giving France a political constitution, and believed that an assembly could decree, by majority vote, that this or that nation should no longer have this or that government but some other. Now, this idea is the height of extravagance, and nothing to equal it has ever come out of all the *Bedlams* in this world. So these men give the impression only of feebleness, ignorance, and *disappointment*. No feeling of admiration or horror can equal the kind of angry pity that the constituent *Bedlam* inspires. The laurels of villainy belong of right to the Jacobins, but posterity will award those for folly to the Constitutionals.

The legislators have all felt that human reason could not stand alone and that no purely human institution could last. This is why they have, so to speak, interlaced politics and religion, so that human weakness, strengthened by a supernatural support, could be overcome. . . .

The excellence and durability of great political institutions are proportionate to the closeness of the union of politics and religion within them. . . .

CHAPTER IX. CONTINUATION OF THE SAME SUBJECT

In his evil book on the rights of man, Paine said that a constitution is antecedent to government; that it is to government what laws are to the courts; that it is visible and material, article by article, or else it does not exist: so that the English people has no constitution, its government being the product of conquest and not of the will of the people.[9]

It would be difficult to get more errors into fewer lines. Not only can a people not give itself a constitution, but no assembly, a small number of men in relation to the total population, can ever carry through such a task. . . .

There has never been, there will never be, there cannot be a nation constituted a priori. Reason and experience join to prove this great truth. What eye is capable of comprehending all the circumstances that must fit a nation to a particular constitution? How especially can a number of men be capable of this effort of intelligence? Unless they refuse to see the truth, they must agree that this is impossible; and history which should decide all these questions again supports theory. A small number of free nations have shone in history, but not one of them has been constituted in Paine's manner. Every particular form of government is a divine construction, just like sovereignty in general. A constitution in the philosophic sense is thus only the political way of life bestowed on each nation by a power above it; and, in an inferior sense, a constitution is only the assemblage of those more or less numerous laws which declare this way of life. It is not at all necessary for these laws to be written. On the contrary, it is particularly to constitutional laws that the maxim of Tacitus, *pessimae republicae plurimae leges*, can be applied. The wiser and more public-spirited a nation is, and the more excellent its constitution, the fewer written constitutional laws it has, for these laws are only props, and a building has no need of props except when it has slipped out of vertical or been violently shaken by some external force. . . .

What Paine and so many others regard as a fault is therefore a law of nature. The *natural* constitution of a nation is always anterior to its *written* constitution and can dispense with it. There has never been and can never be a written constitution made all at once, particularly

[9] Paine, *Rights of Man* (Everyman edition, London, 1954), pp. 48–49.

by an assembly, and the very fact that it is written all at once proves it false and impractical. Every constitution is properly speaking a *creation* in the full meaning of the word, and all *creation* is beyond men's powers. A written law is only the declaration of an anterior and unwritten law. Man cannot bestow rights on himself; he can only defend those which have been granted to him by a superior power; and these rights are *good customs,* good because they are not written and because no beginning or author can be assigned to them. . . .

CHAPTER X. THE NATIONAL SOUL

Human reason left to its own resources is completely incapable *not only of creating but also of conserving any religious or political association,* because it can only give rise to disputes and because, to conduct himself well, man needs beliefs, not problems. His cradle should be surrounded by dogmas; and, when his reason awakes, all his opinions should be given, at least all those relating to his conduct. Nothing is more vital to him than *prejudices.* Let us not take this word in bad part. It does not necessarily signify false ideas, but only, in the strict sense of the word, any opinions adopted without examination. Now, these kinds of opinion are essential to man; they are the real basis of his happiness and the palladium of empires. Without them, there can be neither religion, morality, nor government. There should be a state religion just as there is a state political system; or rather, religion and political dogmas, mingled and merged together, should together form a *general* or *national mind* sufficiently strong to repress the aberrations of the individual reason which is, of its nature, the mortal enemy of any association whatever because it gives birth only to divergent opinions.

All known nations have been happy and powerful to the degree that they have faithfully obeyed this national mind, which is nothing other than the destruction of individual dogmas and the absolute and general rule of national dogmas, that is to say, useful prejudices. Once let everyone rely on his individual reason in religion, and you will see immediately the rise of anarchy of belief or the annihilation of religious sovereignty. Likewise, if each man makes himself the judge of the principles of government you will see immediately the rise of civil anarchy or the annihilation of political sovereignty. Government is a true religion; it has its dogmas, its mysteries, its priests; to submit it to individual discussion is to destroy it; it has life only through the national mind, that is to say, political faith, which is a *creed*. Man's primary need is that his nascent reason should be curbed under a double yoke; it should be frustrated, and it should lose itself in the national mind, so that it changes its individual existence for another communal existence, just as a river which flows into the ocean still exists in the mass of water, but without name and distinct reality.

What is patriotism? It is this national mind of which I am speaking; it is individual *abnegation*. Faith and patriotism are the two great thaumaturges of the world. Both are divine. All their actions are miracles. Do not talk to them of scrutiny, choice, discussion, for they will say that you blaspheme. They know only two words, *submission* and *belief*; with these two levers, they raise the world. Their very errors are sublime. These two infants of Heaven prove their origin to all by creating and conserving; and if they unite, join their forces and together take possession of a nation, they exalt it, make it divine and increase its power a hundredfold. . . .

But can you, insignificant man, light this sacred fire that inflames nations? Can you give a common soul to several million men? Unite them under your laws? Range them closely around a common center? Shape the mind of men yet unborn? Make future generations obey you and create those age-old customs, those conserving *prejudices,* which are the father of the laws and stronger than them? What nonsense! . . .

CHAPTER XII. APPLICATION OF THE PRECEDING PRINCIPLES TO A
PARTICULAR CASE—CONTINUATION

There is no doubt that, in a certain sense, reason is good for nothing. We have the scientific knowledge necessary for the maintenance of society; we have made conquests in mathematics and what is called natural science; but, once we leave the circle of our needs, our knowledge becomes either useless or doubtful. The human mind, ever restless, proliferates constantly succeeding theories. They are born, flourish, wither, and fall like leaves from the trees; the only difference is that their year is longer.

And in the whole of the moral and political world, what do we know, and what are we able to do? We *know* the morality handed down to us by our fathers, as a collection of dogmas or useful prejudices adopted by the national mind. But on this point we owe nothing to any man's individual reason. On the contrary, every time this reason has interfered, it has perverted morality.

In politics, we *know* that it is necessary to respect those powers established we know not how or by whom. When time leads to abuses capable of altering the root principle of a government, we *know* that it is necessary to remove these abuses, but without touching the principle itself, an act of delicate surgery; and we *are able* to carry through these salutary reforms until the time when the principle of life is totally vitiated and the death of the body politic is inevitable. . . .

Wherever the individual reason dominates, there can be nothing great, for everything great rests on a belief, and the clash of individual opinions left to themselves produces only skepticism which is destructive of everything. General and individual morality, religion, laws, revered customs, useful prejudices, nothing is left standing, everything falls before it; it is the universal dissolvent.

Let us return again to basic ideas. Any *institution* is only a political edifice. In the physical and the moral order, the laws are the same; you cannot build a great edifice on narrow foundations or a durable one on a moving or transient base. Likewise, in the political order, to build high and to build for centuries, it is necessary to rely on an opinion or a belief broad and deep: for if the opinion does not hold the majority of minds and is not deeply rooted, it will provide only a narrow and transient base.

Now, if you seek the great and solid bases of all possible institutions of the first and second order, you will always find religion and patriotism.

And if you reflect still further, you will find that these two things are identical, for there is no true patriotism without religion. You will see it shine out only in the ages of belief, and it always fades and dies with it. Once man divorces himself from the divinity, he corrupts himself and everything he touches. His actions are misguided and end only in destruction. As this powerful binding force weakens in the state, so all the conserving virtues weaken in proportion. Men's characters become degraded, and even good actions are paltry. A murderous selfishness relentlessly presses on public spirit and makes it fall back before it, like those enormous glaciers of the high Alps that can be seen advancing slowly but frighteningly on the area of living things and crushing the useful vegetation in their path.

But once the idea of the divinity is the source of human action, this action is fruitful, creative, and invincible. An unknown force makes itself felt on all sides, and animates, warms, vivifies all things. However much human ignorance and corruption have soiled this great idea with errors and crimes, it no less preserves its incredible influence. . . .

CHAPTER XIII. A NECESSARY EXPLANATION

I must forestall an objection. In reproaching philosophy for the harm it has done to us, does one not run the risk of going too far and of being unjust in regard to it by swinging to an opposite extreme?

No doubt it is necessary to guard against enthusiasm, but it seems that in this respect there is one sure rule for judging philosophy. It is useful when it does not leave its own domain, that is, the sphere of the natural sciences. Here all its efforts are useful and merit our gratitude. But, once it sets its foot inside the moral sphere, it should remember that it is no longer on its own ground. It is the general mind that holds sway in this sphere, and philosophy, that is to say, the individual mind, becomes noxious and thus culpable if it dares to contradict or bring into question the sacred laws of their sovereign, that is to say, the national dogmas. Therefore, when it enters the domain of this sovereign, its duty is to act in concert with it. This distinction, whose accuracy I do not think can be contested, shows us the confines of philosophy. It is good when it remains within its own domain or when it enters a sphere higher than its own only as an ally or even as a subject; it is hateful when it enters as a rival or an enemy. . . .

I know that philosophy, ashamed of its dreadful successes, has decided to disavow loudly the excesses which we are witnessing, but it cannot escape the criticisms of the wise like this. Happily for humanity, the same men seldom possess both fatal theories and the power to put them into practice. But what does it matter to me that Spinoza lived peacefully in a Dutch village? What does it matter to me that the weak, timid, and reticent Rousseau never had the wish or the power to stir up revolt? What does it matter to me that Voltaire defended Calas to get his name in the papers? What does it matter to me that, during the appalling tyranny that has fallen on France, the philosophers, frightened for their heads, have withdrawn into prudent seclusion? Once they put forward maxims capable of spawning every crime,

these crimes are their work, since the criminals are their disciples. . . .
The tiger that rips men open is following his nature; the real criminal
is the man who unmuzzles him and launches him on society. . . .

BOOK TWO

ON THE NATURE OF SOVEREIGNTY

CHAPTER I. THE NATURE OF SOVEREIGNTY IN GENERAL

Every species of sovereignty is absolute of its nature, however the
powers are organized, whether vested in one pair of hands or divided.
In the last analysis, it will always be an absolute power which is able to
commit evil with impunity, which is thus from this point of view *despotic* in the full force of the term and against which there is no defense
other than rebellion.

Wherever sovereign powers are divided, the conflicts of these different powers can be looked at as the deliberations of a single sovereign, whose reason weighs up the *pros* and the *cons*. But once a
decision is made, the situation is the same in both cases and the will of
any sovereign whatever is always invincible.

However sovereignty is defined and vested, it is always one, unviolable and absolute. Take, for example, the English government: the
kind of political trinity which makes it up does not stop sovereignty
from being one, there as elsewhere. The powers balance each other,
but, once they are in agreement, there is then only one will which cannot be thwarted by any other legal will, and Blackstone was right to
claim that the English king and Parliament together can do anything.

The sovereign cannot therefore be judged: if he could be, the
power possessing this right would be sovereign and there would be two
sovereigns, which implies contradiction. The sovereign can no more

modify than alienate itself: to *limit* is to *destroy* it. *It is absurd and contradictory for the sovereign to recognize a superior. . . .*[10]

The real problem, then, is not to prevent the sovereign from *willing without restriction*, which is contradictory, but of preventing him from *willing unjustly. . . .* While I might be forced to agree that one has the *right* to murder Nero, I would never accept that one has the right to judge him; for the law by virtue of which he would be judged would have been made either by himself or by some other person, which would suppose either a law made by a sovereign against himself or a sovereign above the sovereign, two equally inadmissible suppositions.

When considering governments in which the powers are divided, it is easy to believe that the sovereign can be judged, because of the activity of each power which acts on the others and, increasing its activity on certain unusual occasions, brings about secondary insurrections which are much less dangerous than insurrections properly speaking, in other words, "popular." But it is necessary to guard against a fallacy into which it is easy to fall if one looks at only one of the powers. It is necessary to envisage them in their entirety and to ask oneself if the sovereign will resulting from their joint wills can be impeded, thwarted, or punished.

One will find in the first place that every sovereign is despotic and that, with regard to them, only two courses can be taken, obedience or insurrection. It is possible to maintain, as a matter of fact, that although all sovereign wills are equally absolute, they are not equally blind or vicious, and that republican or mixed governments are superior to monarchies precisely because in them the decisions of the sovereign are generally wiser and more enlightened. This is in fact one of the principal ideas which should serve as a basis for the important examination of the superiority of one form of government over the other.

One will find in the second place that it is just the same to be *subject* to one sovereign as to another.

CHAPTER II. MONARCHY

It can be said in general that all men are born for monarchy. This form of government is the most ancient and the most universal. . . . Monarchical government is so natural that, without realizing it, men

[10] *Social Contract*, Book iii, Chap. xvi.

identify it with sovereignty. They seem tacitly to agree that, wherever there is no king, there is no real *sovereign*. . . .

This is particularly striking in everything that has been said on both sides of the question that formed the subject of the first book of this work. The adversaries of divine origin always hold a grudge against *kings* and talk only of *kings*. They do not want to accept that the authority of kings comes from God: but it is not a question of *royalty* in particular but of *sovereignty* in general. Yes, all sovereignty derives from God; whatever form it takes, it is not the work of man. It is one, absolute and inviolable of its nature. Why, then, lay the blame on royalty, as though the inconveniences which are relied on to attack this system are not the same in any form of government? Once again, it is because royalty is *the natural government* and because in common discourse men confuse it with sovereignty by disregarding other governments, just as they neglect the exception when enunciating the general rule. . . .

Man must always be brought back to history, which is the first and indeed the only teacher in politics. Whoever says that man is born for liberty is speaking nonsense. If a being of a superior order undertook the *natural history* of man, surely he would seek his directions in the history of facts. When he knew what man is and has always been, what he does and has always done, he would write; and doubtless he would reject as foolish the notion that man is not what he should be and that his condition is contrary to the laws of creation. The very expression of this proposition is sufficient to refute it.

History is experimental politics; and just as, in the physical sciences, a hundred books of speculative theories disappear before a single experiment, in the same way in political science no theory can be allowed if it is not the more or less probable corollary of well-attested facts. If the question is asked, "What is the most natural government to man," history will reply, *It is monarchy*.

This government no doubt has its drawbacks, like every other, but all the declamations that fill the books of the day on these kinds of abuses can only rouse pity for their authors. It is pride and not reason which gives rise to them. Once it is rigorously established that nations are not made for the same government, that each nation has that which is best for it, above all that "liberty is not open to every nation, and that the more we ponder on this principle laid down by Montesquieu, the more apparent its truth appears,"[11] we can no longer understand what the diatribes against the vices of monarchical government are about. If their aim is to make the unfortunate people who are destined to bear the disadvantages feel them more sharply, it is a most barbaric pastime; if their aim is to urge men to revolt against a government made for them, it is a crime beyond description.

But the subjects of monarchies are by no means reduced to taking refuge from despair in philosophic meditations; they have something better to do, which is to gain full knowledge of the excellence of their government and to learn not to envy others. . . .

Let us go on to examine the principal characteristics of monarchical government. . . .

Monarchy is a *centralized* aristocracy. At all times and in all places, aristocracy dominates. Whatever form is given to governments, birth and wealth always take the first rank, and nowhere is their rule more harsh than where it is not founded on the law. But in a monarchy the king is the center of this aristocracy: the latter, here as elsewhere, still rules, but it rules in the name of the king, or, if you like, the king is guided by the understanding of the aristocracy. . . .

Avoiding all exaggeration, it is certain that the government of a single man is that in which the vices of the sovereign have the least effect upon the governed.

A very remarkable truth was spoken recently at the opening of the republican Lycée in Paris. "In absolute governments, the faults of the ruler can scarcely ruin everything at the same time, because his single will cannot do everything; but a republican government is obliged to be essentially reasonable and just, because the general will, once it goes astray, carries everything with it."[12]

This observation is most just: it is far from true that the will of the king does everything in a monarchy. It is supposed to do everything, and that is the great advantage of this government: but, in fact, its utility is almost wholly in centralizing advice and knowledge. Religion, laws, customs, opinion, class, and corporate privileges restrict the sovereign and prevent him from abusing his power; it is striking that kings have even been much more often accused of lacking will than of overexerting it. It is always the king's council that rules. But

---

[11] *Ibid.*, Book iii, Chap. viii.

[12] Speech given at the opening of the republican Lycée, December 31, 1794, by M. de la Harpe (*Journal de Paris*, 1795, No. 114, p. 461).

the *pyramidal* aristocracy that administers the state in monarchies has particular characteristics which deserve our attention.

In every country and under every possible government, the great officers always belong to the aristocracy, that is, to nobility and wealth, most often united. In saying that this *must be so*, Aristotle put forward a political axiom which simple good sense and the experience of the whole of history cannot allow us to doubt. This privilege of aristocracy is really a natural law.

Now, it is one of the greatest advantages of monarchical government that in it the aristocracy loses, as much as the nature of things allows, all those features offensive to the lower classes. It is important to understand the reasons for this.

1. This kind of aristocracy is legal; it is an integral part of government, everyone knows this, and it does not waken in anyone's mind the idea of usurpation and injustice. In republics, on the other hand, the distinction between persons exists as much as in monarchies, but it is harder and more offensive because it is not the work of the law and because popular opinion regards it as a continual rebellion against the principle of equality admitted by the constitution. . . .

2. Once the influence of a hereditary aristocracy becomes inevitable (and the experience of every age leaves no doubt on this point), the best course to deprive this influence of the elements that rub against the pride of the lower classes is to remove all insurmountable barriers between the families within the state and to allow none of them to be humiliated by a distinction that they can never enjoy.

Now this is precisely the case in a monarchy resting on good laws. There is no family that the merit of its head cannot raise from the second to the first rank. . . .

3. And this order of things appears still more perfect when it is remembered that the aristocracy of birth and office, already softened by the right belonging to every family to enjoy the same distinctions in its turn, is stripped of everything possibly offensive to the lower orders by the universal supremacy of the monarch, before whom no citizen is more powerful than another; the man in the street, who is insignificant when he measures himself against a great lord, measures the lord against the sovereign, and the title of *subject* which brings both of them under the same power and the same justice is a kind of equality that stills the inevitable pangs of self-esteem. . . .

In the government of several, sovereignty is by no means A UNITY;

and although the parts making it up form A UNITY, it is far from the case that they make the same impression on the mind. The human imagination does not grasp a unity that is only a metaphysical abstraction; on the contrary, it delights in separating each element of the general unity, and the subject has less respect for a sovereignty whose separate parts are not sufficiently above him. It follows that, in these kinds of government, sovereignty has not the same *intensity* or, in consequence, the same moral force. . . .

Let us abandon all prejudice and party spirit, renounce exaggerated ideas and all the theoretical dreams fostered by the French fever, and European good sense will agree on the following propositions:

1. The king is sovereign; no one can share sovereignty with him, and all powers emanate from him.

2. His person is inviolable; no one has the right to depose or judge him.

3. He has not the right to condemn to death, or even impose any corporal punishment. The power that punishes derives from him, and that is sufficient.

4. If he imposes exile or imprisonment in cases in which reason of state prevents a judicial hearing, he should not be too secretive or act too much without the advice of an enlightened council.

5. The king cannot judge in civil cases; only the judges, in the name of the sovereign, can pronounce on property and contracts.

6. Subjects have the right, by means of certain differently composed bodies, councils, or assemblies, to denounce abuses to him and legally to communicate to him their *grievances* and their *very humble* remonstrances.

It is in these sacred laws, the more truly constitutional since they are written only in men's hearts, and more particularly in the paternal relationship between prince and subjects, that can be found the true character of European monarchy.

Whatever the intense and blind pride of the eighteenth century says about it, this is all we need. These elements, combined in different ways, produce all sorts of nuances in monarchical government. It can be seen, for example, that the men charged with carrying to the foot of the throne the representations and grievances of subjects can form *bodies* or *assemblies;* that the members who compose these assemblies or bodies can vary in number, in rank, in the nature and extent of their powers; that the method of election, the frequency and length of sessions, and so on, alter the number of these combinations: *facies non omnibus una*; but always you will find the same general character: that is, chosen men carrying legally to the father the complaints and the views of the family: *nec diversa tamen.* . . .

How many faults power has committed! And how steadfastly it ignores the means of conserving itself! Man is insatiable for power; he is infinite in his desires and, always discontented with what he has, loves only what he has not. People complain of the despotism of princes; they ought to complain of the despotism of *man*. We are all born despots, from the most absolute monarch of Asia to the infant who smothers a bird with its hand for the pleasure of seeing that there exists in the world a being weaker than itself. There is not a man who does not abuse power, and experience shows that the most abominable despots, if they manage to seize the scepter, are precisely those who rant against despotism. But the Author of nature has set bounds to the abuse of power: He has willed that it destroys itself once it goes beyond its natural limits. Everywhere He has written this law; in the physical as in the moral world, it surrounds us and makes itself constantly heard. Look at this gun: up to a certain point, the longer you make it, the more effective it will be; but once you go at all beyond this limit, its effectiveness will be reduced. Look at this telescope; up to a certain point, the bigger you make it, the more powerful it will be; but go beyond that, and invincible nature will turn all your efforts to perfect the instrument against you. This is a crude image of power. To conserve itself, it must restrain itself, and it must always keep away from that point at which its most extreme effort leads to its own death.

Certainly I do not like *popular* assemblies any more than the next man; but French folly ought not to turn us aside from the truth and wisdom of the happy mean. If there is any indisputable maxim, it is that, in all mutinies, insurrections, and revolutions *the people always start by being right and always end by being wrong*. It is not true that every nation should have its *national assembly* in the French sense; it is not true that every individual is eligible for the national council; it is not even true that everyone can be an elector without any distinction of rank or fortune; it is not true that this council should be colegislative; finally it is not true that it ought to be composed the same way in different countries. But because these exaggerated claims are false, does it follow that no one has the right to speak for the common good in the name of the community and that we are prevented from acting wisely because the French have acted so foolishly? I do not understand this conclusion. . . .

CHAPTER III. ON ARISTOCRACY

Aristocratic government is a monarchy in which the throne is vacant. *Sovereignty there is in regency.*

The regents who administer sovereignty being hereditary, it is totally separated from the people, and in this, aristocratic government approaches monarchy. It cannot, however, reach it in vigor; but from the point of view of wisdom, it has no equal. It can be said in general that all nonmonarchic governments are aristocratic, for democracy is only elective aristocracy. . . .

Leaving aside the natural aristocracy that results from physical strength and talent, which it is unprofitable to discuss, there are only two sorts of aristocracy, elective and hereditary. . . . But, since elective monarchy is the weakest and most unstable of governments, and since experience has shown us clearly the superiority of hereditary monarchy, it follows by an indisputable analogy that hereditary aristocracy is preferable to elective. . . .

All in all, hereditary aristocratic government is perhaps the most advantageous to what is called the *people.* Sovereignty is sufficiently concentrated to inspire respect in them; but, as it has fewer needs and less splendor, it asks less of them. If sometimes it is timid, this is because it is never imprudent. . . .

CHAPTER IV. DEMOCRACY

Pure democracy does not exist any more than absolute despotism. "If you use the strict meaning of the term," says Rousseau admirably, "a true democracy has never existed and will never exist. It is against the natural order for the majority to govern and the minority to be governed."[13]

The idea of a whole people being sovereign and legislative is so contrary to good sense that the Greek political writers, who should know a little about liberty, never talked about democracy as a legitimate government, at least when they meant to express themselves

[13] *Social Contract,* Book iii, Chap. iv.

exactly. Aristotle especially defines democracy as the *excess of the republic*, just as despotism is the excess of monarchy.

If there is no such thing as a democracy, properly speaking, the same can be said of a perfect despotism, which is equally a hypothetical model. "It is wrong to think that there has ever been a single authority despotic in every respect; there has never been nor will there ever be such a system. The widest power is still bounded by some limits."[14]

But nothing stops us, in order to clarify our ideas, from considering these two forms of government as two theoretical extremes which every possible government resembles to a greater or lesser degree.

In this strict sense, I believe I can define democracy as *an association of men without sovereignty*.

"When the whole people," says Rousseau, "decides for the whole people, it considers only itself. . . . Then the matter on which a decision is made is general, like the will which makes it; it is this act that I call a LAW."[15]

What Rousseau calls eminently *law* is precisely what is incapable of bearing the name. . . .

As a nation, like an individual, cannot possess coercive power over itself, it is clear that, if a democracy in its theoretical purity were to exist, there would be no sovereignty within this state: for it is impossible to understand by this word anything other than a repressive power that acts on the *subject* and that is external to him. It follows that this word *subject*, which is a relative term, is alien to republics, because there is no sovereign, properly speaking, in a republic and because there cannot be a *subject* without a *sovereign*, just as there cannot be a *son* without a *father*.

Even in aristocratic governments, in which sovereignty is much more palpable than in democracies, the word *subject* is nevertheless avoided, and other, less rigid, terms, which involve no exaggeration, are found.

In every country there are voluntary associations of men who have united for some self-interested or charitable purpose. These men have voluntarily submitted themselves to certain rules which they observe as long as they find it advantageous. They even submit themselves to certain punishments imposed when they have broken the regulations

---

[14] Montesquieu, *Grandeur et décadence des Romains*, Chap. xxii.
[15] *Social Contract*, Book ii, Chap. vi.

of the association. But these regulations have no authority other than the will itself of those who have drawn them up, and, when there are dissidents, there is no coercive force among them to restrain these dissidents.

A just idea of a true democracy can be gained by magnifying the idea of such corporations. The ordinances emanating from a people constituted in such a way would be rules, and not laws. Law is so little the will of all that the *more* it is the will of *all*, the *less* it is *law*: so that it would cease to be law if it was the work of *all* those who ought to obey it, without exception.

But a purely voluntary state of association exists no more than does a pure democracy. One only starts from this theoretical power in order to understand; and it is in this sense that one can claim that sovereignty is born the moment when the sovereign begins not to be *the whole people* and that it grows stronger to the degree that it becomes less *the whole people*.

The spirit of voluntary association is the constitutive principle of republics, and has necessarily a prime cause; it is *divine*, and no one can produce it. The degree to which it is mixed in sovereignty, the common base of all governments, determines the *physiognomy* of non-monarchical governments.

The observer, and particularly the foreign observer who lives in a republican country, can distinguish very well the effects of these two principles. Sometimes he feels sovereignty and sometimes the communal spirit that serves as a supplement to it. Public power acts less, and above all is less apparent, than in monarchies, seeming to mistrust itself. A certain collective feeling, which is easier to feel than to define, dispenses sovereignty from acting in a host of circumstances in which it would intervene elsewhere. A thousand small things come about of their own accord, and order and agreement show themselves on all sides for no apparent reason. Communal property is respected even by the poor, and everything, even the general propriety, gives the observer food for thought.

A republican nation being thus less governed than any other, it can be seen that the acts of sovereignty must be supplemented by public spirit, so that the less a nation has wisdom to see the good and virtue to follow it of itself, the less fitted it is for a republic.

The advantages and disadvantages of this kind of government are quickly discovered. At its best, it eclipses all others, and the marvels it works seduce even the calmest and most judicious of observers. But, in the first place, it is suitable only for very small nations, for there is no need to demonstrate that the formation and maintenance of the spirit of association becomes more difficult as the number of associates grows.

In the second place, justice has not that calm and smooth action that we ordinarily see in monarchies. In democracies, justice is sometimes weak and sometimes impassioned. It is said that, under these governments, no head can resist the sword of the law. This means that, the punishment of an illustrious criminal or accused person being a real joy for the plebs who by this console themselves for the inevitable superiority of the aristocracy, public opinion strongly favors this kind of sentence; but if the criminal is obscure, or in general if the crime wounds neither the pride nor the immediate interests of the majority of individuals, this same opinion resists the action of justice and paralyzes it.

In a monarchy, the aristocracy is only a prolongation of royal authority, and thus partakes to a certain degree in the inviolability of the monarch. This immunity (always very much below that of the sovereign) is graduated so that it is held by fewer persons as it grows in extent.

In a monarchy, immunity, differently graduated, belongs to the minority, in a democracy to the majority. In the first case it shocks the plebs; in the second it pleases them. I believe it to be good in both cases, that is to say, I believe it to be a necessary element in both governments, which comes to the same thing, for what constitutes a government is always good, at least in an absolute sense.

But it is another matter when one government is compared to another. It is then a question of weighing the benefits and inconveniences to humanity of different social systems.

It is from this point of view that I believe monarchy to be superior to democracy in the administration of justice; and I am talking not only of criminal but also of civil justice. The same weakness can be observed in the one as in the other.

The magistrate is not sufficiently above the citizen; he has the air of an arbitrator rather than of a judge; and, forced to act cautiously even when he speaks in the name of the law, it is obvious that he does not believe in his own power. His strength lies only in the adherence of his equals, because there is either no sovereign or it is not strong enough. . . .

In general, justice is always weak in democracies when it acts alone, and always cruel or irresponsible when it relies on the people.

Some political writers have maintained that one of the advantages of republican government was the ability the people possess to confide the exercise of its authority only to men worthy of it. No one, they claim, can choose better than the people: where their interests are concerned, nothing can seduce them, and merit alone decides them.

I fancy that this idea is largely delusory. Democracy could not last a moment if it was not tempered by aristocracy, and above all by hereditary aristocracy, which is perhaps more indispensable to this government than to monarchy. In a republic, the right to vote gives neither prestige nor power. When Rousseau tells us, in the introduction to the *Social Contract,* that, in his quality as a citizen of a free state, he is personally *sovereign,* even the most benevolent reader is inclined to laugh. Men count for something in a republic only to the degree that birth, marriage, and high talents give them influence; the simple citizen counts for nothing. . . .

In times of peace, the people allow themselves to be led by their rulers: then they are wise because they act little; they choose well because the choice is made for them. When they are content with the power they derive from the constitution and, without venturing to make use of this power, rely on the understanding and wisdom of the aristocracy, when on the other side the rulers, sufficiently restrained by the fear of being deprived of the exercise of power, use it with a wisdom which justifies confidence, this is when republics shine. But when respect on the one side and fear on the other disappear, the state slides quickly toward ruin. . . .

However, I do not want to claim that monarchical government is any less open to mistakes in its choice of men; but the eternal declamation on the errors of blind patronage are much less well founded than is commonly imagined. In the first place, if it is pride that complains, kings always choose badly, for there is not a malcontent who does not prefer himself without question to the most happy choice. Moreover, too often kings are accused when it is the people who should be accused. In periods of general degeneracy, men complain that merit does not succeed; but where is it then, this ignored merit? They are obliged to point it out before accusing the government. During the last two French reigns, it is true that very mediocre men have been vested with high responsibilities; but to which men of merit were they preferred? Now that the most complete revolution the world has seen has broken all the chains which could bind the talents captive, where are they? You might perhaps find them, but they will be joined to profound immorality; but it is the sensible spirit of self-preservation of states that has barred talents of this kind from high offices. Moreover, as the Scriptures put it, there is a certain cleverness that works only for ill. This is the talent that has devastated France for five years. If you look carefully, you will find no or very little real political talent among even the most prominent men who have appeared on this bloody and tearful stage. They have been very good at doing evil; this is the only praise that can be bestowed on them. Happily the most famous of them have been writers; and, when all passions have been buried in the grave, posterity will discover from their indiscreet pages that the most monstrous errors dominated these pride-ridden men and that the previous government which rejected, curbed, and punished them was, without knowing it, fighting for its own life.

It is therefore because France was degenerating, because she was deficient in talents, that the kings seemed to welcome too much the mediocrity brought forward by intrigue. There is a very gross error, into which we nevertheless fall every day without realizing it. Although we recognize the hidden hand which guides all things, yet so important does the action of secondary causes seem to us that we fairly commonly reason as if this hand did not exist. When we contemplate the play of intrigue around thrones, words like *chance, good luck, bad luck, fortune* naturally present themselves, and we say them a little too quickly without perceiving that they make no sense.

Without doubt, man is free; he can make mistakes, but not sufficiently to derange general plans. We are all bound to the throne of God by a pliant chain which reconciles the self-propulsion of free agents with divine supremacy. Unquestionably, a certain king might in a certain age prevent a real talent from occupying a position made for it, and this unfortunate capacity can be more or less extensive. But, in general, there is a secret power that carries each individual to his place; otherwise the state could not continue. We recognize in a plant some unknown power, some single form-giving force which creates and conserves, which moves unwaveringly toward its end, which appropriates what is useful to it and rejects that which would harm it, which carries even to the last fibril of the last leaf the sap that it needs, and fights with all its might against the diseases of the vegetable world. This force is still more obvious and more wonderful in the animal kingdom. How blind we are! How can we deny that the body politic has also its law, its soul, its form-giving force, and believe that everything is dependent on the whims of human ignorance? If the moral mechanism of states were revealed to us, we would be freed of a host of errors: we would see, for instance, that the man who appears to us to be fitted for a certain position is a *disease* which the life force pushes to the surface, while we deplore the *misfortune* that stops him from invading the sources of life. We are misled every day by the words *talent* and *genius;* often these qualities are absent where we think we see them, and often also they belong to dangerous men. . . .

To hear these defenders of democracy talk, one would think that the people deliberate like a committee of wise men, whereas in truth judicial murders, foolhardy undertakings, wild choices, and above all foolish and disastrous wars are eminently the prerogatives of this form of government.

But who has ever said worse of democracy than Rousseau, for he declares point-blank that it is made only for a society of Gods.[16] It remains to be seen how a government which is made only for *gods* can yet be proposed to *men* as the only legitimate government, for if this is not the meaning of the social contract, the social contract has no meaning.

But this is not all: "How many things," he says, "difficult to bring together are required by this government. First, a very small state, in which the people can easily assemble, and where each citizen can easily know all the others; second, great simplicity of manners to prevent a multiplicity of problems and difficult discussions; then a high degree of equality in rank and fortune without which equality in rights and authority would not last for long; finally, little or no luxury."[17]

At this point, I shall consider only the first of these conditions. If democracy is suitable only for very small states, how can this form of government be put forward as the only legitimate form of government and as, so to speak, a *formula* capable of resolving all political problems? . . .

I do not know why Rousseau was willing to admit that democracy

---

[16] *Ibid.*, Book iii, Chap. iv.
[17] *Ibid.*

involves some small disadvantages, but he had a very simple way of justifying it, which is to judge it only by its theoretical perfection and to regard its disadvantages as small and insignificant anomalies which do not deserve careful attention.

"The general will," he says, "is always right and always tends to the public utility, but the deliberations of the people have not always the same rightness. . . . The people are never corrupted, but they are often misled, and it is only then that they appear to will what is evil."[18]

Drink, Socrates, drink; and console yourself with these distinctions: the good people of Athens only *appear* to will what is evil. . . .

CHAPTER V. THE BEST SPECIES OF GOVERNMENT

Rousseau saw quite correctly that no one should ask what is the best form of government in general, since none is suitable for every nation. Each nation has its own, as it has its own language and character, and this government is the best for it. The consequence of which is obviously that all theories of social contract are pipedreams. . . . Since none of the varying circumstances depend on men, it follows that the consent of the people plays no part in the formation of governments. . . . The question is not to know what is the best form of government but which nation is best governed according to the principles of its government. . . .

CHAPTER VI. CONTINUATION OF THE SAME SUBJECT

The best government for each nation is that which, in the territory occupied by this nation, is capable of producing the greatest possible sum of happiness and strength, for the greatest possible number of men, during the longest possible time. I venture to believe that the justice of this definition cannot be denied and that it is by following it that comparison between states from the point of view of their governments becomes possible. In fact, although it is impossible to ask *What is the best form of government?* nothing stops us asking, *Which nation is relatively the most numerous, the strongest, and the happiest, over the greatest period of time, through the influence of the government suitable to it ?*

What peculiarity of mind prevents us from using in the study of

[18] *Ibid.*, Book ii, Chap. iii.

politics the same methods of reasoning and the same general hypotheses which guide us in the study of other sciences?

In physical research, if there is a problem of estimating a variable force, we take the average quantity. In astronomy in particular we always talk of *average distance* and *average time*. To judge the merit of a government, the same method should be used.

Any government is a variable force that produces effects as variable as itself, within certain limits. To judge it, it should not be examined at a given moment, but over the whole of its existence. Then to judge the French monarchy properly, a sum of the virtues and vices of all the French kings should be made, and divided by sixty-six: the result is an *average king*; and the same is true of other monarchies.

Democracy has one brilliant moment, but it is a moment and it must pay dearly for it. The great days of Athens might, I agree, inspire desires in the subject of a monarchy, languishing in such and such a period under an inept or wicked king. Nevertheless, we would be greatly mistaken if we claimed to establish the superiority of democracy over monarchy by comparing moment for moment, because, in this way of judging, we neglect among other things the consideration of duration, which is a necessary element of these sorts of calculation.

In general, all democratic governments are only transitory meteors, whose brilliance excludes duration. . . .

In discussing the different kinds of government, the general happiness is not sufficiently considered, although it should be our sole criterion. We should have the courage to face a glaring truth which would cool our enthusiasm for free constitutions a little; this is that, in every republic over a certain size, what is called *liberty* is only the total sacrifice of a great number of men for the independence and pride of a small number. . . .

Properly speaking, all governments are monarchies which differ only in whether the monarch is for life or for a term of years, hereditary or elective, individual or corporate; or, if you will (for it is the same idea in other terms), all governments are aristocratic, composed of a greater or smaller number of rulers, from democracy, in which this aristocracy is composed of as many men as the nature of things permits, to monarchy, in which the aristocracy, inevitable under every government, is headed by a single man topping the pyramid and which undoubtedly constitutes the most natural government for man.

But of all monarchies, the hardest, most despotic, and most intolerable is King *People.* Again history testifies to the great truth that the liberty of the minority is founded only on the slavery of the masses and that republics have never been anything but multimember sovereigns, whose despotism, always harder and more capricious than that of kings, increases in intensity as the number of subjects grows. . . .

CHAPTER VII. REFLECTIONS ON THIS SUBJECT

What do all these philosophers want, since nothing that exists or has existed can please them? They do not want any government, since there is no government which does not lay claim to obedience. It is not this or that authority which they detest, but authority itself; they cannot endure any. . . .

It is enough to recall the excellent phrase of Rousseau, who was always right when he spoke against himself: "If I consult philosophers, each has only his own voice." Deadly enemies of every kind of association, possessed of a repellent and solitary pride, they agree on only one point, the fury of destruction. Since each wishes to replace what displeases him by his own visions which are agreeable to him alone, the result is that all their power is negative and that all their efforts to build are ineffective and ridiculous. Misguided man, learn once for all to recognize these dangerous tricksters; leave them to admire themselves on their own and rally to the national reason which is never mistaken. Remember that every nation has, in its laws and ancient customs, everything it needs to be happy as far as it can be and that by using these ancient laws as the basis for all your reconstruction you can reveal all your perfectibility without giving way to fatal innovations.

Raise your mind again to higher thoughts. The eternal reason has spoken, and its infallible oracles have shown us in pride "the beginning of all evils." This terrible principle is rampant throughout Europe, since these same philosophers have relieved you of your father's faith. Hatred of authority is the scourge of our day: there is no remedy for this ill except in the sacred maxims you have been made to forget. Archimedes knew well that, to raise the world, you need a fulcrum outside the world.

To overthrow the moral world, the enemies of all order have hit on this fulcrum. Atheism and immorality stir up revolt and insurrection. . . .

In general, we know almost nothing about the unity of things, and in this we are to be excused, but we cannot be excused for being ignorant that this unity exists. The imaginary world of Descartes represents fairly well the reality of the political world. Every nation is a particular vortex at once impelling and impelled; the *whole* is nothing but the totality of these vortices, and nations are between themselves just like the individuals who compose them. Each member of these great families we call *nations* has received a character, faculties, and a mission peculiar to himself. Some are destined to slip in silence along the path of life without their passage being noted. Others herald their progress, and nearly always they are rewarded by fame rather than happiness. Individual talents are infinitely diversified with a divine magnificence, and the most brilliant are not the most useful; but every one has some use, every one is in its place; all play a part in the general organization, all move unswervingly toward the end of the association. . . .

It is the same of nations as of individuals. All have a character and a mission that they fulfill without realizing it. Some are learned and others are conquerors; and again there is an infinite diversity of general characteristics. Among conquering nations, some are purely destructive whilst others seem to destroy only to make room for creations of a new kind. . . .

No nation owes its character to its government, any more than its language. On the contrary, it owes its government to its character, which in fact is always reinforced and perfected subsequently by political institutions. If you see a nation decline, this is not because its government is bad; it is because this government, which is the best for that nation, dies like all human works, or rather it is because the national character is worn out. Then nations must undergo a political rebirth, or perish. . . .

The Pope

BOOK ONE

OF THE POPE IN HIS RELATIONS WITH
THE CATHOLIC CHURCH

CHAPTER I. INFALLIBILITY

What has not been said about infallibility considered from a theological point of view! It would be difficult to add new arguments to those that the defenders of this high prerogative have accumulated in order to support it with unshakable authorities and to relieve it of those phantoms with which the enemies of Christianity and unity have been pleased to surround it, in the hope of making it hated at least, if they could not do worse.

But I am not sure if it has been sufficiently noticed, in this great question as in so many others, that religious truths are only general truths manifested and made divine within the religious sphere, so that it is impossible to attack one without attacking a law of the world.

Infallibility in the spiritual order and sovereignty in the temporal order are two completely synonymous words. Both give voice to that high power which rules over all other powers, from which they derive, which governs and is not governed, which judges and is not judged.

When we say that *the Church is infallible*, it is very important to notice that we do not ask for it any particular privilege: we ask only that it should enjoy the right common to all possible sovereignties, which all necessarily act as if infallible. For every government is absolute, and the moment it can be resisted under the pretext of error or injustice, it no longer exists.

No doubt sovereignty takes different forms. It does not speak in Constantinople as it does in London, but in both places when it has spoken in its peculiar way, the *bill* is as much without appeal as the *fetfa*.

The same is true of the Church. In one way or another, it must be governed, like any other association whatever; otherwise there would be no more cooperation, no more cohesion, no more unity. This government is therefore of its nature infallible, that is to say, *absolute*, or else it would no longer govern.

In the judicial sphere, which is only an aspect of government, it is obvious that we must resort to a power that judges and is not judged, precisely because it speaks in the name of that supreme power of which it is considered to be the organ and the voice. View it as you will, give this high judicial power whatever name you like, there must always be within it one person to whom it cannot be said, *You have erred*. Of course, the condemned man is always displeased with his sentence and never doubts the iniquity of the court, but a disinterested and farsighted view makes light of these vain complaints. It recognizes that there is a limit beyond which no one must go; it knows that interminable proceedings, appeals without end, and uncertainty about property rights are, if it can be put like this, more unjust than injustice.

The only question, then, is to know where sovereignty resides in the Church, for once it is recognized, it is no longer permissible to appeal from its decisions.

Now, nothing is more evident, to reason as much as to faith, than that the universal Church is monarchical. The very idea of *universality* supposes this form of government, whose absolute necessity arises from the double ground of the number of its subjects and the geographical extent of its jurisdiction.

So, all Catholic writers worthy of the name agree unanimously that the structure of the Church is monarchical but sufficiently tempered by aristocracy to be the best and most perfect of governments. . . .

In the sixteenth century, the rebels attributed sovereignty to *the Church*, that is to say, to the people. The eighteenth century only transferred these maxims to politics; it is the same system, the same theory, down to its last details. What difference is there between *the*

Church of God, guided solely by his word, and the great republic one and indivisible, solely governed by laws and by deputies of the sovereign people? None at all. It is the same folly revived in another age under a different name. . . .

Once monarchical government is established, infallibility is no more than a necessary consequence of *supremacy*, or rather it is exactly the same thing under two different names. But, although this identity is obvious, men have never seen or wanted to see that the whole question depends on this truth; and, since this truth in its turn depends on the very nature of things, it has no need at all of the support of theology; so that, by claiming unity to be necessary, logically if not in practice error could not be opposed to the Supreme Pontiff, just as it cannot be opposed to temporal sovereigns who have never laid claims to infallibility. In fact, it is the same thing in practice to be above error and to be above being accused of it. Thus, even if it were agreed that no divine promise had been made to the Pope, he would, as the highest court of appeal, be no less infallible or taken to be such; for every judgment against which there is no appeal is and should be held to be just in every human association and under every conceivable form of government.

Whoever had the right to tell the Pope he is mistaken would, for the same reason, have the right to disobey him, which would destroy supremacy (or infallibility). . . . For, if the body politic is not to crumble, there can be no appeal from a permanent and necessary government to an intermittent power. . . .

CHAPTER II. COUNCILS

It is useless to have recourse to councils in order to preserve unity and maintain a visible tribunal. Let us begin by an observation that does not admit of the least doubt, *that a periodic or intermittent sovereignty is a contradiction in terms,* for sovereignty must be perpetually alive, watchful, and active. *For it, slumber is the same as death.* . . .

CHAPTER IV. ANALOGIES DERIVED FROM TEMPORAL POWER

Councils can be useful. Their existence would be sanctioned by natural law even if they were not by ecclesiastical law, there being nothing so natural, particularly in theory, as that every human association should assemble in the only way it can, that is, through representatives presided over by a chief, to make laws and watch over the interests of the community. I do not quarrel at all with this; I say only that an intermittent representative body, especially if it is spasmodic and not periodic, is by the very nature of things always and everywhere incompetent to govern; and that, during its sessions themselves, it has no existence or legitimacy except through its chief. . . .

BOOK TWO

OF THE POPE IN HIS RELATIONS WITH TEMPORAL SOVEREIGNTIES

CHAPTER I. A FEW WORDS ON SOVEREIGNTY

Since man is both moral and corrupt, just in his understanding but perverse in his will, he must necessarily be governed; otherwise he would be at once social and antisocial, and society would be at once necessary and impossible.

The courts show us the absolute necessity of sovereignty; for man must be governed, precisely as he must be judged and for the same reason, that is because, wherever there is no *adjudication,* there is *conflict.*

On this point, as on so many others, man could not imagine anything better than what exists, that is to say, a power that leads men through general rules made, not for this case or for this man, but for all cases, for all times and for all men.

What makes sovereignty and consequently society possible is that man is righteous, at least in intention, so long as his own interests are not involved. For the cases in which sovereignty is liable to do wrong voluntarily are always, in the nature of things, much rarer than those in which it is not, just as, to follow the same analogy, in the administration of justice the cases in which judges are tempted to betray their trust are necessarily rare in relation to those in which they are not. If it were otherwise, the administration of justice as well as sovereignty would be impossible.

Even the most dissolute of rulers does not prevent the prosecution of public crimes in his courts, provided that his own personal interests are not involved. But, as he is the only man above the law, the general laws can always be enforced even if he himself unfortunately sets the most dangerous examples.

As man is thus necessarily in society and necessarily governed, his will plays no part in the establishment of government; for, when the people have no choice and when sovereignty results directly from human nature, sovereigns do not exist *by grace of the people,* sovereignty being no more the result of their will than society itself.

It has often been asked whether the king was made for the people or the people for the king. It seems to me that this question reveals very little thought. The two propositions are false taken separately and true taken together. The people is made for the sovereign, and the sovereign for the people: and both the one and the other are made in order that there may be a sovereignty.

The mainspring of a watch is not made for the balance wheel, nor the balance wheel for the mainspring, but each for the other, and both to show the time.

There is no sovereign without a nation, just as there is no nation without a sovereign. The nation owes more to the sovereign than the sovereign to the nation, for it is indebted for its social existence and all the benefits that flow from it, whereas the prince owes to sovereignty nothing but empty splendor which has nothing in common with happiness and even almost always excludes it.

CHAPTER II. INCONVENIENCES OF SOVEREIGNTY

Although sovereignty has no greater or more general interest than that of exercising justice, and although the cases in which it is tempted to abandon justice are much less numerous than those in which it sustains it, yet they are unfortunately frequent; and the particular personality of certain sovereigns may increase these inconveniences to a point that there is scarcely any other way of finding them supportable than by comparing them to those which would be present if the sovereign did not exist.

It was then impossible that men should not from time to time have made some attempts to take shelter from the excesses of this extensive prerogative; but on this point the world is divided by two sharply different theories.

The daring race of Japhet has not ceased, if it can be put like this, *to gravitate* toward what is called *liberty,* that is to say, a state in which the governors are as much restricted and the governed as little restricted as is possible. Always on guard against his masters, the European has sometimes deposed them, at others set up laws against them. He has tried everything and exhausted every imaginable governmental system to dispense with rulers or to restrain their power.

The countless progeny of Sem and Cham have taken another road. From the earliest times to our own, it has said to the individual, *Do everything you want and, when we grow tired of it, we shall slaughter you.* Besides, it has never been either able or willing to comprehend what a republic is; it understands nothing about the balance of powers, about those rights and fundamental laws of which we are so proud. Among them, the richest man is the most complete master of his own actions; yet the owner of a huge movable fortune, absolutely free to carry it where he wishes and assured moreover of complete safety on European soil, even when he sees the approach of the noose or the dagger, prefers them to the miserable fate of dying of boredom among us.

Doubtless no one would dream of recommending to Europe the public law of Asia and Africa, concise and clear as it is; but since in Europe power is always being feared, discussed, attacked, or transferred, since nothing is so intolerable to our pride as despotic government, the greatest problem in European eyes is to discover *how sovereign power can be restrained without being destroyed.*

The easy reply has been, *Fundamental laws and a constitution are needed.* But who is to establish these fundamental laws and who is to enforce them? The body or individual with this power would be sovereign, since he would be stronger than the sovereign; so that by the very act of establishing the constitution, he would dethrone the sovereign. If the constitutional code is a concession by the sovereign, the question is reopened. Who will stop one of his successors from violating it? The right of resistance must be attributed to a body or an individual, otherwise it can be exercised only by revolution, a terrible remedy worse than any abuse.

Moreover, we do not find that the many attempts made to restrict sovereign power have ever succeeded in such a way as to inspire the desire to imitate them. Only England, favored by its island position and by a national character that lends itself to such experiments, has been able to carry through something of this sort, but time has yet to prove its constitution. . . .

A great and powerful nation has just made the greatest effort ever made to gain liberty, but what has it achieved? It has put a small *b* in place of a capital *B* on the throne and replaced allegiance by servitude among the people, at the cost of covering itself in ridicule and shame. . . .

As everyone knows, Catholic doctrine forbids every kind of rebellion without distinction, and in defense of this doctrine our writers give sufficiently good arguments on political and even on philosophical grounds.

Protestantism, on the other hand, starting from the sovereignty of the people, a doctrine it has carried from religion to politics, sees in the theory of *nonresistance* only the final degradation of man. Dr. Beattie can be quoted as representative of his whole party. He calls the Catholic theory of *nonresistance* a *detestable doctrine*. He holds that, when there is any question of resisting sovereignty, men ought to decide *according to those instinctive sentiments of morality whereof men are conscious, erroneously ascribing them to blood and spirits, or to education and habit.*[1] He reproaches his famous compatriot Dr. Berkeley for having belittled this interior power and having believed that *man, as a rational being, ought to be guided by the dictates of sober and impartial reason.*[2]

I admire these fine maxims a great deal, but they have the defect of throwing no light to enable the mind to decide on the difficult occasions when theories are completely useless. For the sake of argument, I accept that men have agreed that they have the right to resist the sovereign power and to confine it within certain limits, yet this is still inconclusive, for there remains the problem of *when* this right can be exercised and *who* are entitled to exercise it.

The most ardent supporters of the right of resistance agree (and

[1] Beattie, *On Truth* (London), Part ii, Chap. ii, p. 408.
[2] *Ibid.*

who could not?) that it can be justified only by tyranny. But what is tyranny? Can a single act, if atrocious, be called tyranny? If there must be more than one, how many are needed, and of what kind? What power in the state has the right to decide *that the circumstances justify resistance?* If such a tribunal exists beforehand, it is thus already a part of the sovereign power and, by acting against the other part, destroys it. If it did not already exist, by what tribunal is this tribunal to be set up? Moreover, can men exercise a right, even if just and incontestable, without weighing against it the disadvantages which may result from it? All history teaches us that revolutions started by the wisest men are ended by fools, that their authors are always their victims, and that the efforts of nations to create or increase their liberty almost always result in their enslavement. Extreme dangers rise on every side.

But, it will be said, do you want then to unleash the tiger and reduce yourself to passive obedience? . . . I have never claimed that absolute power does not involve great disadvantages, whatever form it may take. On the contrary, I explicitly recognize the fact, and do not think of attenuating the disadvantages. I say only that we are placed in a dreadful dilemma.

CHAPTER III. IDEAS OF ANTIQUITY ON THE GREAT PROBLEM

It is not within human power to create a law which will have no need of any exception. This impossibility stems both from the weakness of men, who cannot foresee everything, and from the very nature of things, for circumstances vary to the point that some, of their own impetus, go beyond the scope of the law, whilst others, arranged by rough gradations into general categories, cannot be expressed by a general term which is not false in some of its meanings.

The result is that in every legal code it is necessary to have a dispensing power, for, wherever law cannot in certain instances be waived, it will be violated.

But every violation of the law is dangerous or fatal for the law itself, whereas every dispensation strengthens it. For men cannot ask for it to be waived without rendering homage to it and acknowledging that no man has, of himself, any power against it.

The law that prescribes obedience to sovereigns is a general law like any other; it is good, just, and necessary in *general*. But if Nero rules, it may *appear* to be defective.

Then why should there not be in such cases dispensation from the general law, based on completely unforeseen circumstances? Is it not better to ask with full knowledge of the case and in the name of authority than to fall upon the tyrant with blind impetuosity, which has all the symptoms of a crime?

But to whom should we apply for this dispensation? Sovereignty is for us a sacred thing, an emanation of divine power which nations of all ages have placed under the care of religion but which Christianity above all has taken under its particular protection by ordering us to view the sovereign as the representative and the image of God himself; and so it was not absurd to think that no other authority was competent to release us from the oath of allegiance than that of the high spiritual power unique in the world, whose sublime prerogatives form part of revelation.

Since the oath of allegiance exposed men to all the horrors of tyranny unless it was restricted, and since resistance exposed them to all the evils of anarchy unless it was regulated, dispensation from this oath pronounced by the spiritual sovereignty very naturally presented itself to the human mind as the only way of containing temporal authority without obliterating its character.

Besides, it would be a mistake to believe that, on this hypothesis, dispensation from the oath would contradict the divine origin of sovereignty. The contradiction would be less in evidence as, since the dispensing power would be supposed to be preeminently divine, there would be no hindrance to another power being subordinated to it in certain respects and in unusual circumstances.

The forms of sovereignty are, moreover, not everywhere the same: they are determined by fundamental laws, the true bases of which are never written. Pascal aptly said that he *would detest as much the destruction of liberty where God has put it as its introduction where it does not exist.* For this is not a question of monarchy but of sovereignty, which is very different.

It is essential to notice this in order to escape a fallacy into which it is very easy to slip. In this or that place, *sovereignty is limited*; therefore it proceeds from the people.

In the first place, there is no such thing as limited sovereignty, accurately speaking. All are absolute and infallible, since it is nowhere permissible to say that they are mistaken. When I say that *no sovereignty is limited,* I mean *if it is constitutionally exercised,* and this qualification should be noted carefully. For, from two different points of view, it is equally true to say that *every sovereignty is limited* and that *no sovereignty is limited*. It is limited in that no sovereign power can do everything; it is not limited in that, within its legitimate circle traced by the fundamental laws of each country, it is always and everywhere absolute, and no one has the right to call it unjust or mistaken. Thus its legitimacy consists, not in conducting itself in such and such a way within the constitutional process, but in not stepping outside that process. This has not always been given sufficient attention. It will be said, for example, that in England *sovereignty is limited*: nothing could be more mistaken. It is *royalty* that is limited in this famous country. Now, royalty is not the whole sovereignty, at least in theory. But when the three powers which make up sovereignty in England are in agreement, what can they do? Blackstone's answer must be accepted—EVERYTHING. And what can legally be done against them? NOTHING. Thus the question of divine origin can be raised in London as well as in Madrid and elsewhere, and everywhere it presents the same problem, although the forms of sovereignty vary from country to country.

In the second place, the maintenance of constitutional procedures according to the fundamental laws alters neither the nature nor the rights of sovereignty. Are judges of the supreme court who deprive a father of the right to bring up his children because of his intolerable cruelty to be thought of as encroaching on parental authority or denying its divine basis? In containing a power within proper limits, the court does not contest either its legitimacy or its character or its legal extent; on the contrary, it solemnly acknowledges them.

In the same way, the Sovereign Pontiff would not contradict divine law by releasing subjects from their oath of allegiance. He would simply claim that sovereignty is a divine and sacred authority which can be controlled only by another similarly divine authority, but of a superior order, and specially vested with this power in certain out-of-the-ordinary instances. . . .

CHAPTER IV. FURTHER CONSIDERATIONS ON THE SAME SUBJECT

The defenders of the right of resistance have too often avoided putting the question honestly. In fact, it is by no means a question of settling *if*, but *when* and *how* it is permissible to resist. The problem is entirely practical and, put in this form, it is a frightening one. But if the right to resist were changed to the right to prevent, and belonged to a power of another order rather than to the subject, there would not be the same disadvantages, for in this situation there could be resistance without revolution and without any violation of sovereignty. . . .

CHAPTER V. DISTINGUISHING CHARACTERISTICS OF THE POWER EXERCISED BY THE POPES

The Popes have struggled sometimes with sovereigns, but never with sovereignty. The very act by which they released subjects from the oath of fidelity declared sovereignty inviolable. The Popes warned peoples that no human power could derogate from sovereignty, whose authority could be suspended only by a wholly divine power; so that their anathemas, far from ever departing from the rigor of Catholic doctrines on the inviolability of sovereigns, had on the contrary no effect other than to give them a new sanction in the eyes of the people. . . .

Experience is thus in perfect agreement with reasoning. The excommunications of the Popes have not inflicted any harm on sovereignty in the popular mind; on the contrary, by repressing it in certain matters, by making it less harsh and overbearing, by frightening it for its own good of which it was ignorant, they have nurtured respect for it; they have wiped from its brow the old mask of brute force and put in its place that of regeneration; they have made it holy to make it inviolable; a new and important proof, among a thousand others, that papal power has always been conservative. . . .

It may be observed that, in regard to sovereigns, modern philosophers have followed a diametrically opposite path to that which the Popes have marked out. The latter have consecrated the office by attacking persons; the former, in contrast, have often and even servilely flattered the person who hands out places and pensions, while destroying, so far as they could, the office, by making sovereignty look odious or ridiculous, by claiming that it derived from the people, by forever seeking to restrain it by the people. . . .

CHAPTER IX. JUSTIFICATION OF PAPAL POWER

Writers of the last century fairly often make use of a very expeditious method of judging institutions. They imagine a purely ideal order of things, good in their eyes, and treat this as a firm foundation on which to build judgments of realities. . . .

We must start from a general and incontestable principle, namely, *that every government is good when it has been established and has existed for a long time without being disputed.*

General laws alone are eternal. All the rest vary, and never does one time resemble another. No doubt man will always be governed, but never in the same way. Other customs, other knowledge, other beliefs will necessarily lead to other laws. Names can also be misleading in this sphere as in so many others, for they are liable both to express similarities between contemporaneous things without expressing their differences, and to designate by the same word things that time has changed. For example, the word *monarchy* can cover two governments, either contemporaneous or separated by time, which are more or less different, so that we cannot assert about the one all that can properly be asserted about the other. . . .

Every possible form of government has shown itself in the world, and every one is legitimate when once it has been established; this cannot be criticized by reasoning from hypotheses divorced from facts.

Now, one indisputable fact, attested by all the monuments of history, is that the Popes, in the Middle Ages and even long before that time, exercised a considerable power over temporal sovereigns, that they judged and excommunicated them on some solemn occasions, and that often they even declared the subjects of these princes released from their oath of allegiance to them.

When men speak of *despotism* or *absolute government*, they rarely know what they are talking about. No government can do everything. By virtue of a divine law, there is always by the side of every sovereignty some power or other that acts as a check. It may be a law, a custom, conscience, a Pope, or a dagger, but there is always some curb. . . .

Now, the authority of the Popes was the power chosen and constituted by the Middle Ages to balance the temporal power and make it bearable for men. . . .

In the Middle Ages, nations had *within themselves* only worthless or despised laws and *corrupt customs*. This indispensable *check* had therefore to be sought *from without*. It was found, and could only be found, in papal authority. What happened, therefore, was only what ought to have happened.

BOOK THREE

OF THE POPE IN HIS RELATIONS WITH THE CIVILIZATION AND HAPPINESS OF PEOPLES

CHAPTER II. CIVIL LIBERTY OF MANKIND

We have seen that the Sovereign Pontiff is the natural head, the most powerful promoter, the great *Demiurgus* of universal civilization; his powers in this respect are limited only by the blindness or bad faith of princes. The Popes have no less deserved the gratitude of humanity by the extinction of slavery, which they have ceaselessly fought against and which they will inevitably stamp out without fuss, without upheaval, and without danger wherever they are allowed to.

It was a singular absurdity of the last century to judge everything according to abstract rules without regard to experience; and this absurdity is all the more striking as at the same time this very century never stopped crying out against all philosophers who started from abstract principles instead of seeking them in experience.

Rousseau is exquisite when he starts his *Social Contract* with the resounding maxim *Man was born free, and everywhere he is in chains.* What does he mean? Apparently he does not intend to speak of the fact, since in this very phrase he affirms that EVERYWHERE *man is in chains.* Then it is a question of *right*, but this is what is necessary to prove *in opposition to the fact.*

The foolish assertion *Man was born free* is the opposite of the truth. Until the establishment of Christianity, and even until this religion had sufficiently penetrated men's hearts, slavery was everywhere and always considered as a necessary part of the government and the political system of nations, in republics as in monarchies, without it occurring to any philosopher to condemn it or to any legislator to abolish it by a constitutional or other law.

One of the most profound philosophers of antiquity, Aristotle, as is well known, went so far as to say *that there were men who were born slaves*, and nothing is more true than this. I know that in our age he has been blamed for this assertion, but it would be better to understand than to criticize him. His proposition is based on the whole of history which is experimental politics, and on the very nature of man, who produced history.

Those who have sufficiently studied this unfortunate nature recognize that *man in general*, if reduced to his own resources, *is too wicked to be free.*

If each man looks in his own heart to see the nature of man, he will accept that, wherever civil liberty belongs to everyone, there is no longer any means of governing men as national bodies *without some extraordinary help.*

It follows that slavery was constantly the natural state of a very great part of humanity up to the establishment of Christianity, and, as general good sense felt the necessity of this order of things, it was never contested either legally or theoretically.

A great Latin poet put a terrible maxim into the mouth of Caesar: *Humanity was made for a few men.*[3]

No doubt, in the sense the poet gives to it, this maxim appears Machiavellian and shocking, but, from a different point of view, it is quite justified. Everywhere small minorities have ruled majorities, for, without a more or less strong aristocracy, sovereignty is no longer powerful enough. . . .

It would be superfluous to prove at length what everyone knows, *that the world, up to the Christian Era, has always been covered with slaves and that the sages never condemned this custom.* This proposition is unshakable.

But eventually the divine law appeared on earth. Immediately it took possession of the heart of man, and changed it in a manner calculated to excite the eternal admiration of every true observer. This religion started to labor especially and tirelessly for the abolition of slavery, something that no other religion, no legislator, no philosopher had ever dared to undertake or even imagine. Christianity, acting divinely, for the same reason acted slowly; for all legitimate operations, of what-

---

[3] *Humanum paucis vivit genus.* Lucan, *Pharsalia.*

ever sort they may be, are always carried through imperceptibly. Wherever noise, tumult, impetuosity, and destructiveness are found, one can be sure that crime and folly are at work. . . .

Wherever another religion than ours holds sway, slavery is the rule, and wherever this religion weakens, the nation becomes, in exact proportion, less susceptible of general liberty.

We have just seen the social structure shattered to its foundations because there was too much liberty in Europe and no longer sufficient religion. There will be still more upheavals, and good order will not be thoroughly consolidated until either slavery or the true religion is restored.

Government alone cannot govern. This maxim will appear the more uncontestable, the more it is thought about. Government therefore needs, as an indispensable agent, either slavery, which diminishes the number of effective wills within the state, or divine power, which by a kind of spiritual *graft* destroys the natural harshness of these wills and enables them to act together without harming each other.

The New World has given an example that completes the demonstration. What have Catholic missionaries, that is to say the envoys of the Pope, not done to extinguish servitude, to console, to restore, to ennoble humanity in those vast territories?

Wherever this power is allowed to act, it will produce the same results. But let not the nations who disregard it take it into their heads, even if they are Christian, to abolish slavery if it still exists among them; the inevitable consequence of this blind imprudence would be a great political calamity.

But it should not be imagined that the Church, or the Papacy (*for they are both one*), has no other aim in the war it has declared on slavery than the political improvement of man. For this power, there is a higher object, and that is the perfecting of morality of which political improvement is simply a derivation. . . .

The great bulk of mankind is thus *naturally* in bondage, and cannot be rescued from this state except by *supernatural* means. With slavery, there is no morality properly speaking; without Christianity, no general liberty; and without the Pope, no true Christianity, that is to say, no active, powerful, converting, regenerating, conquering, *perfecting* Christianity. It was, therefore, for the Supreme Pontiff to proclaim universal liberty; he has done so, and his voice has resounded through the whole world. He alone made this liberty possible in his character of sole head of that religion which was alone capable of moderating wills and which could deploy its full strength only through him. Today, one would have to be blind not to see that every European sovereignty is weakening. On every side, they are losing men's confidence and love. Sects and the spirit of individualism are multiplying in a frightening manner. Wills must be either purified or enslaved. Dissenting rulers in whose states servitude prevails must preserve it or perish. The others will have to restore servitude or unity....

Essay
on the Generative Principle of
Political Constitutions

I

One of the gravest errors of a century which embraced them all was to believe that a political constitution could be written and created a priori, whereas reason and experience agree that a constitution is a divine work and that it is precisely the most fundamental and essentially constitutional elements in a nation's laws that cannot be written.

II

Frenchmen have often been asked as a joke *in what book the Salic Law was written*; but Jérôme Bignon replied exactly to the point, very probably without understanding how aptly, *that it was written in the hearts of Frenchmen*. Indeed, supposing that a law of this importance exists only because it is written, it is certain that whatever authority has written it will have the right to annul it; the law would not therefore have that aura of sanctity and immutability that distinguishes truly constitutional laws. The essence of a fundamental law is that no one has the right to abolish it: but how is it beyond human power if it has been made by someone? The agreement of a people is impossible, and, even if it were, an agreement is not a law and obliges no one unless there is a superior authority guaranteeing it. *Locke* sought the characteristic of law in the expression of combined wills, an unlucky chance to choose the precise characteristic that excludes the idea of *law*. As a matter of fact, combined wills form a *settlement* and not a *law*, which necessarily and obviously presupposes a superior will enforcing obedience. "In the Hobbesian system (which has been so successful in our day under the pen of Locke), the authority of civil laws derives solely from a contract; but if there is no natural law which obliges men to carry out the laws that have been made, of what use are they? Promises, engagements, and oaths are mere words; it is as easy to break these weak links as to forge them. Without the dogma of a law-giving God, all moral obligation is chimerical. On the one hand power, on the other powerlessness, this is the only bond uniting human societies."[1]

What a wise and profound theologian has said here of moral obligation applies with equal force to political or civil obligation. Law is properly *law* and has a genuine sanction only if it is taken as emanating from a superior will; so that its essential feature is *that it is not the will of all*. Otherwise laws would, as has just been said, be *only settlements*; and, as the author just quoted added, "Those who have been free to make contracts have not renounced the power of revoking them; and their descendants, who played no part in them, are still less bound to observe them." Consequently, primordial good sense, happily anterior to sophisms, has everywhere sought the sanction for laws in a power above men, either by recognizing that sovereignty derives from God, or by revering certain unwritten laws as God's word.

III

The editors of the Roman laws have included in the first chapter of their collection a very remarkable fragment of Greek jurisprudence. *Among the laws which govern us*, says this passage, *some are written and others are not*. Nothing could be simpler and nothing more profound. Is there any Turkish law expressly permitting the sovereign to send a man to his death immediately without the intermediate decision of a court? Is there any *written* law, even a religious one, which forbids this to the sovereign of Christian Europe? Yet the Turk is no more surprised to see his ruler order an immediate execution than to see him go to the mosque. Like all of Asia and even all of antiquity, he believes that the immediate power of life and death is a legitimate appendage of sovereignty. But our kings shudder at the very idea of condemning a man to death; for, in our eyes, such a condemnation would be a vile murder, and yet I doubt if it would be possible to for-

---

[1] Bergier, *Traité historique et dogmatique de la religion*, Book III, Chap. IV, paragraph 12.

bid them this power through a written fundamental law without it leading to greater evils than those which one wished to prevent.

IV

The search in Roman history for an answer to the question of what were precisely the powers of the Senate will be unsuccessful, at least in establishing any exact limits to this power. It is easy to see in general that the powers of the populace and of the Senate balanced each other and that they never ceased to struggle against each other: it is clear that patriotism or lassitude, feebleness or violence ended their dangerous battles, but we do not know more than this. Witnessing these great scenes of history, one sometimes feels tempted to believe that things would have gone much better if there had been precise laws circumscribing these powers; but this would be very wrong. Laws like this, forever endangered by unforeseen cases and unlikely exceptions, would not have lasted six months or would have undermined the Republic.

V

The English constitution is an example nearer to us and consequently more striking. If it is examined closely, it can be seen that *it works only by not working* (if this play on words is excused). It maintains itself only by exceptions. *Habeas corpus*, for example, has been suspended so often and for such long periods that it could be argued that the exception has become the rule. Suppose for a moment that the authors of this famous Act had attempted to lay down the cases when it could be suspended, they would by that deed have destroyed it. . . .

VII

In spite of this, we are still told of written constitutions and constitutional laws made a priori. It is impossible to conceive how a rational man can believe in such chimeras. If any scheme was carried through in England to give the cabinet a formal constitutional status by law and thus to regulate and circumscribe rigorously its privileges and powers, together with the precautions necessary to limit its influence and prevent it from abusing it, the state would be undermined.

The real English constitution is the public spirit, admirable, unique, infallible, and above praise, which leads, conserves, and protects all—what is written is nothing.

VII

At the end of the last century, loud complaints were made about a statesman who conceived the idea of introducing this same English constitution (or what went under the name) into a convulsed kingdom that was demanding any constitution whatever with a kind of madness. If you like, he was wrong, so far at least as one can be wrong when acting in good faith, which it is reasonable to suppose he was and as I believe wholeheartedly. But who then has the right to condemn him? *Vel duo, vel nemo.* He did not assert a wish to destroy anything of his own authority: he wanted only, he said, to substitute something which seemed to him to be reasonable for something that was no longer wanted and that, even by that fact, no longer existed. Moreover, if the principle is accepted (as in fact it was) *that a man can create a constitution,* this minister (who was certainly a man) had the right to create his as much as anyone else and more than some. Was opinion at all divided on this point? Was it not everywhere believed that a constitution is as much a work of the imagination as an ode or a tragedy. Had not *Paine* asserted, with a profundity which enraptured the universities, *that a constitution does not exist if one cannot put it in one's pocket?* The eighteenth century, which questioned nothing, had no doubts of itself: that is the rule; and I do not believe that it produced a single youth of any talent whatever who had not made three things by the time he left school—a new system of education, a constitution, and a society. If therefore a mature and talented man, deeply versed in economics and contemporary philosophy, had undertaken only the second of these projects, this in itself would have convinced me of his extreme moderation: but I must admit that he seems to me to be a veritable prodigy of wisdom and modesty when, putting experience (at least as he saw it) in place of foolish theories, he humbly demanded a constitution on the English model instead of drawing one up himself. It will be said that *even this was not possible.* I agree, but he did not know this; and how could he have known? Who was there who could have told him?

IX

The more you examine the part human action plays in the formation of political constitutions, the clearer it becomes that it is effective only in an extremely subordinate role or as a simple instrument; and I do not believe that any doubt at all remains of the incontrovertible truth of the following propositions:

1. That the fundamentals of political constitutions exist before all written laws.
2. That a constitutional law is and can be only the development or the sanction of a preexistent and unwritten right.
3. That the most essential, the most intrinsically constitutional, and the really fundamental is not written and even should not be if the state is not to be imperiled.
4. That the weakness and fragility of a constitution is in direct relationship to the number of written constitutional articles.

X

We are misled on this point by a fallacy so natural that it entirely escapes our attention. Because a man acts, he believes he acts by himself; and because he is conscious of his liberty, he forgets his dependence. As far as the physical order is concerned, he listens to reason; and although he can, for example, plant an acorn, water it, and so on, yet he is capable of admitting that he does not make oaks, since he sees that the tree grows and perfects itself without human interference and that, moreover, he has not made the acorn; but, in the social order in which he is a participant and actor, he begins to believe that he is really the direct author of everything that happens through him: in a sense, the trowel believes himself to be the architect. Doubtless, man is intelligent, free, and sublime, but he is nonetheless an *implement of God.* . . .

XI

Nothing is better known than Cicero's simile on the subject of the Epicurean system, which wished to construct a world with atoms moving haphazardly in a vacuum. *It is more credible,* said the great orator, *that letters thrown into the air could arrange themselves on falling so as to form a poem.* This idea has been repeated and praised thousands of times; yet I know of no one who has thought of supplying the missing corollary. Suppose that printing type thrown by the handful from the top of a tower fell to earth to form Racine's *Athalie*, what would be the conclusion? *That some intelligence has governed the fall and the arrangement of the type.* No other conclusion could sensibly be reached.

XII

Consider, now, any political constitution whatever, that of England, for example. Certainly it has not been made a priori. Never have statesmen gathered together and said: *Let us create three powers, balance them in such and such a manner,* and so on: no one has thought this. The constitution is the work of circumstances, and the number of these circumstances is infinite. Roman, ecclesiastic, and feudal law, Saxon, Norman and Danish customs, every kind of class privilege, prejudice and ambition, wars, revolts, revolutions, conquests and crusades, all the virtues, vices, sciences, errors and passions; all these elements, acting together and forming by their intermixture and interaction endlessly multiplying combinations, have finally produced after many centuries the most complex unity and the most delicate equilibrium of political forces the world has ever known.

XIII

However, since these elements, so cast into space, have fallen into such meaningful order without a single man among the multitude who have acted on this huge stage knowing what relation his actions had with the whole scheme of things or what the future was to be, it follows that these elements were guided in their fall by an unerring hand, superior to man. Perhaps the greatest folly of a century of follies was to believe that fundamental laws could be written a priori, whereas they are obviously the work of a power above men, and the very act of writing them down, later on, is the surest sign that their real force has gone.

XIV

It is very remarkable that God, having deigned to speak to men, has himself made these truths clear in the two revelations which we owe to his goodness. A very clever man, to my mind one of the most outstanding of our age because of the bitter struggle revealed in his writings between the most terrible prejudices of the age, of sect, of habit, and the purest intentions, the most righteous sentiments, the most sensitive understanding; this man has decided *"that a teaching coming direct from God, or given solely on his command, must have been man's first assurance of the existence of this Being."* The truth is precisely the opposite because the prime characteristic of this teaching is not to reveal directly either the existence or the attributes of God, but to presuppose the whole of this knowledge, without our understanding why or how. Thus it does not tell us: *There is* or *You will believe in only one God eternal, omnipotent,* and so on. It says (and these are its first words) in a purely narrative form, *In the beginning, God created . . .;* by which it supposes that this dogma is known before writing.

XV

Let us pass on to Christianity, the greatest of all imaginable institutions, since it is entirely the work of God and is made for all men in all ages. We will find it subject to the general law. To be sure, its divine author could very well himself have written or have had things written, yet he did neither, at least in a legislative form. The New Testament, coming after the death of the legislator and even after the establishment of his religion, offers a narrative, warnings, moral precepts, exhortations, orders, threats, and so on, but certainly not a collection of dogma set out in an imperative form. In telling the story of the Last Supper when God loved us up to the end, the evangelists had a good opportunity to direct our beliefs by writing; however, they refrained from declaring or ordaining anything. It is well said in this splendid story: *Go forth and teach;* but not *teach this or that.* If the scriptural historian sets out a dogma, it is simply as something already known. The creeds which have since appeared are professions of faith which serve to collect our thoughts or to contradict momentary errors.

We read there *We believe* and not *You believe*. We recite them as individuals; we sing them in church, *on the lyre and organ*,[2] as real prayers, since they are forms of submission, confidence, and faith addressed to God, and not orders addressed to men. It would be very amusing to hear the *Confession of Augsburg* or the *Thirty-nine Articles* set to music!

Far from the first creeds containing a statement of all our dogmas, on the contrary, Christians of those days would have regarded it as a serious crime to state them all. The same is true of the Holy Scriptures; no idea has been more mistaken than the attempt to find in them the whole of Christian dogma; there is not a single line in these writings which lays down or even hints at a plan to construct a code or a dogmatic declaration of all the articles of faith.

XVI

Moreover, if a people possesses one of these *codes of belief*, three things are certain:

1. That the religion of this people is false;
2. That it has written out its religious code in a bout of fever;
3. That in a little while it will be made fun of even in this nation, and that it can have neither power nor durance. Such as, for example, the famous Articles, *which are signed more than they are read and read more than they are believed*.[3] Not only does this list of dogmas count for nothing, or very nearly, in the country of its birth, but besides it is evident even to a foreigner that the illustrious possessors of this piece of paper find it nothing but an embarrassment. They would like very much to see it go, since it irritates the national good sense enlightened by time, and since it recalls to them an unhappy beginning: but the *constitution is written*.

XVII

Doubtless, these same Englishmen would never have demanded the Great Charter if the nation's rights had not been violated, but also they would never have demanded it if these rights had not existed

---

[2] Psalms 150:4.
[3] *Mémoires de Gibbon* (Paris [1797]) t. i, Chap. vi.

before the Charter. It is as true of the Church as of the State: if Christianity had never been attacked, it would never have written out its dogma in order to determine it: but also dogma has never been determined by writing unless it existed previously in its natural state, which is the spoken word.

The true authors of the Council of Trent were the two great Reformers of the sixteenth century. Their followers, more calm now, have since proposed to us that we delete this fundamental law because it contains some words difficult for them to accept; and they have tried to tempt us by showing us that this is the price for a reunion which would make us accomplices rather than friends; but this request is neither theologically nor philosophically justified. They themselves formerly brought into the language of religion these words which weary them. Let us hope that they learn today to pronounce them. Faith, if sophistical opposition had never forced it to write, would be a thousand times more angelic; it weeps over these decisions that revolt has forced it to make and that were always unfortunate, since they presuppose doubt or attack and could have been required only in the midst of the most dangerous upheavals. The state of war elevated venerable ramparts around the truth: they doubtless protect it, but they hide it; they make it unassailable, but at the same time even less accessible. This is not what truth, which would like to clasp humanity in its arms, asks for.

XVIII

I have talked of Christianity as a system of belief: I am now going to consider it as a sovereign power, in its most numerous association. There it is monarchical, as everyone knows, and this must be so, since, by the very nature of things, monarchy becomes the more necessary as the association becomes the more numerous. It has not been forgotten that an impure mouth has nevertheless brought itself into favor nowadays when it said *that France was geometrically monarchical.* It would be indeed difficult to express more happily a more unshakable truth. But if the extent of France of itself excludes any other kind of government, for greater reason that sovereignty which, by the very nature of its constitution, will always have subjects on every point of the globe, cannot be other than monarchical; and experience reinforces theory on this point. This being granted, it might be thought that the prerogatives of the head of such a monarchy would be more rigorously determined and circumscribed than any others. This, however, is the opposite to what has taken place. If you read the innumerable books spawned by external attacks and even by a kind of civil war which has its advantages as well as disadvantages, you will see that they all base their arguments on fact; and it is very remarkable that the supreme tribunal has continually allowed disputes over the question that presents itself to every mind as the most fundamental in the constitution without ever having wished to settle it by a formal law; which must be so, if I am not greatly mistaken, precisely because of the fundamental importance of the question. . . .

XIX

These ideas, taken in their general aspects, are not foreign to the philosophers of antiquity: they well understood the weakness, I almost said the nullity, of writing in great institutions; but no one has better seen or expressed this truth than Plato, who is always the first on the path to all the great truths. According to him, first of all, "the man who owes all his education to written discourses *has always just the appearance of wisdom.*" "The spoken word," he adds, "is to writing what a man is to his portrait. The creations of the painter strike us as being lifelike, yet *if you question them, they preserve a solemn silence.* It is the same with a book, *which does not know what to say to one man or to hide from another.* If it is attacked or insulted needlessly, it cannot defend itself, *for its father is never there to protect it.* So that whoever imagines himself able to establish a clear and durable doctrine by the written word alone is a great fool. If he did possess the real seeds of truth, he would take great care not to believe that, *with a little black liquid and a pen,* he could make them take root among men, protect them against inclement weather, and induce in them strong growth. As for the man who undertakes to write *laws or civil constitutions,* imagining that, because he has written them down, he has been able to give them the proper clarity and stability, he disgraces himself, whatever he is, whether private citizen or legislator, and whatever men say; for he has thereby shown that he is equally ignorant of inspiration and madness, justice and injustice, good and evil. Such ignorance is disgraceful even if he has the applause of the whole of the vulgar masses."[4]

Plato, *Phaedrus,* 275–277.

XX

Having heard the *wisdom of nations,* it will be useful, I think, to listen again to Christian philosophy.

"Doubtless it would have been most desirable, the most eloquent of Greek Fathers has said, for us to have had no need of writing and for the divine precepts to have been written only in our hearts by grace, as they are written by ink in our books; but, as we have lost this grace through our own fault, let us then, of necessity, seize a *plank in place of a ship,* without forgetting however the superiority of the first state. God never revealed anything to the Elect of the Old Testament; he always talked to them directly, for he saw the purity of their hearts; but once the Hebrew people were thrown into the abyss of vice, books and laws became necessary. This course was resumed under the influence of the new revelation; for Christ did not leave a single writing to his Apostles. In place of books, he promised them the Holy Spirit. *It is it,* he said to them, *that will inspire what you will have to say.*[5] But, because in the course of time, guilty men revolted against dogmas and morality, it was necessary to resort to books."

XXI

The whole truth is to be found in these two authorities. They show the profound stupidity (it is permissible to talk like Plato, who never lost his temper), the profound stupidity, as I say, of those poor people who imagine that legislators are men, that laws are pieces of paper and that nations can be created *by ink.* They show, to the contrary, that writing is always a sign of weakness, ignorance, or danger; that the more perfect an institution, the less it writes; so that the institution which is certainly divine has no written document as its basis, showing us that every written law is only a necessary evil produced by human infirmity or malice, and that it is nothing at all if it has not received a previous and unwritten sanction.

XXII

It is here that one must grieve over the fundamental fallacy of a system that has so unfortunately divided Europe. The partisans of

[5] Matthew 10:19.

this system have said: *We believe only in the word of God.* . . . What an abuse of words! What a strange and fatal ignorance of divine works! We alone believe in *the spoken word* while our *dear enemies* persist in believing only in *the written word*: as if God could or would have changed the nature of things that he has ordained, and invested writing with a life and efficacy that it has not. Is not then the Holy Scripture *written?* Has it not been produced by *a pen and a little black liquid? Does it know what must be said to one man and hidden from another?* Did not Leibnitz and his servant read there the same words? Can this writing be other than the *portrait of the Word?* And, although infinitely worthy of regard in this respect, does it not need to *maintain a divine silence?* Finally, if it is attacked or insulted, *can it defend itself in the absence of its father?* Glory be to truth! If the eternally living *spoken word* does not give life to writing, it will never become *the Word*, that is to say *life*. Let others then invoke as much as they like the SILENT WORD, we shall peacefully laugh at this *false god*, ever waiting with a gentle impatience for the moment when its partisans will leave their illusions and throw themselves in our arms, extended now for three centuries.

XXIII

Every right-thinking person will end by being convinced on this point, however little he reflects on an axiom equally striking for its importance and universality. This is that NOTHING GREAT HAS GREAT BEGINNINGS. No exception to this law will be found in the whole of history. *Crescit occulto velut arbor oevo*; this is the eternal motto of every great institution; and it follows that every false institution writes a great deal, as it is sensible of its weakness and seeks to buttress itself. From this truth results the inevitable consequence that no great and real institution can be founded on a written law, since men themselves, successive instruments of the institution, do not know what it is to become, and since gradual growth is the true sign of durability in every possible order of things. A remarkable example of this is to be found in the power of the Sovereign Pontiffs, whom I do not intend to consider here in a dogmatic light. Since the sixteenth century, a host of scholars have made prodigious efforts of erudition to establish, by going to the earliest days of Christianity, that the Bishops of Rome were not in the first centuries what they have since become; thus assuming as an agreed point that everything that is not found in primitive ages is an abuse. However (and I say this in no spirit of contention and without meaning to shock anyone), they show in this as much philosophy and true learning as if they sought in a babe in arms the real dimensions of a full-grown man. The sovereignty of which I am now talking was born like others and has grown like others. It is pitiful to see powerful minds straining themselves to prove that maturity is an abuse by citing infancy, whereas the very idea of any institution being adult at birth is essentially an absurdity, a true logical contradiction. If the enlightened and generous enemies of this power (and certainly it has many of this kind) look at the question from this point of view, as I beg them with respect to do, I have no doubt that all those objections drawn from antiquity will vanish before their eyes like a light mist.

As for abuses, I must not spend time on them here. I shall say only, since I have raised the subject, that there is plenty to rebut the declarations that the last century has given us on this great subject. A time will come when the Popes about whom there is the most protest, such as Gregory VII, for example, will everywhere be regarded as the friends, teachers, and saviors of mankind, as the true constituent geniuses of Europe.

No one will doubt this once French intellectuals have become Christian and English intellectuals Catholic, which must assuredly come about one day.

XXIV

But what penetrating words can we now use to make ourselves heard in an age infatuated with writing and suspicious of the spoken word, to the point of believing that men can create constitutions, languages, and even sovereignties; in a century for which every reality is a falsehood and every falsehood a reality, which does not see even what is happening beneath its eyes, which feeds on books and goes to seek ambiguous lessons in Thucydides and Titus Livius, while entirely closing their eyes on the truth that shines in the newspapers of the time?

If the wishes of a common mortal were worthy of obtaining from Providence one of those memorable decrees which shape the great crises of history, I would ask it to inspire in some powerful nation that had offended it gravely the arrogant intention of constituting itself politically, starting at the very foundations. If, in spite of my unworthiness, I was allowed the ancient intimacy of the patriarchs, I would say: "Grant it everything! Give it spirit, knowledge, wealth, courage, above all an unlimited confidence in itself and that adaptable and enterprising genius which is not checked or intimidated by anything. Wipe out its ancient government; take away its memory; slay its affections; spread terror around it; blind or freeze its enemies; arrange for it to be victorious on all its frontiers at once, so that none of its neighbors can meddle in its affairs or trouble it in its plans. Let this nation be distinguished in science, rich in philosophy, sated with human power, free from all prejudices, all ties, every superior influence, lest one day it might be able to say, *I lacked this or I was hampered by that*; finally let it act freely with this plenitude of means so that it becomes, under your unfailing protection, an eternal lesson for humanity."

XXV

Doubtless one cannot expect a conjunction of circumstances which would literally be a miracle; but events of a similar order, if less remarkable, have shown themselves here and there in history, even in the history of our own day; and although they have not, to serve as an example, that ideal force that I just now asked for, nonetheless they point some important lessons.

Less than twenty-five years ago, we witnessed a serious attempt to regenerate a great but mortally sick nation. This was the first draft of a great work, and the *preface*, so to speak, of the frightening book that we have since had to read. Every precaution had been taken. . . . Alas, all human wisdom was at fault, and everything ended in death.

XXVI

It has been said: *But we know the causes of the failure of the undertaking.* How so? Do you want God to send angels in human form, charged with destroying a constitution? It will always be very necessary for secondary agents to be employed; this or that, what does it matter? Every tool is useful in the hands of the great craftsman; but so blind are men that if tomorrow some constitution-mongers came again to organize a people and to constitute it with *a little black liquid*, the crowd would again lose no time in believing in the promised miracle. Once more, it would be said, *Nothing is lacking*; *all is foreseen*; *all is written*; whereas, the very fact that all had been foreseen, discussed, and written would demonstrate the worthlessness and insubstantiality of the constitution.

XXVII

I think I have read somewhere *that there are very few sovereignties able to justify the legitimacy of their origins.* Admitting the justice of this claim, it does not imply the least blemish on the successors of a ruler against whose actions many objections might be raised: the shadows which to a greater or lesser degree fall across the origins of his authority should be regarded only as an inconvenience, a necessary consequence of a law of the moral world. If it was otherwise, it would follow that a sovereign could reign legitimately only by virtue of a deliberation of the whole people, that is to say, *by grace of the people;* which will never happen, for nothing is more true than what has been said by the author of *Considerations on France*: *that the people will always accept masters and will never choose them.* It is always necessary for the origin of sovereignty to appear as being outside the sphere of human control; so that the very men who appear to be directly involved are nevertheless only circumstances. As for legitimacy, if it seemed ambiguous in its beginning, God has explained himself through his prime minister in the affairs of this world, *time.* It is nevertheless quite true that certain contemporary portents do not mislead us much when we are in a position to observe them; but the details of this will be followed through in another work.

XXVIII

Everything therefore brings us back to the general rule: *Man cannot make a constitution, and no legitimate constitution can be written.* The corpus of fundamental laws that must constitute a civil or religious society have never been and never will be written. This can be done only when the society is already constituted, yet it is impossible to spell out or explain in writing certain individual articles; but almost always these declarations are the effect or the cause of very great evils, and they always cost the people more than they are worth.

XXIX

To this general rule *that no constitution can be written or made a priori*, only one exception is known; that is the law of Moses. It alone was, so to speak, cast like a statue and written down to the smallest detail by a prodigy who said, "Let it be," without his work ever having to be corrected, made good, or modified, either by himself or by others. . . .

XXX

But, since every constitution is divine in its origin, it follows that man cannot do anything unless he relies on God, in which case he becomes an instrument. This is a truth to which the whole of humanity has constantly rendered the most striking witness. If we refer to history, which is experimental politics, we shall see there continually the cradle of nations surrounded by priests and hear a constant call to God for help in human weakness. Myth, much truer than ancient history for trained eyes, adds to this proof. It is always an oracle who founds communities; it is always an oracle who announces divine protection and the successes of the founding heroes. Above all, kings, leaders of nascent empires, are continually designated and almost stamped by Heaven in some extraordinary way. How many frivolous men have laughed at the Holy Ampulla, without thinking that it is a hieroglyphic which only needs interpreting.

XXXI

The coronation of kings springs from the same roots. There has never been a ceremony or, more properly, a profession of faith more significant and worthy of respect. The finger of the Pontiff has always touched the brow of the new sovereign. The many writers who have seen in these august rites nothing but ambitious designs, and even the open alliance of superstition and tyranny, have spoken against truth, almost all even against their conscience. This subject merits examination. Sometimes sovereigns have sought coronation, and sometimes coronation has sought sovereigns. Others have been seen to reject coronation as a sign of dependence. We know enough of the facts to be able to judge sufficiently soundly; but it would be necessary to distinguish carefully between different men, periods, nations, and religions. Here it is sufficient to insist on the general and universal opinion which invokes the divine power in the establishment of empires.

XXXII

The most famous nations of antiquity, above all the most serious and wisest, such as the Egyptians, the Etruscans, the Spartans, and the Romans, were precisely those with the most religious constitutions; and the length of empires has always been proportionate to the influence that the religious principle has acquired in the political system. "The towns and nations most devoted to a cult of divinity have always been the most durable and the wisest, just as the most religious ages have always been the most distinguished by genius."[6]

XXXIII

Nations have never been civilized except by religion. No other force known has a hold on primitive man. Without recourse to antiquity, which is very decisive on this point, we see a striking proof of it in America. We have been there for three centuries with our laws, arts, sciences, culture, commerce, and wealth; how have we helped the indigenous population? In no way. We are destroying these unfortunate people with the sword and spirits; we are gradually pushing them back into the deserted interior, until in the end they will be wiped out completely, the victims of our vices as much as of our cruel superiority.

XXXIV

Has any philosopher ever dreamed of leaving his native land and his pleasures to go to the American forests in chase of savages, to prise them from vice and to give them a moral code?[7] They have done much better; they have written splendid books to prove that the savage is the *natural* man and that we can wish for nothing happier than to resemble him. Condorcet has said that *the missionaries have carried into*

[6] Xenophon: *Memorabilia*, Book i, Chap. iv.

[7] As a matter of fact, Condorcet promised us that the philosophers would undertake tirelessly the civilization and welfare of the barbarian nations (*Esquisse d'un tableau historique de l'esprit humain*, p. 335). We shall wait till they really intend to start.

Asia and America only shameful superstitions.[8] Rousseau has said, with a truly inconceivable compounding of folly, that *the missionaries seemed to him scarcely wiser than the conquerors.*[9] Finally, their leader has had the impudence (but what had he to lose?) to throw the most vulgar ridicule on these pacific conquerors of whom antiquity would have made gods.[10]

XXXV

These are, however, the very missionaries who have worked such remarkable wonders over human power and even over the human will. They alone have traversed the vast American continent from one end to the other to raise the human spirit. They alone have done what politics had not even dared to imagine. But none of them can equal the missions in Paraguay: there has been seen there most markedly the exclusive power and authority of religion in civilizing men. This prodigious effort has been praised, but not sufficiently: the spirit of the eighteenth century and another accessory spirit have managed to stifle in part the voice of justice and even that of admiration. Perhaps one day (since it can be hoped that great and noble works will again be taken up), in the heart of some affluent town set in an old savannah, a statue will be raised to the father of these missionaries. One will be able to read on its pedestal:

TO THE CHRISTIAN OSIRIS

whose envoys have traversed the earth to snatch men from misery, from savagery and from brutality, by teaching them the arts of agriculture, giving them laws, and showing them how to know and serve God, NOT BY THE FORCE OF ARMS, of which they had no need, but by gentle persuasion, moral songs, AND THE POWER OF HYMNS, so that they were believed to be angels.

XXXVI

Now, when it is remembered that this legislating monastic order which held sway in Paraguay by the sole authority of virtues and talents, without ever departing from the humblest submission to even

---

[8] *Ibid.,* p. 335.
[9] *Lettre à l'archevêque de Paris.*
[10] Voltaire, *Essai sur les moeurs et l'esprit.*

the most distant legitimate authority; that this order, as I say, at the same time tackled in our prisons, our hospitals, and our leper colonies all the most horrible and repulsive aspects of destitution, illness, and despair; that these same men, who went at first call to sit in the straw by the side of poverty, were at home in the most polished circles; that they went on to the scaffolds *to say the last words* to the victims of human justice, and from these theaters of horror hastened into the pulpits to thunder before kings; that they brought the artist's brush to China, the telescope to our observatories, the Orphean lyre to the midst of savages, and that they had educated the whole of Louis XIV's age; when it is remembered finally that a hateful coalition of perverse ministers, delirious judges, and ignoble sectarians has been able in our time to destroy this amazing institution and to congratulate themselves on their deed, one can believe in that madman who exultantly stamped on a watch, saying to it, *That will stop you from making a noise.* But what am I saying? A madman is not guilty.

XXXVII

I have had to dwell principally on the formation of empires as the most important subject; but all human institutions fall under the same rule, and all are useless or dangerous if they do not rest upon the foundation of all existence. This principle being incontestable, what are we to think of a generation that has thrown everything into confusion, down to the very bases of the social structure, in making education purely scientific? It would be impossible to make a more serious mistake, for every educational system that does not rest on religion will fall in the twinkling of an eye or will disgorge nothing but poison into the state, *religion being*, as Bacon has well put it, *the preservative that saves sciences from putrefaction.*

XXXVIII

It is often asked *why there is a school of theology in every university*. The reply is easy: *It is so that universities will continue to exist and that teaching will not corrupt itself.* Originally there were only schools of theology, which other *faculties* joined like subjects around a queen. The structure of public education, resting on this base, lasted until our own day. Those who have overturned it in their countries will repent of it vainly for a long time. To burn a town, only a child or a madman is needed; to rebuild it, architects, material, workmen, money and, above all, time are necessary.

XXXIX

Those who have been happy to corrupt old institutions while preserving their external forms have perhaps done as much damage to mankind. Already the influence of modern universities on morals and national spirit in a considerable part of the European continent is widely recognized. In this respect, the English universities have retained more reputation than the others; perhaps because the English know better when it is proper to be silent and when to be satisfied; perhaps also because public opinion, which has an extraordinary power in that country, has been able to protect these ancient colleges from the general disease better than elsewhere. However, they must go under, and already the evil heart of Gibbon has yielded some strange secrets to us on this point. In short, not to leave generalities, if one does not rely on ancient maxims, if education is not given back to the priests, and if science is not put everywhere in second place, the evils that await us are incalculable; we shall be brutalized by sciences, and that constitutes the lowest point of brutalization.

XL

Not only is creation not one of man's proper functions; it does not seem as if our *unassisted* power extends to the reform of established institutions. Nothing is plainer to man than the existence of two opposed forces which ceaselessly battle in the universe. There is no good that evil does not defile and debase; there is no evil that good does not restrain and attack, in impelling all things toward a more perfect state. These two forces are everywhere present. They can be seen equally in the growth of plants, in the generation of animals, in the formation of languages and of empires (two inseparable things), and so on. Human power extends perhaps only to removing or combating evil to free the good from it and to restore to the good the power to grow according to its nature. The celebrated Zanotti has said, *It is difficult to change things for the better.*[11] This thought hides a profound

---

[11] Quoted in *Transunto delle R. Academia di Torino*, 1788–89, p. 6.

meaning under the appearance of extreme simplicity. It accords completely with another saying of Origen, which is alone worth a whole volume. *Nothing*, he said, *can be changed for the better in social matters without divine help.*[12] All men feel the truth of this, without being able themselves to express it. It is from this that follows the unconscious aversion of all right-thinking men to innovations. The word *reform*, in itself and before any scrutiny, will always be suspect to the wise, and the experience of every age justifies this kind of instinct. It is too well known what has been the fruit of the finest speculations in this line.

XLI

To apply these generalizations to a particular case, it is from the sole consideration of the grave danger of innovations based on simplified human theories that, without believing that I am in a position to hold a reasoned opinion on the great question of parliamentary reform which has so deeply and for such a long time stirred English minds, I nevertheless feel led to believe that this idea is dangerous and that, if the English surrender to it too readily, they will repent of it. *But*, say the partisans of reform (for this is the great argument), *the abuses are striking and incontestable: can a formal abuse, a vice, be constitutional?* Yes, indisputably it can be; for every political constitution has its essential faults which spring from its nature and which cannot be separated from it; and what should make every reformer hesitate is that these faults can change with circumstances; so that by showing that they are new, one has not thus shown that they are not necessary. What sensible man will not therefore be scared to undertake such work? Social harmony is subject to the law of *temperament*, as is harmony properly speaking *in the musical scale*. Get the *fifths* carefully in tune and the *octaves* will clash, and *vice versa*. Discord being therefore inevitable, rather than removing it, which is impossible, it is necessary to *temper* it, by distributing it. Thus in both cases, *fault is an element in possible perfection.* This proposition is only apparently paradoxical. *But*, it will perhaps still be said, *what is the rule to distinguish an accidental fault from that which belongs to the nature of things and which is impossible to eliminate?* Men to whom nature has given only

[12] Origen, *Against Celsus*, Book i, Chap. xxvi.

ears put this kind of question, and those with an ear for music shrug
their shoulders.

XLII

It is still more necessary to take care, when it is a question of abuses,
to judge political institutions only by their constant effects and never
by any of their causes, which are not important, still less by certain collateral disadvantages (if it can be so expressed) which can easily
engross shortsighted views and prevent them from seeing things as a
whole. In fact, cause, according to the hypothesis that seems to be
proved, not having any necessary logical relation to effect, and the
drawbacks of a good institution in itself being, as I have just said, only
the necessary discord in the musical scale, how can institutions be
judged on the basis of their causes and disadvantages? Voltaire, who
talked of everything for a whole age without once piercing below the
surface, reasoned curiously on the sale of judicial offices which took
place in France; and perhaps no example could show more accurately
the truth of the theory I am expounding. *The proof,* he said, *that this
sale is an abuse is that it has been produced only by another abuse.*[13]
Voltaire is not merely mistaken here, since all men are liable to error.
He is shamefully mistaken. This is a complete reversal of common
sense. *Everything that springs from an abuse is an abuse!* On the contrary, it is one of the most general and most evident of the laws of the
hidden yet apparent power which operates and makes itself felt on all
sides that the remedy for an abuse springs from the abuse itself and
that an evil, carried to a certain point, is necessarily its own destroyer;
for evil, which is no more than a negative, has the same dimension and
duration as the being to which it is attached and which it devours. It
is like a cancer which can fulfill itself only by destroying itself. But
then a new reality necessarily rushes into the place of that which has
just disappeared; *since nature abhors a vacuum,* and good—But I
am wandering too far from Voltaire.

XLIII

The error of this man comes from the fact that this great writer,
divided between twenty sciences, as he has somewhere said himself,

[13] *Précis du siècle de Louis XV,* Chap. xlii.

and moreover continually occupied with instructing the world, had only very rarely the time to think. "A voluptuous and spendthrift court, reduced to extremities by its wastefulness, conceived the idea of selling judicial offices, and thus created (what it would never have done freely and with full knowledge of the case) it created, I say, a rich, immovable and independent judiciary; in this way the infinite power *playing over the world*[14] makes use of corruption to create incorruptible courts (as much as it allows to human weakness)." In truth, nothing is more plausible than this to a true philosopher, nothing conforms more to human experience and to that indisputable law which lays down that the most important institutions are never the result of deliberation but of circumstances. The problem is now almost resolved when it is posed, as happens to every problem. *Could a country such as France be served better than by hereditary judges?* If this is agreed, as I assume, it immediately becomes necessary to propose a second problem like this: *The judiciary being necessarily hereditary, is there a more advantageous method of constituting it in the first place and subsequently of recruiting to it than that which adds millions at the very least to the state funds, and which guarantees at the same time the wealth, the independence and even the nobility* (of every kind) *of the higher judiciary?* If the sale of offices is considered only as a means of making them hereditary, every impartial mind is struck by the truth of this view. This is not the place to develop the point; but enough has been said to show that Voltaire did not even see it.

XLIV

Let us now suppose at the head of affairs a man such as he, combining in perfect harmony superficiality, incapacity, and temerity. He will not fail to act according to his foolish theories of laws and abuses. He will borrow to the last halfpenny to reimburse officeholders, to the last shilling to reimburse creditors: he will prepare the public mind by paying for a host of writings insulting the judiciary and sapping public confidence in it. Soon patronage, a thousand times more foolish than chance, will begin its endless career of folly; the man of distinction, no longer seeing in heredity a counterweight to overwhelming labors, will stand down for ever; and the high courts will be open to adventurers without name, wealth, or reputation, in place of that respected

[14] Proverbs, 8:31.

judiciary, in which virtue and knowledge had become, like rank, hereditary, a true priesthood envied by foreign nations up to the time when the cult of philosophy, having excluded wisdom from all the places it used to visit, ended its splendid exploits by expelling it from its true home.

XLV

This is a true reflection of the majority of reforms: because not only does creation not belong to man, but even reformation belongs to him in only a secondary manner and with a host of severe restrictions. Starting from these incontestable principles, each man can judge his country's institutions with complete certainty; above all he can appreciate all those *creators*, those *legislators*, those *restorers* of nations so dear to the eighteenth century, whom posterity will regard with pity, perhaps even with horror. Houses of cards have been built both in and outside Europe. Details would be odious, but certainly no disrespect is shown to anyone by simply asking men to deliberate and judge at least on the basis of events, even if they persist in refusing any other kind of instruction. Man in harmony with his Creator is sublime and his action creative; equally, once he separates himself from God and acts alone, he does not cease to be powerful, since that is a privilege of his nature, but his acts are negative and lead only to destruction.

XLVI

In the whole of history, there is not a single fact that contradicts these maxims. No human institution can last if it is not supported by the hand which supports all things, that is to say, if it is not specially consecrated to Him in its origins. The more it is penetrated by the divine principle, the more durable it will be. How curiously blind are the men of our age! They boast of their enlightenment and are totally ignorant, since they know nothing of themselves. They know neither what they are nor what they can do. A boundless pride leads them continually to overthrow everything they have not themselves made; and to bring about new creations, they cut themselves off from the principle of all existence. Jean-Jacques Rousseau, however, has himself very well said: *Petty and vain man, confess to me your weakness and I will show you your strength.* In fact, once man has recognized his incapacity, he has taken a great step forward, for he is then very near to seeking a support with which he can do all things. This is precisely the opposite of what the last century did. (Alas, it has ended only in our calendars!) Examine all its undertakings, any of its institutions, and you will see it constantly engaged in separating them from the Divinity. Man believed himself to be an independent being, and professed a real practical atheism, more dangerous perhaps and more culpable than a theoretical atheism.

XLVII

Distracted by its vain sciences from the only science that really concerns him, he believed that he had the power of *creation,* whereas he has not even that of *naming.* He, who has not the power even of making an insect or a blade of grass, believed that he was the immediate author of sovereignty, the most important, sacred, and fundamental thing in the moral and political world, and that, for example, such and such a family reigns because such and such a people has willed it; while he is surrounded by incontrovertible proofs that every sovereign family reigns because it is chosen by a superior power. If he does not see these proofs, it is because he closes his eyes or scrutinizes too closely. He believed that it is he who invented languages; whereas again all that lies with him is to see that every human language is *learned* and never *invented,* and that no conceivable hypothesis based on human power can explain with the least appearance of probability either the formation or the diversity of languages. He believed that he could constitute nations, that is to say, in other words, *that he could create that national unity by virtue of which one nation is distinguishable from another.* Finally, he believed that, since he had the power of creating institutions, he had with greater reason the power of borrowing them from other nations and transplanting them ready made in his own country, with the name that they had abroad, to enjoy them like those foreigners with the same advantages. French sources provide me with a very apt example of this point.

XLVIII

Several years ago the French took it into their heads to establish in Paris certain races that were seriously called in some writings of the day Olympic Games. The reasoning of those who invented or revived this splendid name was not subtle. *There were,* they said to themselves, *foot and horse races on the banks of the Alpheius; there are foot and horse races on the banks of the Seine; so it is the same thing.* Nothing could be simpler; but without asking them why they did not think of calling these games *Parisian* instead of *Olympic,* there would be many other observations to make. To initiate the Olympic Games, oracles were consulted: gods and heroes played a part in them; they were never started without sacrifices and other religious ceremonies being performed; they were regarded as the great public assemblies of Greece, and nothing was more dignified. But did the Parisians, before they set up their races *revived from the Greeks,* go to Rome, *ad limina apostolorum,* to consult the Pope? Before starting off their daredevils to amuse the shopkeepers, did they sing a high mass? What great political viewpoint had they been able to associate with these races? What names were given to their founders?—But this is more than enough; the most ordinary good sense at once feels the meaninglessness and even the absurdity of this imitation. . . .

XLIX

For myself, I *believe,* and indeed I *know,* that no human institution can last if it has not a religious base; *and moreover* (I beg that particular attention be paid to this), *if it has not a name taken from the national language and self-generated, without any previous or known deliberation.*

L

The theory of names is again a subject of great importance. Names are not purely arbitrary, as has been claimed by so many men *who have lost their own names.* God calls himself *I am,* and every creature is called *I am so and so.* Since the name of a sacred being is necessarily relative to its function, which is its distinctive quality, it follows, that among the ancients, the greatest honor for God was *polyonymy,* that is to say, a *plurality of names,* which gives proof of a plurality of functions or of extensive power. Ancient mythology shows us Diana, while still a child, demanding this honor from Jupiter; and in the verse

THE GENERATIVE PRINCIPLE OF POLITICAL CONSTITUTIONS

attributed to Orpheus, she is complimented by the name of *démon polyonyme* (spirit of many names). Which means, at bottom, that God alone has the right to bestow a *name*. Indeed, he has *named* everything, since he has created everything. He gave names to the stars; he named the angels and of these last names Scripture mentions only three, but all three are related to the intended purpose of these agents. It is the same with men whom God wished to name himself, and whom Scripture has made known to us in a sufficiently large number; in every case, names are related to functions. Has it not been said that in his Kingdom to come he would give to the victors a NEW NAME,[15] suited to their deeds? And have men, *made in the image of God*, found a more solemn way of rewarding victors than by giving them *a new name*, the most honorable of all being in men's eyes the name of the vanquished nations. Whenever a man is supposed to change his way of life and to assume a new character, very often he receives *a new name*. This is revealed in baptism, in confirmation, in the enrollment of soldiers, in the entry into religious orders, in the enfranchisement of slaves, and so on; in a word, the name of every being expresses what he is, and in this way there is nothing arbitrary about it. The common expression *He has a name, he has no reputation* (*Il a un nom, il n'a point de nom*) is very apt and meaningful, for no man can be placed among those *called to assemblies and who have a name*,[16] if his family is not marked with the sign that distinguishes it from other families.

LI

What is true for individuals is true for nations; there are those that *have no name*, in either sense. Herodotus observes that the Thracians would have been the most powerful nation in the world if they had been united: *but*, he adds, *this unity is impossible because they are divided into groups with different names.*[17] This is an acute remark. There are also some modern nations *which have no name* and there are others which have several; but *polyonymy* is as unfortunate for nations as it was believed to be honorable for gods.

[15] Revelation 3:12.
[16] Numbers 16:2.
[17] Herodotus, Book V, 3.

LII

Names therefore being far from arbitrary and being derived in their origin, like all things, more or less immediately from God, it should not be thought that man has the right to name without restriction even those things of which he has some right to regard himself as the author, and to impose names on them according to the idea he has formed of them. God has reserved for himself in this respect a kind of original jurisdiction impossible to ignore. *My dear Hermogenes, the imposition of names is an important matter, and cannot belong to the evil or even the common man. . . . This right belongs only to the maker of names, that is to say, as it seems, to the legislator alone; but a legislator is the rarest of all human beings.*[18]

LIII

However, man likes nothing so much as to give names. That is what he does, for example, when he applies conventional epithets to things, a talent which distinguishes the great writer and above all the great poet. The happy imposition of an adjective renders a noun illustrious, makes it celebrated in this new combination. . . . Man will never lose the memory of his original powers; it can even be said that, in a certain sense, he will always exercise them; but how much has his degradation restricted them. Here is a law true as God who made it:

It is forbidden to man to give great names to the things of which he is the author and which he believes to be great; but if he has acted legitimately, the great thing will ennoble the vulgar name and it will become great. . . .

LV

Another reason, which, if less important, still has its value, must oblige us to mistrust all pretentious names imposed a priori. It is that, man's conscience almost always warning him against the imperfection of the work he has just produced, rebellious pride, while it cannot mislead itself, seeks at least to mislead others by inventing an honorable

[18] Plato, *Cratylus* 388e.

name that assumes precisely the opposite merit; so that this name, instead of giving a true witness to the excellence of the work, is really confession of the blemish that characterizes it. . . .

LVI

But, as I have said, all this is only secondary: let us return to the general principle that *man has not, or has no longer, the right to name things* (at least in the sense I have given). What is especially significant is that the names most worthy of respect have in every language an origin in common speech. The name is never adapted to the thing itself: in every case the thing adds luster to the name. The name must *grow*, so to speak; otherwise it is inappropriate. What does the word *throne* mean originally? a *seat*, or even a *stool*. What does *scepter* mean? a walking stick. But the *stick* of kings was soon distinguished from all the others, and this name, in its *new* meaning, has lasted for three thousand years. Is there anything nobler in literature and yet humbler in its origins than the word *tragedy?* And the now almost stinking word *flag*, raised and ennobled by warriors' lances, what a varied fate has it had in our own language. Many other words come in varying degrees to the support of the same principle, such as, for example, *senate, dictator, consul, emperor, church, cardinal, marshal.* Let us end by considering the names *constable* and *chancellor*, given to two high offices of modern times; the first meant originally only the *keeper of the stables*, and the second, *the man who stood behind a grille* (so as not to be overwhelmed by a crowd of supplicants).

LVII

There are therefore two infallible rules for judging all human creations, whatever they may be, *origin* and *name;* and properly understood these two rules are easily applied. If the origin is purely human, the structure must be unsound; the more the human interference and the greater the role of deliberation, science, and *above all writing*, in a word of human means of every kind, the more fragile will be the institution. It is primarily by this rule that the work of kings or assemblies in civilizing, establishing, or regenerating nations must be judged.

LVIII

For the opposite reason, the more divine an institution in its origin, the more durable it is. It is as well to point out, for the sake of clarity, that the religious principle is in essence creative and conservative, in two ways. In the first place, as it is the most effective influence on the human mind, it can stimulate prodigious efforts. So, for example, a man persuaded by his religious beliefs that it is very advantageous to him that after his death his body should be preserved as far as possible as it was in life, without any prying or profane hand being able to touch it, such a man, having brought the art of embalment to perfection, will end by constructing the pyramids of Egypt. In the second place, the religious principle, already so strong because of what it effects, is still stronger because of what it prevents, through the respect with which it surrounds everything it takes under its wings. If a pebble is consecrated, that immediately becomes a reason for keeping it from those who might mislay or misuse it. The world is full of proofs of this truth. For example, Etruscan vases, preserved by the sanctity of the tomb, have in spite of their fragility come down to us in greater numbers than marble or bronze statues of the same period. If therefore you wish to *conserve* all, *consecrate* all.

LIX

The second rule, that of names, is to my mind neither less clear nor less decisive than the first. If a name is imposed by an assembly; if it is established by a previous deliberation, so that it precedes the thing to which it applies; if the name is pompous; if it is as portentous as the object it should represent; finally, if it is taken from a foreign language, and especially an ancient language, it is completely useless and both the name and the thing it stands for will certainly disappear in a short time. The opposite conditions are a mark of the legitimacy and consequently the durability of the institution. It is very necessary to guard against dealing with this subject superficially. The true philosopher must never lose sight of language, a barometer that registers faithfully *good and bad weather*. To keep to my present subject, the unlimited introduction of foreign words, above all when applied to national institutions of every kind, is certainly one of the surest signs of a people's degradation.

LX

If the formation of empires, the progress of civilization, and the unanimous agreement of all history and tradition is still not sufficient to convince us, the death of empires will complete the proof begun by their birth. Just as it is the religious principle that has created all things, so it is the absence of this same principle that has destroyed all things. The Epicureans, who could be called the *ancient unbelievers,* first degraded and soon destroyed every government which had the misfortune to tolerate them. Everywhere *Lucretius* heralded *Caesar.*

But all past experience dwindles to nothing beside the astonishing example furnished by the last century. Still drunk with its heady fumes, men in general are far from having sufficient composure to look at this example in its true light and especially to draw from it the necessary conclusions; it is therefore essential to scrutinize this terrible epoch with every care.

LXI

There have always been religions in this world, and there have always been the ungodly to fight them; also, blasphemy has always been a sin; for, since every false religion must contain some element of truth, every blasphemous doctrine must attack some divine truth more or less distorted; *but true blasphemy can exist only in the bosom of a true religion*; and inevitably blasphemy has never been able to produce in the past the evils it has produced in our own day, for its culpability is always relative to the general standard of enlightenment. It is by this rule that the eighteenth century must be judged, for it is from this point of view that it differs from every other. It is often said *that every age is alike and that all men have always been the same;* but it is very necessary to guard against believing these generalizations invented by laziness or superficiality to escape from real thought. On the contrary, every age and every nation has a particular and distinctive character which must be carefully considered. No doubt there have always been vices in the world, but these vices can differ in quantity, in nature, in dominant quality, and in intensity. Although there has always been impiety, there had never been, before the eighteenth century and in the heart of the Christian world, *an insurrection against God*; above all there had never been seen before a sacrilegious conspiracy of all the talents against their author. Now, this is what we have seen in our own day. Comedy has vied with tragedy in blasphemy, and the novel with history and natural philosophy. The men of this age have prostituted their talents to irreligion, and, to use the admirable phrase of the dying St. Louis, THEY HAVE WAGED WAR AGAINST GOD WITH HIS GIFTS. The impiety of the ancient world is never angry; sometimes it is reasonable, ordinarily it is lighthearted, but it is never bitter. Even Lucretius scarcely ever descends to an insult; and although his somber and melancholy temperament leads him to see things in their darkest colors, yet, even when he attacks religion for having produced great evils, he remains composed. The ancient religions were not sufficiently worthwhile to merit the anger of contemporary skeptics.

LXII

When *the good tidings* were proclaimed in the world, the attack became more violent, yet its enemies always kept within certain limits. Only occasionally do they appear in history, and then always isolated. There is never any combination or formal alliance; never did they unleash the fury that we have witnessed. Even Bayle, the father of modern skepticism, does not resemble in the slightest his successors. In his most flagrant errors, he shows no spirit of proselytization, still less any tone of irritation or partisan spirit; he denies less than he doubts; he gives arguments for and against; often he speaks even more eloquently for the good than for the bad cause.

LXIII

It was not therefore until the first half of the eighteenth century that irreligion really became a force. At once it spread everywhere with incredible speed. From the palace to the cabin, it crept everywhere and infected everything; it followed secret channels and had a hidden but effective action so that the closest observer, although he sees the effects, cannot always discover the causes. By its enormous prestige, it made itself loved even by those of whom it was the deadliest enemy; and the authority which it was about to destroy stupidly embraced it before receiving the deathblow. Soon a simple theory became a formal association, which rapidly graduated into a conspiracy and finally into a great organization covering Europe.

LXIV

Then for the first time the unique character of eighteenth century atheism revealed itself. It no longer speaks in the cold tone of indifference, still less with the biting irony of skepticism; there is a deadly hatred, a tone of anger and often of fury. The writers of this age, at least the most outstanding, no longer treat Christianity as an inconsequential human error, but hunt it like a mortal enemy: it becomes a fight to the end, a war to the death; and what would seem unbelievable, if we did not have sad proofs of it before our eyes, is that many of these self-styled philosophers raised their hatred of Christianity to a personal hatred of its divine Author. They really detest him as a living enemy is detested. Two men above all, who will be for ever cursed by posterity, have distinguished themselves by a kind of wickedness which might seem beyond the powers of even the most depraved human nature.

LXV

However, the whole of Europe having been civilized by Christianity, and its ministers having gained an important place in the politics of every country, civil and religious institutions had been intermingled and even amalgamated to a surprising degree; so that it could be said with more or less truth of every European state what Gibbon said of France, *that this Kingdom had been made by bishops*. It was therefore inevitable that the philosophy of the age did not hesitate to vilify the social institutions identified with the religious principle. This is what happened; every government and institution in Europe displeased it, precisely *because* they were Christian; and *in proportion to* the influence of Christianity, a malaise of opinion, a general discontent seized men's minds. In France especially, this philosophic fury no longer recognized any limits; and soon many voices were joined in one chorus which was heard at the heart of sinful Europe:

LXVI

"Depart from us, God![19] Must we for ever tremble before priests, and receive from them whatever instruction they care to give us? Throughout Europe, truth is hidden by the smoke of incense; it is time that it emerged from this fatal cloud. We shall no longer speak of you to our children; it is for them, when they become men, to decide if you are and what you are and what you ask of them. All things displease us, because your name is written on all things. We wish to destroy everything and to re-create it without your help. Depart from our councils of state, our schools, our homes; we shall be better off alone, reason will be a sufficient guide. Depart from us, God!"

How has God punished this abominable delirium? He has punished it as he created the world, by a single phrase. He has said: LET IT BE—and the political world collapsed.

This is how the two proofs join to convince even the least farseeing minds. On the one side, the religious principle presides over every political creation; and on the other everything crumbles once it withdraws.

LXVII

Europe's sin is to have closed men's eyes to these great truths, and it is because it has sinned that it suffers. Yet it still rejects the true light and ignores the hand that punishes it. Very few men in this materialist generation are capable of knowing the *time*, the *nature*, and the *enormity* of certain crimes committed by individuals, nations, and sovereigns, still less of understanding the kind of expiation these crimes necessitate and the wonderful miracle that forces evil to clean with its own hands the place that the eternal architect has already surveyed for his awesome works. The men of this age have made up their minds. *They have sworn to bow their eyes to the earth.*[20] But it would be useless, perhaps even dangerous, to go into greater detail. We are enjoined *to speak the truth in love.*[21] It is more necessary on certain occasions not to speak it except with respect; and, in spite of every

[19] Job 21:14.
[20] Psalms 17:11.
[21] Ephesians 4:15.

imaginable precaution, the way would be difficult for even the calmest and best intentioned of writers. The world, moreover, always holds an innumerable host of men so perverse, so profoundly corrupted, that, if they have been allowed to doubt certain things, they will also take the opportunity to redouble their wickedness and make themselves, so to speak, as guilty as the rebel angels. Rather let them grow more like brutes, if this is possible, so that, as less than men, their guilt will be the less. Blindness is no doubt a terrible punishment; yet sometimes it still allows the perception of love: this is all that can usefully be said at this time.

The
Saint Petersburg
Dialogues

FIRST DIALOGUE

THE KNIGHT: You believe, then, that the wicked are not happy? I too would like to believe this, yet I hear it said every day that they succeed in everything. If this were really the case, I would be a little angry that Providence had reserved the punishment of the wicked and the reward of the just entirely for another world; it seems to me that a little on account on both sides, in this life, would have done no harm. . . .

THE COUNT: For long there have been complaints of Providence in the distribution of good and evil, but I confess that these difficulties have never been able to make the least impression on my mind. I see with the certainty of intuition, and I humbly thank this Providence for it, that on this point man misleads himself in the full meaning of the phrase and in its natural sense.

I should have liked to be able to say with Montaigne, *Man fools himself*, for this is exactly right. It is quite true: man *fools himself*; he is his own dupe; he takes the sophisms of his naturally rebellious heart (alas, nothing is more certain) for real doubts born of his understanding. If occasionally superstition *believes in belief*, as it is accused of, more often still, you can be sure, pride *believes in disbelief*. In both cases, man *fools himself*, but in the second this is much worse.

183

In a word, gentlemen, there is no subject on which I feel more strongly than the temporal rule of Providence: it is therefore with complete conviction and profound satisfaction that I shall reveal to two men whom I love dearly some useful thoughts I have gathered through an already long life entirely devoted to serious studies.

THE KNIGHT: I will listen to you with the greatest pleasure, and I have no doubt our common friend will give you the same attention, but allow me, I beg you, to start by contradicting you before you begin. Do not accuse me of *replying to your silence,* for it is just as if you had already spoken, and I know very well what you are going to say to me. Without any doubt, you were about to start where the preachers end, *with the life eternal.* "The guilty are happy in this world, but will be tormented in the next; the just, on the other hand, suffer in this but will be happy in the next." This is a commonplace. And why should I hide that this peremptory reply does not satisfy me fully? I hope you will not suspect me of wishing to destroy or weaken this valuable argument, but it seems to me that it would not be harmed at all if it was associated with others.

THE SENATOR: If our friend is indiscreet or too precipitous, I confess that I am at fault like him and as much as he, for I was also about to quarrel with you before you had broached the question; or, more seriously, I should like to ask you to leave the beaten tracks. I have read several of your ascetic writers of the first rank, whom I honor deeply, but, while giving them all the praise they deserve, it pains me that, on this great question of the ways of divine justice in this world, they almost all seem to accept criticisms of the fact and to admit that there is no way of justifying divine Providence in this life. If this proposition is not false, it seems to me at least to be extremely dangerous, for there is grave danger in allowing men to believe that virtue will be rewarded and vice punished only in another life. Skeptics, for whom this world is everything, ask for nothing better, and the masses themselves must take the same line: man is so muddled, so dependent on the things immediately before his eyes, that every day even the most submissive believer can be seen to risk the torments of the after-life for the smallest pleasure. What will be the case with those who do not believe or whose belief is weak? Let us then rely as much as you like on the future life, which answers every objection, but if a truly moral regime exists in this world, and if even in this life crime should go in fear, why relieve it of this fear?

THE COUNT: Pascal observes somewhere that *the last thing that is discovered in writing a book is to know what should be put first.* I am not writing a book, my friends, but I am beginning a discourse that may well be long and should have had the opportunity to think about its beginning. Fortunately, you have saved me the trouble of deliberation by telling me where I should start.

The familiar expression that should be addressed only to a child or an inferior, *You do not know what you are saying,* is nevertheless the compliment that a man of good sense has the right to make to the crowd who meddle in discussions of the thorny questions of philosophy. Have you ever heard a soldier complain that in war wounds are suffered only by honest men and that it is sufficient to be a rascal to be invulnerable? I am sure the answer is no, for in fact everyone knows that the bullet does not choose the person it hits. It would be quite proper to lay down at least a perfect parallel between the evils of war in relation to soldiers and the evils of life in general in relation to all men; and this parallel, exact as I assume, is alone sufficient to overcome a difficulty based on a manifest falsehood; for it is not only false but obviously false *that crime in general prospers and virtue suffers in this world*: on the contrary, it is very evident that good and evil are a kind of lottery in which each, without distinction, can draw a winning or a losing ticket. The question therefore should be changed to, *Why, in the temporal world, are the just not exempt from the evils which can afflict the guilty; and why are the wicked not deprived of the benefits that the just can enjoy?* But this question is entirely different from the other, and I should even be astonished if the simple statement of it does not show you its absurdity; for it is one of my favorite ideas that the upright man is very commonly informed, by an inner sentiment, of the falsity or truth of certain propositions before any examination, often even without having made the studies necessary to be in a position to examine them with full knowledge of the case.

THE SENATOR: I am so much of your opinion, and so drawn to this doctrine, that I have perhaps exaggerated it by carrying it into the natural sciences; yet I can, at least to a certain point, invoke experience in this respect. More than once, in questions of physics or natural history, I have been shocked, without knowing quite why, by certain accepted opinions, which in one case at least I have had the pleasure subsequently of seeing attacked and even ridiculed by men deeply versed in these very sciences, in which as you know I have few pretensions. Do you think it necessary to be the equal of Descartes to make fun of these flurries? If anyone tells me that this earth we inhabit is only a bit of the sun drawn off some millions of years ago by some erratic comet hurtling through space; or that animals are made like houses by putting this by the side of that; or that geological strata are only the result of some chemical action, and a hundred other splendid theories of this kind that have been spread abroad in our time, must I be very well read and very reflective, should I have been to four or five universities to feel that these theories are absurd? I shall go further: I believe that in those very questions pertaining to the exact sciences or which appear to rest entirely on experience, this rule of the intellectual conscience is far from worthless for those who are not initiated in this kind of knowledge; which is what has led me to doubt, I confess to you in confidence, several things which commonly pass as certain. The explanation of tides by lunar and solar attraction, the decomposition and recomposition of water and other theories that I could quote to you and that are accepted today as dogmas are repelled by my mind, and I feel led to the inevitable conclusion that some day a scholar of good faith will come to teach us that we were in error on these important subjects or that they were not understood. Since friendship carries this right, you might say to me, *This is pure ignorance on your part.* I have said this to myself a thousand times. But tell me in your turn why I should not be equally intractable about other truths. I believe them on the word of the masters, and never does a single idea *against the faith* occur to my mind.

Where then does this internal feeling that revolts against certain theories originate? These theories are based on arguments that I am unable to counter, and yet this conscience of which we talked still says, *Quodcunque ostendis mihi sic, incredulus odi....*

THE COUNT: I shall not examine at this point to what degree one can rely on this internal feeling that the Senator so justly calls *intellectual conscience.*

Still less will I allow myself to discuss the particular example to which he has applied it; these details would carry us too far from our subject. I shall say only that righteousness of heart and habitual purity of intention can have hidden effects and results that extend very much further than is commonly imagined. I am therefore very disposed to believe that among men such as those who now hear me, the secret instinct we were just talking about will very often guess correctly even in the natural sciences; but I am led to believe it well-nigh infallible in questions of theoretical philosophy, morality, metaphysics, and natural theology. It is well worthy of the supreme wisdom, which has created and regulated all things, to have excused man from deep learning in everything that really matters to him. I have thus been right to affirm that once the question occupying us was posed exactly, the internal agreement of every right-thinking person had necessarily to precede discussion. . . .

I repeat that I have never understood this eternal argument against Providence drawn from the misfortune of the just and the prosperity of the wicked. If good men suffered because they are good, and likewise the wicked prospered because they are wicked, the argument would be incontrovertible; it falls to the ground once it is assumed that good and ill fortune are distributed indiscriminately among all men. But false opinions are like false money, struck first of all by guilty men and thereafter circulated by honest people who perpetuate the crime without knowing what they are doing. Impiety first noised this objection abroad; frivolity and good nature have repeated it; but in truth it is nothing. I return to my first analogy: a good man is killed in war; is this an injustice? No, it is a misfortune. If he has gout or gravel, if his friend betrays him, if he is crushed under a falling building, this is again a misfortune, but nothing more, since all men without distinction are subject to these kinds of bad fortune. Never lose from sight this great truth: *A general law, if it is not unjust to all, cannot be unjust to an individual.* You have not a certain illness, but you could have it; you have it, but you could be free from it. Whoever has perished in a battle could have escaped; whoever returns from it could have remained. All are not dead, but all were there to die.

Consequently more injustice: the just law is not that which takes effect on everyone but that which is made for everyone; the effect on such and such an individual is no more than an accident. To find difficulties in this order of things, they must be loved for their own sake; unfortunately they are loved and sought out; the human heart, always in revolt against the authority that constricts it, tells stories to the mind, which believes them; we accuse Providence in order to be freed from accusing ourselves; we raise objections to it that we would be ashamed to raise against a sovereign or even an official whose wisdom we would assess. How strange that it is easier for us to be just toward men than toward God!

It seems to me, gentlemen, that I would abuse your patience if I went any further in proving to you that the question is ordinarily wrongly put, and that really *they know not what they are saying* when they complain that vice is happy and virtue unhappy in this world; whereas, even on the assumption most favorable to the grumblers, it is patently proved that evils of every kind fall on humanity like bullets on an army, without any distinction of persons. Now, if the good man does not suffer *because he is good*, and if the wicked man does not prosper *because he is wicked*, the objection vanishes and good sense has reasserted itself.

THE KNIGHT: I admit that, if the distribution of physical and external evils alone is considered, the objection drawn from it against Providence is obviously based on inattention or bad faith, but it seems to me that the impunity of crimes is much more significant. This is the great scandal and the point on which I am most curious to hear what you say.

THE COUNT: It is not yet time, Knight. You have decided in my favor a little too quickly on the evils that you call *external*. If I have up to now assumed, as you have taken it, that evils are distributed equally among all men, this was only for the sake of argument, for in truth this is not the case. But before going any further, let us be careful not to stray from our path; there are questions which are so interconnected that it is easy to slide from one to another without being aware of it. So, for example, the question *Why do the just suffer?*, leads imperceptibly to another, *Why does man suffer?* Yet the last is quite different, being a question about the origins of evil. Let us then start by abjuring all equivocation. That *evil exists on the earth* is alas a truth that needs no proof, but, it should be added, *it is there very justly, and God could not have been its author.* This is another truth that we here do not, I hope, doubt and that I can dispense with proving since I know to whom I am speaking.

THE SENATOR: I wholeheartedly profess the same belief without any reservation, but this profession of faith demands an explanation precisely because of its scope. Saint Thomas said with the laconic logic that marked him, *God is the author of the evil which punishes, but not of the evil which defiles.*[1] He is certainly right in one sense, but it is necessary to understand him aright. God is the author of the evil *which punishes*, that is to say, of physical evil or pain, as a sovereign is

[1] Aquinas, *Summa Theologica*, Part 1, Qu. 49, Art. iii.

the author of punishments inflicted under his laws. In a remote and indirect sense, God himself hangs men and breaks them on the wheel, since all authority and every legal execution derives from him; but in the direct and immediate sense, it is the robber, the forger, the murderer who are the real authors of this *evil which punishes*. It is they who build the prisons, who raise the gallows and the scaffolds. In all this the sovereign acts, like Homer's Juno, *of his free will, but very unwillingly*.[2]

It is the same with God (while still excluding any rigorous comparison which would be blasphemous). Not only can he not in any sense be the author of moral evil or of sin; he cannot even be taken to be originally the author of physical evil, which would not exist if rational creatures had not made it necessary by abusing their liberty. Plato said, and nothing is more immediately obvious, *The good person cannot wish to injure anyone*.[3] But as no one will ever think of holding that the good man ceases to be so because he justly punishes his son or kills an enemy on the battlefield or sends a ruffian for punishment, let us, as you have just said, Count, guard against being less equitable toward God than toward men. Every right-thinking person is convinced by intuition that evil cannot proceed from an all-powerful being. This was the infallible feeling that formerly taught Roman good sense to join, as if by a necessary link, the two august titles of MOST GOOD and MOST POWERFUL. This wonderful expression, although born of paganism, appeared so right that it passed into our religious vocabulary, so discerning and exclusive. I shall even say that it has occurred to me more than once that the ancient inscription IOVI OPTIMO MAXIMO could be placed in full on the pediments of your Latin churches, for what is IOV-I but IOV-AH?

THE COUNT: You know well that I have no wish to dispute anything you have just said. Without doubt, *physical evil could come into the world only through the fault of free beings; it can be there only as a remedy or an expiation, and consequently God cannot be its direct author*; these are for us indisputable dogmas. Now I come back to you, Knight. You agreed just now that it was unjustifiable to quarrel with Providence over the distribution of good and evil but that the scandal lies above all in the impunity of sinners. I doubt, however, if you can give up the first objection without abandoning the second, for

[2] *Iliad*, IV, 43.
[3] *Timaeus*, 29e.

if there is no injustice in the distribution of pains, on what will you base the complaints of virtue? The world being governed only by general laws, you do not claim, I imagine, that, if the foundations of the terrace on which we are now speaking were suddenly thrown into the air by some underground disturbance, God would be obliged to suspend in our favor the laws of gravity because this terrace holds three men who have never murdered or stolen; we would certainly fall and be crushed. The same thing would happen if we were members of the Bavarian Illuminés or of the Committee of Public Safety. Do you wish that, when it hails, the fields of the just man should be spared? This indeed would be a miracle. But if by chance this just man was to commit a crime after the harvest, it would then be necessary for the corn to rot in his barns; here would be another miracle. So that each moment would require a new miracle, and miracles would become the ordinary order of events, or in other words there could be no more miracles, for the exception would be the rule and disorder order. To set out such ideas is enough to refute them.

What misleads us still more often on this point is that we cannot stop ourselves from ascribing to God, without our perceiving it, our own ideas on the dignity and importance of individuals. In relation to us, these ideas are very proper, since we are all subject to the established order in society, but, when we apply them to the general order of the universe, we are like that queen who said, *You can well believe that God thinks more than once about damning people like us.* Elizabeth of France mounts the scaffold, Robespierre follows the next moment. In coming into the world, the angel and the monster were subjected to all the general laws which regulate it. No terms are strong enough to describe the crime of the villains who spilled the most pure and noble blood in the world, yet, in relation to the general order of things, there is no injustice; it is still a misfortune implicit in the human condition, nothing more. *Every man, as a man, is subject to all the misfortunes of humanity*: the law is universal and so is not unjust. To suggest that a man's worth or position should shield him from the action of an iniquitous or misguided court of law is the same as wanting them to protect him from apoplexy, for example, or even from death.

Notice however that in spite of these general and inevitable laws it is very far from the truth that this assumed equality, on which I have insisted up to now, actually exists. As I said, I have supposed it for the sake of argument; but nothing is more false, as you will see.

Start first of all by leaving the individual out of account: the general law, visible and visibly just, is that *The greatest amount of happiness, even temporal, belongs, not to the virtuous man, but to virtue.* If it were otherwise, there would be neither vice nor virtue, merit nor demerit, and in consequence no moral order. Supposing that each virtuous action was repaid by some temporal advantage, the act, no longer having any higher purpose, could not merit a reward of this kind. Supposing on the other hand that, by virtue of a divine law, a thief's hand was to drop off when he committed a theft, men would refrain from stealing as they refrain from putting their hands under a butcher's chopper; and moral order would disappear completely. To reconcile this order (the only one possible for rational beings, as is shown by experience) with the laws of justice, it is necessary for virtue to be rewarded and vice punished, even in this world, but not always or immediately. It is necessary that much the greater share of temporal happiness should be alloted to virtue and that a proportional share of unhappiness should fall to vice, but that the individual should never be sure of anything, as is in fact the case. Any other hypothesis will lead you directly to the destruction of the moral order or to the creation of another world.

To come now to detail, let us start with human justice. Wishing men to be governed by men at least in their external actions, God has given sovereigns the supreme prerogative of punishing crimes, in which above all they are his representatives. . . .

This formidable prerogative of which I have just spoken results in the necessary existence of a man destined to inflict on criminals the punishments awarded by human justice; and this man is in fact found everywhere, without there being any means of explaining how; for reason cannot discern in human nature any motive which could lead men to this calling. I am sure, gentlemen, that you are too accustomed to reflection not to have pondered often on the executioner. Who is then this inexplicable being who has preferred to all the pleasant, lucrative, honest, and even honorable jobs that present themselves in hundreds to human power and dexterity that of torturing and putting to death his fellow creatures? Are this head and this heart made like ours? Do they not hold something peculiar and foreign to our nature? For my own part, I do not doubt this. He is made like us externally; he is born like us but he is an extraordinary being, and for him to exist in the human family a particular decree, a FIAT of the creative power is necessary. He is a species to himself. Look at the place he holds in public opinion and see if you can understand how he can ignore or affront this opinion! Scarcely have the authorities fixed his dwelling-place, scarcely has he taken possession of it, than the other houses seem to shrink back until they no longer overlook his. In the midst of this solitude and this kind of vacuum that forms around him, he lives alone with his woman and his offspring who make the human voice known to him, for without them he would know only groans. A dismal signal is given; a minor judicial official comes to his house to warn him that he is needed; he leaves; he arrives at some public place packed with a dense and throbbing crowd. A poisoner, a parricide, or a blasphemer is thrown to him; he seizes him, he stretches him on the ground, he ties him to a horizontal cross, he raises it up: then a dreadful silence falls, and nothing can be heard except the crack of bones breaking under the crossbar and the howls of the victim. He unfastens him; he carries him to a wheel: the shattered limbs interweave with the spokes; the head falls; the hair stands on end, and the mouth, open like a furnace, gives out spasmodically only a few blood-spattered words calling for death to come. He is finished: his heart flutters, but it is with joy; he congratulates himself, he says sincerely, *No one can break men on the wheel better than I.* He steps down; he stretches out his blood-stained hand, and justice throws into it from a distance a few pieces of gold which he carries through a double row of men drawing back with horror. He sits down to a meal and eats; then to bed, where he sleeps. And next day, on waking, he thinks of anything other than what he did the day before. Is this a man? Yes: God receives him in his temples and permits him to pray. He is not a criminal, yet it is impossible to say, for example, that he *is virtuous, that he is an honest man, that he is estimable,* and so on. No moral praise can be appropriate for him, since this assumes relationships with men, and he has none.

And yet all grandeur, all power, all subordination rests on the executioner: he is the horror and the bond of human association. Remove this incomprehensible agent from the world, and at that very moment order gives way to chaos, thrones topple, and society disappears. God, who is the author of sovereignty, is the author also of chastisement: he has built our world on these two poles; *for Jehovah is the master of the two poles, and on these he makes the world turn.*[4]

Thus there is in the temporal sphere a visible and divine law for

[4] 1 Samuel 2:8.

the punishment of crime, and this law, as stable as the society it upholds, has been carried out invariably from the beginning of time. Evil exists on the earth and acts constantly, and by a necessary consequence it must be continually repressed by punishment; indeed, we see over the whole globe constant action by every government to prevent or punish criminal outrages. The sword of justice has no scabbard; it must always threaten or strike. What then do these complaints about the *impunity of crime* mean? For whom are the knout, the gallows, the wheels, and the stakes? Obviously for the criminal. The mistakes of courts are exceptions that do not shake the rule: I have, besides, several reflections to offer to you on this point. In the first place, these fatal errors are much less frequent than is imagined. If it is allowed to doubt, opinion is always contrary to authority, and the public ear listens avidly to the slightest suggestions of a judicial murder; a thousand individual passions can fortify this general inclination. . . .

That an innocent dies is a misfortune like any other; that is to say, it is common to all mankind. That a guilty man escapes is another exception of the same kind. But it always remains true, generally speaking, *that there is on the earth a universal and visible order for the temporal punishment of crimes*; and I must again draw your attention to the fact that criminals do not by any means cheat justice so often as might be ingenuously supposed in view of the infinite precautions they take to avoid it. There is often in the circumstances that betray the most cunning scoundrels something so unexpected, so surprising, so unforeseeable, that men who are called by their position or reflections to follow this kind of affair tend to believe that human justice is not entirely without a certain supernatural assistance in seeking out the guilty.

Allow me to add one more consideration to bring to an end this chronicle of punishments. Just as it is very possible for us to be wrong when we accuse human justice of sparing the guilty, since those we regard as being such are not really guilty, so it is equally possible on the other side that a man punished for a crime he has not committed has actually merited it by another completely unknown crime. Fortunately and unfortunately, there are several examples of this kind of thing shown by the confessions of criminals, and there are many more, I believe, of which we are ignorant. This last supposition deserves especially close attention, for, although in such a case the judges are extremely blameworthy or unfortunate, Providence, for whom everything, even an obstacle, is a means, makes full use of dishonesty or mistakes to execute the temporal justice we demand; and it is certain that these two suppositions restrict considerably the number of exceptions. You can see, then, how far this assumed equality that I supposed at the beginning is already disrupted by the consideration of human justice alone.

From the corporal punishment inflicted by justice, let us move now to illnesses. Already you have anticipated me. If intemperance of every kind was removed from the world, most illnesses, perhaps even all of them, would be expelled too. Everyone can see this in general and in a confused manner, but it is as well to pursue the matter more closely. If there had been no moral evil on the earth, there would be no physical evil. . . .

For my part, I must agree with the opinion of a recent apologist who held that every illness has its source in some vice proscribed by Scripture, that this holy rule of conduct is the real medicine for the body as much as for the soul, so that in a society of just men following it death would be no more than the inevitable end of a healthy and robust old age; a view that was, I believe, that of Origen. What misleads us on this question is that, when the effect is not immediate, we no longer perceive it, but it is no less real. Once established, illnesses spread, connect up, and amalgamate by a deadly affinity, so that we can suffer today the physical penalty of an excess committed more than a century ago. However, in spite of the confusion resulting from these terrible mistakes, the parallel between crimes and illnesses is plain to every attentive observer. As with sins, there are diseases that are *actual and original, accidental and habitual, mortal and venial.* There are illnesses of anger, of gluttony, of incontinence, and so on. Notice, moreover, that there are crimes which have distinctive characteristics and therefore names in every language, such as murder, sacrilege, and incest, while others can be designated only by general terms such as fraud, injustice, violence, and embezzlement. Likewise there are distinctive illnesses such as dropsy, consumption, and apoplexy, and others which can be designated only by the general names of malaise, discomfort, aches, and nameless fevers. Now, the more virtuous a man, the more he is protected against illnesses *which have names.* . . .

Leaving aside from this discussion everything that could be

regarded as hypothetical, I am still entitled to put this indisputable principle: *Moral vices can increase the number and intensity of illnesses to a degree that it is impossible to fix; and conversely that this dreadful grip of physical evil can be loosened by virtue to a degree that it is equally impossible to fix.* As there is not the slightest doubt of the truth of this proposition, there is no need to go further to justify the ways of Providence even in the temporal sphere, above all if this consideration is joined to that of human justice, since it is clear that from these two points of view the advantage of virtue is incalculable, without giving any reasons or even appealing to religious considerations. . . .

SECOND DIALOGUE

THE COUNT: All pain being a punishment, it follows that no pain can be considered as inevitable and, no pain being inevitable, it follows that every pain can be prevented either by the suppression of the crime which made it necessary or by prayer, which has the power of preventing or mitigating punishment. Since the empire of physical evil can still be restricted indefinitely by this supernatural means, you can see—

THE KNIGHT: Allow me to interrupt you and to be a little impolite, if necessary, in order to force you to be clearer. You are touching here upon a subject which has more than once disturbed me profoundly; but for the moment I shall defer my questions on this point. I should just like to point out to you that, unless I am mistaken, you are confusing the evils immediately due to the faults of those who suffer them with those which an unfortunate heritage has transmitted to us. You said *that we perhaps suffer today for excesses committed more than a century ago*; now, it seems to me that we ought not to be held to account for these crimes, as for those of our first ancestors. I do not believe that faith extends as far as that; and, if I am not mistaken, original sin is quite enough, since this alone has subjected us to all the miseries of this life. It seems to me, then, that the physical ills which come to us by heredity have nothing to do with the temporal government of Providence.

THE COUNT: I pray you to notice particularly that I did not by any means insist on this sad heredity and that I did not give it to you as a direct proof of the justice Providence exercises in this world. I talked of it in passing in an incidental observation, but I thank you with all my heart, my dear Knight, for bringing it back to our notice, for it is well worthy of our attention. If I have not made any distinction between illnesses, it is because they are all punishments. Original sin, which explains everything and without which nothing can be explained, unfortunately repeats itself at every moment of time, although in a secondary manner. Since you are a Christian, I do not believe that this idea, when it is explained to you exactly, will shock your mind at all. Doubtless, original sin is a mystery, yet if man examines it closely he will find that this mystery, like the others, has its understandable sides, even to our limited intelligence.

Let us leave on one side the theological question of *imputation*, which we have not touched, and confine ourselves to the common view, which agrees so well with our most natural ideas, *that every being with the power of propagating itself can produce only a being similar to itself.* The rule has no exception; it is inscribed all over the world. If then a being is degraded, its descendants will no longer be like the original state of this being, but rather like the state to which it has been reduced by whatever cause. This is very plain, and the rule holds in the physical as in the moral order. But it must be noticed that there is the same difference between an *infirm* and an *ill* man as between a *vicious* and a *guilty* man. Acute illness is not transmissible, but that which vitiates the humors becomes an *original malady* that can taint a whole race.

It is the same with moral maladies. Some belong to the ordinary state of human imperfection, but there are certain transgressions or certain consequences of transgression which can degrade man absolutely. These are *original sins* of a second order which nevertheless portray to us, however imperfectly, the first. This is the origin of the savages of whom so many extravagant things have been said and who have especially been used as an eternal text by J. J. Rousseau, one of the most dangerous sophists of his age and yet the most bereft of true knowledge, wisdom, and above all profundity, having an apparent depth that is entirely a matter of words. He has continually taken the savage to be primitive man, whereas the savage is not and cannot be anything other than the descendant of a man detached from the great tree of civilization by some transgression, but of a kind that can no longer be repeated, as far as I can judge, for I doubt if new savages can be created.

As a consequence of the same error, the languages of the savage have been taken for the original languages, whereas they are not and cannot be other than the debris of ancient languages, *ruined*, as it were, and degraded like the men who speak it. Indeed, every degradation, individual or national, is immediately marked by a rigorously proportional degradation in language. How could man lose or even blur an idea without losing the word or the correct usage of the word that expresses it? And, on the other hand, how could he extend or sharpen his thinking without this showing itself at once in his language?

There is therefore an *original illness* just as there is an *original sin*, that is to say, that by virtue of this primitive degradation, we are subject to all kinds of physical suffering *in general*, as by virtue of this same degradation we are subject to all kinds of vices *in general*. This original illness has no other name. It is only the capacity to suffer every disease, as original sin (an abstraction derived from imputation) is only the capacity to commit every crime, which ends the comparison.

But there are, besides, *original* maladies of the second order, as there are *original* transgressions of the second order; that is to say, certain transgressions committed by certain men have been able to degrade them afresh to a greater or lesser degree, and so to perpetuate to a greater or lesser degree in their descendants both vices and maladies. It may be that these great transgressions are no longer possible, but it is no less true that the general principle still operates and that Christianity showed that it possesses vital knowledge when it turned its whole attention and all the force of its legislative and originating power on the legitimate reproduction of man to prevent every harmful transmission from father to son. If I have talked of illnesses without distinguishing those we owe directly to our own sins from those we owe to our fathers' vices, the mistake was slight, since, as I just now said, they are all in truth only punishments of sin. It is only the element of heredity that shocks the reason at first; but until we can talk of it at greater length, let us be satisfied with the general rule that I pointed out at the beginning: *Every being which reproduces itself can produce only something in its own image.*

Here, Senator, I call on your *intellectual conscience*: if a man has indulged in certain crimes or in a certain series of crimes, so that they are capable of altering the moral principle within him, you accept that this degradation is transmissible, as you accept the transmission of scrofulous or syphilitic vice. Besides, I have no need of these hereditary ailments. If you like, look on everything I have said on this subject as a conversational parenthesis; everything else remains unshakable. Taking into account all the considerations that I have set before you, I hope you will not retain any doubts *that the innocent, when he suffers, always suffers only in his quality as a man, and that the great majority of evils fall on crime*; which would be enough for me as a start. Now—

THE KNIGHT: It would be quite useless, at least for me, for you to go any further, for I have heard you no more since you spoke of the savages. You mentioned something in passing about this kind of man that entirely occupies me. Can you prove to me that the languages of savages are the remains and not the rudiments of languages?

THE COUNT: The essence of all intelligence is to know and to love. The limits of knowledge are those of its nature. The immortal being learns nothing: he knows by nature everything he should know. On the other side, no intelligent being can love the bad naturally or by virtue of his nature; for this to be so, it would be necessary for God to have created man evil, which is impossible. If then man is subject to ignorance or evil, this can be only by virtue of some accidental degradation, which can be only the consequence of a crime. The need, the hunger for knowledge, which stirs man, is nothing but the natural tendency of his being that carries him toward his primitive state and shows him what he is.

If I can so express myself, he gravitates toward the areas of light. No beaver, swallow, or bee wishes to know more than its predecessors. All these creatures are happy in the place they occupy. All are degraded, but are ignorant of it; man alone senses it, and this feeling is the proof at once of his grandeur and his misery, of his sublime prerogatives, and his incredible degradation. In the state to which he is reduced, he has not even the sad satisfaction of being unaware of himself: he must continually contemplate himself, and this he cannot do without shame; even his grandeur humiliates him, since the understanding that raises him to the angels serves only to show him the abominable tendencies in himself that degrade him to the brutes. He seeks in the depths of his being some healthy part without being able to find it: evil has stained everything *and man in his entirety is nothing but a malady*.[5] An incredible combination of two different and incompatible powers, a monstrous centaur, he feels that he is the result of some unknown crime, some detestable mixture that has corrupted him even in his deepest nature.

Every intellect is by its very nature the result, single yet in three parts, of a *perception* that apprehends, a *reason* that affirms, and a *will* that acts. The first two powers are only weakened in man, but the third is broken, and like Tasso's serpent *it drags itself along*,[6] completely ashamed of its sad powerlessness. It is in this third power that man feels himself fatally injured. He does not know what he wants; he wants what he does not want; he does not want what he wants; *he would want to want*. He sees in himself something which is not he and is stronger than he. The wise resist and call out, *Who shall deliver me?*[7] The foolish surrender and call their cowardice *happiness*, but they cannot rid themselves of this other will incorruptible of its nature although it has lost its dominance; and remorse, piercing them to the heart, constantly cries out to them, *By doing what you do not want, you consent to the law*.[8] Who could believe that such men could have been molded in this form by the Creator? This idea is so repulsive that philosophy itself, that is, pagan philosophy, hit on original sin. . . .

After all, when the philosophers . . . assure us that the vices of human nature belong more *to the father than to the sons*, it is clear that they are not talking of any generation in particular. If the proposition remains in the air, it has no meaning, so that the very nature of things relates it to an original and thus universal corruption. Plato tells us *that in contemplating himself he does not know if he sees a monster more arrant, more evil than Typhon, or rather a moral, gentle, and beneficent being who partakes of the nature of divinity*. He adds that man, so torn between these opposite natures, cannot act well and live happily *without mastering that power of the soul in which evil resides,*

[5] Hippocrates, *Letter to Demagetus*.
[6] Tasso, *Jerusalem Delivered*, xv, 48.
[7] Romans 7:24.
[8] *Ibid.*, 7:16.

and without setting free that which is the abode and the agent of virtue. This is precisely the Christian doctrine, and original sin could not be more clearly admitted.

What do words matter? Man is evil, horribly evil. Has God created him like this? Emphatically no, and Plato himself hastens to reply *that the good being neither wishes nor does evil to anyone.* We are then degraded—yet how? This corruption Plato saw in himself was obviously not something peculiar to himself, and certainly he did not believe himself more evil than his fellow men. Thus he was saying essentially what David said, *My mother has conceived me in iniquity,* and if these words had been presented to him he would have been able to accept them without difficulty. Now, as every degradation can be only a penalty, and as every penalty presupposes a crime, reason alone is forced to accept original sin. For, since our fatal inclination to evil is a truth of feeling and experience attested by every age, and since this inclination is always more or less victorious over conscience and laws, never having failed to produce on earth transgressions of every kind, man has never been able to recognize and deplore this sorry condition without admitting by the same token the woeful dogma I am expounding to you; for he cannot be *wicked* without being *evil,* nor evil without being degraded, nor degraded without being punished, nor punished without being guilty.

In short, gentlemen, nothing is so well attested, nothing so universally accepted under one form or another, nothing finally so intrinsically plausible as the theory of original sin.

Let me add this—you will not I hope feel it difficult to accept that an originally degraded intelligence is and remains incapable, short of a substantial regeneration, of that ineffable contemplation that our old masters very aptly call *beatific vision,* since it produces and even is eternal happiness, just as you accept that a physical eye which is seriously injured can be incapable of bearing sunlight. Now, this incapacity to enjoy the SUN is, if I am not mistaken, the only consequence of original sin that we are bound to regard as natural and independent of every present transgression. Reason can, it seems to me, reach this point, and I think that it is right to congratulate itself on this without ceasing to be docile.

Having thus studied man in himself, let us pass on to his history.

All mankind springs from Adam and Eve. This truth has been denied like every other—but what does it matter?

We know very little of the time before the Deluge, and, according to some convincing speculations, we should not know more. One consideration only is of interest to me, and we should never lose sight of it. This is that punishments are always proportionate to crimes and crimes always proportionate to the knowledge of the guilty, so that the Deluge presupposes unparalleled crimes and these crimes presuppose knowledge infinitely higher than that which we possess. This is certain, and needs thorough investigation. This knowledge, untrammeled by the evil that has made it so fatal, survived the destruction of humanity in the righteous family. On the nature and the development of humanity, we are bemused by a rank but attractive fallacy: this lies in judging the age in which men saw effects in causes by that in which they rise painfully from effects to causes, in which they even concern themselves only with effects, in which they say that it is useless to concern oneself with causes, in which they do not even know what a cause is. It is constantly repeated, *Just imagine the time it took to get to know such and such a thing!* What incredible blindness! It needed only a moment. If man could know the cause of a single physical phenomenon, he would probably understand all the others. We do not want to see that the most difficult truths to discover are very easy to understand. The solution of the problem of the *annulus* once brought joy to the best geometer of antiquity, but this very solution is now to be found in all the elementary mathematical textbooks and is well within the capacities of a fifteen-year-old.

Plato, talking somewhere of what it is most important for man to know, adds immediately, with that incisive simplicity natural to him, that *these things are easily and perfectly learned if someone teaches them to us.*[9] This is exactly right. It is, moreover, obviously apparent that the first men who repeopled the world after the great catastrophe needed miraculous help to conquer the diverse difficulties facing them. And notice, gentlemen, the splendid character of this argument! Do you want to prove it? Witnesses present themselves on every side: they never contradict one another, whereas witnesses of error are contradictory even when they lie. Listen to what wise antiquity has to say about the first men. It will tell you that they were wonderful men, whom beings of a superior order favored with the most important messages. There is unanimity on this point: initiates, philosophers, poets,

[9] What follows is no less valuable; *but,* he says, *no one will teach us unless God shows him the way.*—*Epinomis* 989d.

history, myth, Asia and Europe speak with one voice. Such complete agreement of reason, revelation, and all human traditions constitutes a proof that cannot reasonably be contradicted. Thus, not only did men start with knowledge, but with a knowledge different from and superior to our own, since it penetrated more deeply, which made it the more dangerous. This is why science at the beginning was mysterious and confined within the temples, where the flame finally burned out when once it had no purpose other than to burn. . . .

It is impossible to think of modern science without seeing it perpetually surrounded by all the apparatus of the mind and every kind of methodological aid. . . . So far as we can penetrate the mists of time to perceive the science of the earliest days, it always emerges free and independent, flying rather than walking, and presenting in its entire person something aerial and supernatural. . . . Yet, although it owed nothing to any man and knew no human support, it is no less the case that it possessed the rarest understanding. If you think of it, this is a convincing proof that ancient science had been freed from the travail imposed on our own and that nothing could be more mistaken than the calculations we make on the basis of modern experience. . . .

If all men spring from the three couples who repeopled the world, and if humanity began with a science, the savage can be, as I have said, nothing more than a branch broken off from the social tree. Although it is incontestable, I could abandon the argument from science and rely on religion alone, which is of itself enough to exclude a state of savagery, however imperfectly. Wherever an altar is found, there civilization exists. The poor man in his hut with straw alone to cover him is doubtless less learned than we are, yet more truly social if he attends his catechism class and profits from it. The most shameful errors, the most despicable cruelties have stained the history of Memphis, Athens, and Rome, but all the virtues together honor the huts of Paraguay. . . . We must then recognize that the state of civilization and science is in a certain sense the natural and primitive state of man. . . . Has not Voltaire himself (and nothing more need be said) admitted that the motto of every nation has always been, *The golden age was the first to show itself on earth*? So every nation has protested in unison against the hypothesis of an original state of barbarism, and surely this protest counts for something.

What does it matter at what point in time such and such a branch was broken from the tree? It has been, and that is enough for me:

there is no doubt about the degradation and, I dare add, no doubt about the cause of the degradation, which could only have been a crime. Once the leader of a people had changed its moral character by some of those grave transgressions which are apparently now no longer possible, since happily we no longer know enough to become guilty to this degree, this leader passed on the curse to his posterity; and since every constant force is by nature accelerative because it is accumulative, this degradation bears constantly on his descendants until finally it makes them into what we call *savages*. It is this final degree of brutalization that Rousseau and his like call *the state of nature*.

Two quite different causes have thrown an obfuscating cloud around the dreadful situation of the savages, one is ancient; the other belongs to our own age. In the first place, in its immense charity the Catholic Church has often, in talking of these men, imposed its desires upon reality. There was only too much truth in the first reaction of the Europeans, who refused in Columbus's time to recognize these degraded men peopling the New World as equals. The priests employed all their influence to contradict this opinion which favored too much the barbarous despotism of the new rulers. They cried out to the Spaniards, "No violence; the Scripture condemns it. If you cannot overthrow the idols in the hearts of these unfortunates, what good is it to destroy their wretched altars? To make them know and love God, you must take up other tactics and weapons." From deserts watered with their sweat and blood, they traveled to Madrid and Rome to ask for edicts and bulls against the pitiless greed which wanted to enslave the Indians. The merciful priest exalted them in order to make them precious; he played down the evil, he exaggerated the good, he stated as truth what he wished to be true; indeed, a reliable witness, Robertson, warns us in his *History of America, that on this subject one must be suspicious of all the writers who belonged to the clergy, seeing that they are in general too favorable to the natives.*

Another source of false judgments about them lies in the philosophy of our own age, which has made use of the savages to support its empty and culpable harangues against the social order; but even the slightest consideration is enough to put us on our guard against the errors of both charity and bad faith. It needs only a glance at the savage to see the curse written not only on his soul but on the external form of his body. He is a deformed child, sturdy and fierce, on whom the light of intelligence throws no more than a pale and fitful beam. A formidable hand weighing on these doomed races wipes out in them the two distinctive characteristics of our grandeur: foresight and perfectibility. The savage cuts the tree down to gather the fruit; he unyokes the ox that the missionary has just entrusted to him, and cooks it with wood from the plow. For over three centuries, he has known us without wanting anything from us except powder to kill his fellows and spirits to kill himself, yet he has never thought of making these things for himself: he relies for them on our greed, which will never fail him.

Just as the meanest and most revolting substances are nevertheless still capable of some degeneration, so the vices natural to humanity are still more corrupt in the savages. He is a thief, he is cruel, he is dissolute, but he is these things in a different way than we are. To be criminals, we surmount our nature: the savage follows it, he has an appetite for crime, and has no remorse at all. While the son kills his father to preserve him from the bothers of old age, his wife destroys in her womb the fruit of their brutal lust to escape the fatigues of suckling it. He tears out the bloody hair of his living enemy; he slits him open, roasts him and eats him while singing; if he comes across strong liquor, he drinks it to drunkenness, to fever, to death, equally deprived of the reason which rules men through fear and the instinct which saves animals through aversion. He is visibly doomed; he is flawed in the very depths of his moral being; he makes any observer tremble: but do we tremble at ourselves, in a way which would be very salutary? Do we think that with our intelligence, our morality, our sciences and our arts we are to primitive man what the savage is to us?

I cannot leave this subject without suggesting to you yet another important point. The barbarian, who is a kind of midway point between the civilized man and the savage, could and still can be civilized by any religion whatever, but the savage, properly speaking, has never been civilized except by Christianity. This is a miracle of the highest order, a kind of redemption, the exclusive prerogative of the true Church. . . . The *savage* must not be confused with the *barbarian*. In the one the germ of life is dying or dead; in the other it has been sown, and needs only time and circumstances to develop itself. At this point his language, which was degraded with the man, is reborn with him and perfects and enriches itself. If one wishes to call this a *new language*, I should agree: the phrase is right in one sense, but a sense very different from that which is taken by the modern sophists when they talk of *new* or *invented* languages.

No language could be invented, either by a single man, who would not be able to compel obedience, or by several men, who would not be able to understand one another. Nothing can be better said about words than what has been said by that which is called THE WORD. They are those *whose goings forth have been from of old, from ever-lasting . . . who shall declare their generation?*[10] Already, in spite of the unhappy prejudices of the age, a natural philosopher—yes, truly, a natural philosopher—has taken upon himself to agree, with a timid intrepidity, *that man first spoke because* SOMEONE *spoke to him.* God bless the word SOMEONE, so useful on difficult occasions. While rendering this tentative effort all the justice it deserves, it is nevertheless necessary to admit that every philosopher of the last century, not even excepting the best, was chickenhearted, afraid of thought. . . .

But before finishing on this subject, I should like to draw your attention to a thought that has always struck me. How is it that in the primitive languages of all the ancient peoples there are words which imply ideas foreign to these peoples? . . . These words . . . are obviously the remnants of more ancient languages that have been destroyed or forgotten. . . .

Reading the modern metaphysicians, you will come across huge generalizations on the importance of symbols and on the advantages of what they call a philosophical language, which should be created a priori or perfected by philosophers. I do not want to throw myself into the question of the origins of language (the same question, incidentally, as that of innate ideas). What I can assure you of, since nothing is clearer, is the astonishing talent of infant nations in forming words and the total inability of philosophers to do likewise. I recall that Plato, in the most refined of ages, drew attention to this talent of nascent peoples. What is astonishing is that it has been said that they proceeded by way of deliberation, by virtue of an established system of agreement, although such a thing is strictly impossible from every point of view. Each language has its genius, and this genius is one and indivisible, so that it excludes any idea of composition, of arbitrary formation and of previous agreement. . . .

Each language, taken separately, mirrors the spiritual realities that were present at its birth, and the more ancient the language, the more

[10] Micah 5:2; Isaiah 53:8.

perceptible are these realities. You will not find any exception to the
observation on which I have insisted so much, which is that the further
back you go toward the ages of ignorance and barbarism which saw
the birth of languages, the more logic and profundity you will find in
the formation of words, and that this talent disappears conversely as
you move toward the ages of civilization and science. . . .

Languages have started, but not *the word*, not even with man. The
one has necessarily preceded the other since *the word* is possible only
through the WORD OF GOD. Every particular language comes into
being like an animal, by birth and development, without which man
would have passed from the state of aphonia to the use of speech. He
has always talked, and it is sublime reason that prompted the Hebrews
to call him a TALKING SOUL. When a new language emerges, it is born
in the heart of a society which already has full possession of a language, and no word is invented arbitrarily in this formation; the new
language uses the materials it finds around it or that it calls from further off; it lives off them, it chews them, it digests them; it never adopts
them without modifying them to some degree. . . .

In all the writings of the time on this interesting matter there has
been continually expressed a wish for a *philosophical language*, but
without any knowledge or even suspicion that the most philosophical
language is that in which there is the least philosophy. Philosophy
lacks two small things to be a creator of words—the intelligence to
invent them and the power to make them used. If it sees a new object,
it leafs through its dictionaries to find an ancient or a foreign word;
and almost always it turns out badly. . . . If the right to create new
expressions belonged to anyone, it would be to the great writers and
not to the philosophers, who are in this respect peculiarly inept: yet
the writers use this right only very sparingly, never in moments of
inspiration and only for making nouns and adjectives; as for *words*
themselves, they hardly dream of offering new ones. Indeed, this idea
of *new languages* should be erased, except only in the sense I have just
explained; or, to put this another way, the spoken word is eternal and
every language is as old as the people who speak it. . . . It is certain
that every nation has had the power of speech and that it has spoken
precisely as much and as well as it thought; for it is equally foolish to
believe either that a symbol can exist for an idea which does not exist
or that an idea can exist without a symbol to express it. . . .

THE KNIGHT: In talking of another subject, you claimed that *the question of the origin of language was the same as that of the origin of ideas.* I would be interested to hear your reasons for this. . . .

THE COUNT: Before anything else, I should like to suggest to you that authority should be the fundamental ground for decision. Human reason is manifestly incapable of guiding men, for few can reason well, and no one can reason well on every subject, so that it is in general wise to start from authority, whatever people say. Just balance the voices on both sides; against the ideas that knowledge originates in sensory perceptions there are Pythagoras, Plato, Cicero, Origen, Saint Augustine, Descartes, Cudworth, Lami, Polignac, Pascal, Nicole, Bossuet, Fénélon, Leibnitz, and the renowned Malebranche, who occasionally went wrong in the pursuit of truth but never abandoned it. I shall not give the names of the spokesmen for the other side, for they offend my tongue. When I am ignorant about a problem, I decide without any reason other than my taste for good company and my aversion for bad.

I would put yet another preliminary argument to you which has much force; this is the hateful results of that absurd system which would wish, so to speak, to materialize the origins of our ideas. To my mind, nothing is more degrading or destructive to the human spirit. Because of it, reason has lost its wings and drags itself along the ground like some filthy reptile; it has dried up the divine source of poetry and eloquence; because of it, all the moral sciences have fallen into a decline.

THE KNIGHT: It is not perhaps for me to dispute the consequences of the system, but as far as its defenders are concerned, it seems to me, my dear friend, that it is possible to cite various respectable names besides those which *offend your tongue.* . . .

THE COUNT: Now, whether universal ideas are innate in us, or whether we derive them from God, or whatever you like, is not relevant, and I do not want at this point to examine it: the negative side of the question is undoubtedly the most important; let us establish first of all that the greatest, noblest, and most virtuous geniuses in the world are agreed in rejecting the origin of ideas in sensory perceptions. It is the holiest, most unanimous, most inspiring protest of the human spirit against the gravest and vilest of errors. . . .

After this short preliminary, Knight, I should like first of all, as you have done me the honor of choosing me to introduce you to this kind of philosophy, to remark that any discussion of the origin of ideas is extremely foolish until the question of the nature of the soul has been decided. Would you allow anyone to claim in the courts an inheritance as a relative, if it were doubtful that he was such? Well, gentlemen, there are equivalents in philosophic discussions to those questions that lawyers call *pre-judicial* which must be cleared up completely before other questions can be considered. If the estimable Thomas was right in the beautiful phrase, *Man lives by his soul, and the soul is thought*, everything has been said; for if thought is the essential nature of man, to ask what is the origin of ideas is to ask what is the origin of the origin.

Here is what Condillac has to say, *I shall be concerned with the human spirit, not with ascertaining its nature, which would be fool-hardy, but only with examining its operations.* Let us not be fooled by this modest hypocrite: every time you see a philosopher of the last century bowing respectfully before some problem and telling us *that the question passes beyond the boundaries of the human mind*, that he will not undertake to resolve it, and so on, you can be sure that on the contrary he fears the problem is only too clear and that he is hurrying to leave it on one side in order to retain the right of causing trouble. I do not know one of these gentlemen to whom the sacred title of *honest man* would be fitting. You can see an example in the point under discussion. Why lie? Why say that one does not want to pronounce on the essential nature of the soul while one is expressly putting forward a view on this point by holding that ideas come to us through the senses, which obviously excludes thought from the category of essences?

I do not see, moreover, that there is any more difficult problem relating to the nature of thought than that of its origin, which is tackled so courageously. *Can thought be conceived as an accident of a substance that does not think?* Or rather, *Can this accident-thought be conceived as knowing about itself, as thinking and meditating on the nature of that which gives rise to it and which does not itself think?* Here is the problem posed in two different forms, and for my part I confess that I do not see it as hopeless; yet one is perfectly free to pass it over on condition of agreeing and even warning people at the head of every work on the origin of ideas that it should be treated as simple *jeu d'esprit*, as a completely airy hypothesis, since the question is not seriously broached so long as the preceding question is not resolved.

I would then point out, Knight, that there is something equivocal in the very title of all the books written in the modern idiom on the origin of ideas, since the word *origin* can apply equally to the cause simply occasioning and exciting ideas and to the cause producing ideas. In the first case, there is no argument since the ideas are assumed to preexist; in the second, it is precisely the same as holding that the substance of an electrical discharge is produced by that which sparks it off.

We should now examine why these writers always talk of the origin of *ideas*, and never of the origin of *thoughts*. There must have been a hidden reason for the preference continually given to one word rather than the other, but this point should not take long to clear up. I would simply say to you, using the words of Plato, whom I am always happy to quote, *Do you and I understand the same thing by this word, "thought"?* For my part, thought is the DIALOGUE THAT THE MIND HOLDS WITH ITSELF.[11]

And this sublime definition alone should show you the truth of what I was just saying, *that the question of the origin of ideas is the same as that of the origin of language,* for thought and language are simply two splendid synonyms, the mind not being able to think without knowing what it thinks, nor being able to know what it thinks without putting it into words, since it must say, *I know.*

So if some follower of modern doctrines comes and says to you that you speak because someone has spoken to you, ask him (but will he understand you?) if, in his view, *understanding* is the same as *hearing,* and if he believes that to *understand* language it is enough to hear the noise that strikes the ear.

For the rest, let us leave this question on one side. If we want to study the main question, I would ask you to look at a very essential preliminary, which is that, even after so much argument, the definition of *innate ideas* is still not properly understood. Is it conceivable that Locke never took the trouble to tell us what he meant by this phrase? Yet this is the exact truth. The French translator of Bacon says, in the course of pouring scorn on *innate ideas,* that he confesses *that he does not remember having known about the square on the hypotenuse when he was in his mother's womb.* Here then is an intelligent man (for Locke was this) who attributes to spiritualistic philosophers the belief that a foetus in its mother's womb knows mathematics, that we can

---

[11] *Theaetetus,* 189–190.

know without learning, or, in other words, learn without learning, and that this is what philosophers call *innate ideas*.

A very different writer with quite a different authority, who honors France today by his superior talents or by the distinguished use he can make of them, thought it a decisive argument against *innate ideas* to ask, "*How*, if God has engraved a certain idea on our minds, could *man* succeed in obliterating it? How, for example, can the idolatrous child, born just like the Christian with the *clear notion* of a single God, yet be reduced to the point of believing in a multitude of gods?"

I would have much to say on this *clear notion* and on the appalling power that, only too really, man possesses to *obliterate more or less his innate ideas* and to *pass on his degradation*. I shall restrict myself here to noticing an obvious confusion of an *idea* or simple *notion* with a *statement of belief*, two things which are nevertheless quite different. It is the first which is *innate* and not the second, for no one, I believe, has thought of saying that there have been *innate* powers of reasoning. The deist says, *There is only one God*, and he is right; the idolater says, *There are several Gods*, and he is wrong, but he is wrong in the same way as a man who makes a mistake in a process of calculation. Does it by any chance follow that the latter has no idea of number? On the contrary, it proves that he possesses it, for without such an idea, he could not even be mistaken. In fact to be mistaken one must state a view, which one cannot do without any use of the verb *to be*, which is the soul of all speech, and every statement of view assumes a preexisting idea. Thus, without the previous idea of a God, there would be neither theists nor polytheists, inasmuch as one can say neither *yes* nor *no* to what one does not know about, and as it is impossible to be mistaken about God without having an idea of God. It is therefore the *notion* or the pure *idea* that is innate and necessarily does not derive from the senses. . . .

THIRD DIALOGUE

THE KNIGHT: Allow me to point out a contradiction to you that has always struck me ever since I entered into the world's bustle, which is also a good teacher, as you know. On the one side, everyone extols the happiness, even in this world, of virtue. . . . But, on the other side, a no less universal voice, from one end of the earth to the other, tells us of *innocence on its knees baring its bosom to crime*. It is said that virtue exists in this world only to suffer, to be martyred by barefaced vice which always goes unpunished. The successes of audacity, fraud, and bad faith are on every tongue, as is the continual disappointment of ingenuous probity. . . .

THE COUNT: Yes, you are no doubt right, humanity dwells on both the happiness and the calamities of virtue. But, in the first place, men could be told, *Since profit and loss seem so evenly balanced, you should, in cases of doubt, decide for that virtue which is so lovable in itself*, especially as this saves us from making such calculations. In fact, you will find this contradiction of which you have just spoken everywhere, since the whole world is subject to two forces. . . . In truth, there is no real contradiction, since it is not the same subject who holds these opposing views. Like us, you have read:

> *My God, what a cruel war is this,*
> *I find two men in myself. . . .*

Well, here is the solution to your problem and to so many others which are only the same basic problem in different forms. It is *a man* who quite rightly praises the advantages of virtue, even in this world, and it is *another man* within the same man who will argue a moment later that virtue exists on earth only to be persecuted, disgraced, butchered by crime. What then has the world shown you? Two men who are in disagreement. There is nothing really astonishing in that, but it is far from the truth that these two men are equal in worth. It is right reason, it is conscience which tells us, with the weight of facts behind it, that in every calling, in every undertaking, in every piece of business, the advantage, other things being equal, always lies on the side of virtue; that health, the first of temporal goods, without which all others are useless, is in part a result of it; that finally it bestows on us an inner contentment a thousand times more precious than all the wealth in the world.

On the other hand, it is rebellious or resentful pride, it is envy, avarice, and impiety which complain of the temporal disadvantages of virtue. It is then no longer *man* who speaks, or rather it is *another man.* . . .

THE SENATOR: It seems to me that the existence and progress of governments cannot be explained by human means, any more than the movement of bodies by mechanical means. *Mens agitat molem.* There is in each state a *directing spirit* . . . that animates it as the soul animates the body and that produces death when it fades out.

THE COUNT: You are rephrasing, in what seems to me a happy manner, a very simple phenomenon, the necessary intervention of a supernatural power. This is recognized in the physical world without anyone contesting the effects of secondary causes. Why not recognize it in the same way in the political world, where it is no less essential? Without accepting its direct intervention, one cannot, as you very rightly say, explain either the creation or duration of governments. It manifests itself in the national unity that constitutes them, in a multiplicity of wills working unconsciously to the same end, showing that they are simply *instruments,* and above all in the wonderful mechanism that makes use of all the circumstances we call accidental, of our very follies and crimes, to maintain and often to establish order. . . .

FOURTH DIALOGUE

THE COUNT: Here is how I was led to talk to you about prayer. Every pain being a punishment, it follows that no pain can be regarded as necessary, since it could have been prevented. On this point, as on so many others, the temporal order is the image of a higher order. Punishments being made necessary only by crimes, and every crime being the act of a free will, every punishment could have been prevented, since the crime need not have been committed. I would add that even after it has been committed, the punishment can still be prevented in two ways; for in the first place the merits of the guilty person or even those of his ancestors can balance his faults, and in the second place his earnest entreaties or those of his friends can disarm the sovereign. . . .

THE KNIGHT: I never mocked my curé when he threatened his parishioners with hailstones or blight because they had not paid their tithes, yet I see an order in the physical world so invariable that I do not really understand how the prayers of these poor little men could have any effect on these phenomena. When a meteorologist is certain, because of a series of exact observations, that so many inches of rain must fall in a certain country each year, he would begin to laugh if he attended public prayers for rain. I am not approving of him; but why hide from you the fact that the jeers of the natural philosopher give me an uneasy feeling which I distrust all the less as I should like to dismiss it? . . .

THE SENATOR: Believe me, my dear Knight, you have just shown us the most perfidious temptation the human mind can face, that of believing in invariable laws of nature. This theory has an attractive appearance, yet it leads directly to the decline of prayer, that is the death of spiritual life, for prayer is the breath of the soul, as M. de Saint-Martin said, I believe. Whoever has ceased to pray no longer lives. *No religion without prayer*, said Voltaire . . .; nothing is more evident, and it necessarily follows, *No prayer, no religion*. This is very nearly the state to which we are reduced. Since men have never prayed except by virtue of a revealed religion (or one recognized as such), they have ceased to pray to the degree that they have approached deism, which is and can be nothing; and now you can see them with their eyes glued to the physical world, occupied solely with physical laws and studies and without any longer the slightest feeling for their natural dignity. Such is the misfortune of these men that they can no longer even desire their own regeneration, not only because of the recognized reason that *what is not known cannot be desired*, but because they find in their moral brutalization some curious but frightful charm, which is an appalling chastisement. In vain are they told what they are and what they will become. Plunged in the divine atmosphere, they refuse to breathe, *whereas if they only opened their mouths, they would draw down the spirit to themselves.*[12] Such is the man who no longer prays; no other proof of the indispensable necessity of public worship is required than that, if it did not check a little the general degradation, we would end up, I honestly believe, no better than animals. Consequently the antipathy of the men of whom I am speaking toward this worship and its ministers is boundless.

Unhappy confidences have taught me that there are those for whom the atmosphere of a church is a kind of poison gas which literally stifles them and forces them to leave; whereas healthy souls feel themselves there refreshed by some spiritual dew which is beyond description, but needs none since no one can fail to recognize it. Vincent de Lerins set out a well-known religious rule, saying that it was necessary to believe what has been believed ALWAYS, EVERYWHERE AND BY ALL. Nothing is so true and so universally true. Man, in spite of his fatal degradation, bears always the evident marks of his divine origin, in that every universal belief is always more or less true. Man may well have covered over and, so to speak, *encrusted* the truth with the errors he has loaded onto it, but these errors are local, and universal truth will always show itself. Now, men have always and everywhere prayed. Doubtless it is possible that they have prayed badly, asking for what they had no need and not asking for what they needed, but this is man's nature; yet they have always prayed, and this is the work of God.

The splendid theory of invariable laws would lead us straight to fatalism and make an automaton of man. As our friend did yesterday, I swear that I do not mean to insult reason. I respect it infinitely in spite of all the harm it has done to us, but it is certain that, every time it is opposed to *common sense*, we should reject it as pernicious. It is reason that has said, *Nothing can happen except what happens, and nothing happens except what must happen.* But good sense has said, *If you pray, something which was to have happened will not happen;* in which common sense was very reasonable, whereas reason lacked common sense. For the rest, it matters little that certain subtle arguments can be raised against proven truths and cannot be answered immediately, for there is no source of gross error more fruit-

---

[12] Psalm 119:131.

ful or more dangerous than rejecting such and such a dogma simply because it raises an objection we cannot resolve.

THE COUNT: You are perfectly right, my dear Senator: no objection can be admitted against the truth, otherwise it would no longer be the truth. Once its character is recognized, the unanswerability of an objection shows nothing more than a defect in the knowledge of those who cannot answer. . . .

It is enough for me to draw from the mass of instances a general theory, a kind of formula which will serve to resolve all particular cases. I would say that "every time a proposition is proved by the kind of proof relevant to it, no objection whatever, *even an unanswerable one, should be countenanced.*" The very inability to reply shows that the two propositions, taken to be true, are not really contradictory; which can always happen when the contradiction is not *in the terms.*

THE KNIGHT: Would you explain that more fully?

THE COUNT: No authority on earth, for example, has the right to claim that *three and one are the same;* for I know the meaning of *one* and *three,* and, since the sense of the terms does not change in the two propositions, to ask me to believe that *one* and *three* are and are not the same is the same as God telling me to believe that God does not exist. But if someone said to me *that three persons partake of one nature,* I am ready to believe it, provided that revelation provides me with a sufficient proof, especially, though not necessarily, if revelation is backed by solid psychological theories and even by the more or less obscure traditions of every nation; it does not matter to me that *three* is not *one,* for this is not here the question, which is to know if *three persons* can have *one nature,* quite another problem.

THE SENATOR: Indeed, in this case where is the contradiction, when it cannot be supported either by the facts, since we do not know them, or by the terms, since they have changed? Allow, then, the stoics to tell us that the proposition *It will rain tomorrow* is as certain and as immutable in the ordained order of things as the proposition *It rained yesterday;* allow them to perplex us, if they can, with the most dazzling sophisms. We shall let them prattle on, for no objection, even an unanswerable one (which I am very far from admitting in this case), can stand against the proof that resides in the innate belief of all men. If you accept what I say, Knight, you will continue when you return to your homeland to say your Rogation-day prayer. In the meantime, it will be as well to pray to God with all your might to bless you by returning you there, in the same way letting them prattle on who would object that it is determined beforehand whether or not you will see your dear country again.

THE COUNT: Although I am, as you have seen, completely convinced that the general sentiments of all men constitute, so to speak, intuitive truths before which all rationalist sophistries fade away, I nevertheless think like you, Senator, that in the present question we are by no means reduced to these intuitions. For, first, if you look at it more closely you will recognize the fallacy without being able to explain it fully. No doubt, the proposition *It rained yesterday* is no more certain than the other, *It will rain tomorrow*, but only *if in fact it must rain*, but this is precisely the point at issue, and one is back where one started.

In the second place, and this is the main point, I do not see these inevitable laws and this inflexible chain of events about which so much is spoken. On the contrary, I see in nature only complex forces, as must necessarily be the case if the functioning of free agents, interacting frequently in this world with the natural laws of matter, is to be accommodated. Just look at the variety of ways and the degree to which we influence the reproduction of animals and plants. Grafting, for example, is or is not a law of nature according to whether man exists or does not exist. You speak, Knight, of a certain precise quantity of rain that falls on each country during the year. As I have never concerned myself with meteorology, I do not know what has been said on this point, although, to tell you the truth, it seems to be impossible that this can be proved, at least not with even an approximate certainty. However that may be, here it can be a question only of an average year; then on what period of time are we to base this average? It could be ten years, it could be a hundred. But I want to pick more quarrels with these theorists. I shall allow that precisely the same amount of water must fall in every country each year; let this be an invariable law; but the distribution of this rain will be, so to speak, the *flexible part* of the law. So you see that even with your *invariable* laws we can still very well have floods and droughts, *general* rains for the world at large, and *exceptional* rains for those who have asked for it.[13]

. . . I can well accept that philosophers of our time all talk constantly about inevitable laws: their aim is simply to prevent man from

[13] Psalm 68:9.

praying, and this is the infallible means of success. This is the reason for the anger of these unbelievers when preachers or moralists are led to tell us that the physical scourges of this world, such as volcanoes, earthquakes, and so on, were divine punishments. They affirm that it was absolutely inevitable that Lisbon should have been destroyed on November 1, 1755, as it was inevitable that the sun should have arisen that same day—a truly splendid theory, very suited to bring man to perfection. I recall how indignant I was one day while reading a lecture that *Herder* addressed somewhere to Voltaire on the subject of his poem about the Lisbon disaster. Seriously he said, "You dare to complain to Providence about the destruction of this town: you are thoughtless, for this is an explicit blasphemy against the *eternal wisdom*. Do you not realize that man, like his beams and his tiles, is a *debtor for his existence*, and that all things in existence must pay their debts? Elements combine, elements come apart; *this is a necessary law of nature*: what then is surprising in this or that event that should give rise to complaints?"

Is not this, gentlemen, a splendid consolation, well worthy of the honest comedian who preached the Scripture in the pulpit and pantheism in his writings? But this is the limit of the wisdom of philosophy. From Epictetus to *the bishop of Weimar* and to the end of time, this will be its unchanging role and *its necessary law*. It is ignorant of the balm of consolation. It withers and hardens the heart, and thinks it has made a man a sage by making him callous. In any case, Voltaire had already replied to his critic in this same poem on the Lisbon earthquake:

> "No, offer no more to my distressed heart,
> These immutable laws of necessity,
> This chain of bodies, minds and worlds;
> Oh, learned dreams and deep illusions!
> God holds the chain and is not bound:
> All is determined by his beneficent choice;
> He is free, he is just, he is merciful."

Up to this point, this could not be better put; but as if repenting of having talked sense, he adds immediately:

> "Why then do we suffer under a just master?
> This is the fatal knot that must be untied."

Here the rash questions begin. *Why then do we suffer under a just master?* The catechism and common sense agree in replying, BECAUSE WE DESERVE IT. *This is the fatal knot wisely untied*, and any deviation from this solution is meaningless. In vain does Voltaire exclaim:

> "Seeing this pile of victims, do you say;
>   God is avenged; their death is the price of their crimes?
> What crime, what fault lies on these children
> Broken and bloody on their mothers' breasts?"

This is bad reasoning, lacking care and close analysis. Doubtless there were children at *Lisbon* as there were at *Herculaneum* in A.D. 79, as there were at Lyons some time previously, or as there were, if you like, at the time of the flood. When God punishes any society for its crimes, he enacts justice as we do it ourselves in this sort of case, without anyone thinking of complaining about it. A town revolts; it massacres the king's representatives; it closes its gates to him; it resists him; it is taken. The king dismantles it and strips it of all its privileges; no one will condemn this judgment on the grounds that there were innocent people in the town. We should never deal with two questions at once. *The town has been punished because of its crime, and without this crime it would not have suffered.* This is a true proposition, independent of any other. Will you then ask me *why innocent people have been included in the same punishment?* This is another proposition to which I am not obliged to reply. I could reply that I have no idea of the reason without weakening in any way the first proposition. I can also reply that the king can do no other, and I would have good grounds for claiming this.

THE KNIGHT: Allow me to ask you this—what would prevent the good king from taking into his protection the inhabitants of the town who remained faithful and taking them to some more fortunate district so that they could there enjoy, not the same privileges, but greater privileges, more fitting to their loyalty?

THE COUNT: That is precisely what God does when innocent people perish in a general catastrophe. But let us go back. I flatter myself that I feel no less sincere a pity than Voltaire for these unfortunate *children broken and bloody on their mothers' breasts;* but it is madness to cite them to contradict the preacher who claims, *God is avenged; these evils are the price of our crimes*, for nothing is in general more true. The question is only to explain why the innocent are included in the penalty directed against the guilty: but, as I have just said to you, this is only an objection, and if we allow truth to submit to difficulties, there is no more philosophy. Moreover, I wonder if Voltaire, who wrote in such haste, took care to treat this as a general question rather than as a particular question relating to the event concerning him on this occasion. I wonder too if he did not ask, without realizing it, *why infants who could not yet be either condemned or praised are subject throughout the whole world to the same evils which can afflict grown men.* For if it is determined that a certain number of infants must perish, I do not see that it matters to them whether they die in one way rather than in another. A man dies whether he is stabbed to the heart or has a brain tumor, but it is said in the first case that he ended his days *by a violent death.* But, to God, there is no such thing as a violent death. A steel blade thrust in the heart is an infirmity like a simple corn that we call a *polypus.*

We must then go to a further question and ask *why it became necessary for a host of infants to be stillborn, for a good half of those born to die before the age of ten and for a great many others still to die before reaching the age of reason. . . .*

Why are these children born and why do they die? What will one day happen to them? These are perhaps unapproachable mysteries, but it is senseless to use the incomprehensible as an argument against the easily comprehensible.

Would you like to hear another sophistry on the same subject? It is Voltaire again who gives it to us and still in the same work:

> "Had Lisbon, which is no more, more vices
> Than London or than Paris steeped in its delights?
> Lisbon is destroyed, and they dance in Paris!"

Good God, does this man want the Almighty to convert every great city into an execution chamber? Or does he want God never to punish because he does not punish always and everywhere and at the same time?

Had then Voltaire been given the divine balance for weighing the crimes of kings and individuals and for fixing punishments at the right time? And what would this rash man have said if, when he was writing these senseless lines, in the middle of the town *steeped in its delights*, he could have seen suddenly, in the not so distant future, the

Committee of Public Safety, the Revolutionary Tribunal and the long pages of the *Moniteur* quite red with human blood?

Doubtless pity is one of the noblest sentiments to honor man, and nothing should be done to kill it, even to weaken it in men's hearts; yet in treating philosophic subjects, every kind of poetry should be carefully avoided and things should be seen as they are. For example Voltaire, in the poem I quoted, shows us *a hundred thousand unfortunates devoured by the earth*; but, first of all, why *a hundred thousand?* Especially as he could have told the truth without spoiling the meter, since in fact only about twenty thousand people died in this horrible catastrophe, many less in consequence than in many battles I could name to you.

It should then be noticed that in these great catastrophes many things are only superficial. For example, the crushing of a child under a rock is a frightful sight to us, but to the child it is much better than dying of smallpox or a painful dental operation. To the reason, it is the same thing no doubt whether three or four thousand men scattered over a wide area perish, or they die all at once in a single catastrophe, in an earthquake or a flood; but to the imagination the difference is enormous. So that it can very well happen that one of those terrible events that we place among the world's greatest scourges is in reality of no account, not just to humanity in general but to a single country.

You can see here a fresh example of those laws, at once flexible and invariable, that rule the universe. If you will let us accept as a proven point that in a given time in a certain country a certain number of men must die, this is what is invariable; but the distribution of life among individuals, as well as the place and time of deaths, constitute what I have called the flexible part of the law, so that a whole town can be destroyed without the general mortality being increased. A scourge can even be just in two ways, by reason of the guilty who have been punished and the innocent who have gained in compensation a longer and happier life. The omnipotent wisdom governing all things has means at its disposal so numerous, so diversified, so wonderful that the part we can comprehend should well teach us to revere the other. A good many years ago, I came across certain mortality statistics gathered in a small province with great care and exactitude. I was not at all surprised to learn from these figures that two serious epidemics of smallpox had not increased the mortality rate in the year when they raged. So much is it true that this hidden force we call *nature* has means of compensation which can scarcely be doubted.

THE SENATOR: A sacred saying says that *pride is the beginning of sin;*[14] I think one could very well add, *and of error.* It misleads us by rousing in us an unfortunate spirit of contention that leads us to seek out difficulties for the pleasure of argument rather than referring them to a proved principle; but, unless I am very much mistaken, the disputants themselves at bottom feel that it is all in vain. How many arguments would be saved if every man was forced to say what he really thought!

THE COUNT: I agree with you entirely, but, before going any further, allow me to point out a peculiar characteristic of Christianity which strikes me in regard to the calamities of which we are speaking. If Christianity were a human artifact, its teaching would vary with human opinions, but since it emanates from the unchangeable Being, it is as unchangeable as he. Certainly this religion, the fount of all· good and true knowledge in the world, whose greatest concern is the advancement of this very knowledge, takes great care not to forbid it to us or to impede its progress. For example, it approves strongly of our inquiring into the nature of all the physical factors that play a part in great natural convulsions. As for itself, in direct relation with God, it scarcely bothers about the agents which execute his orders. It knows that it was created to pray and not to dispute, since it knows with certainty what it needs to know. Whether one approves of it or condemns it, admires or ridicules it, it remains unmoved; and on the ruins of a town destroyed by an earth tremor, it says to the eighteenth century what it would have said to the twelfth:

We beg of you, O Lord, to be pleased to protect us; by your supreme grace make firm once more this earth unsettled by our iniquities, so that every man may recognize in his heart that it is your wrath that imposes punishments on us, as it is your mercy that delivers us from them. . . .

[14] Ecclesiasticus 10:13.

FIFTH DIALOGUE

THE SENATOR: No living creature can have knowledge other than that which is part of its nature and which is entirely relative to its place in the world; and to my mind this is one of the many and unanswerable proofs of innate ideas; for, if there were no ideas of this sort in every cognitive creature, each of them, owing its ideas to its own particular and fortuitous experience, could move outside its proper sphere and overturn the order of things; however, this will never happen. The *half-reasoning* dog, monkey, or elephant will, for example, draw near to the fire and find pleasure in its warmth as we do, but you will never teach them to throw a log on the embers, because fire is alien to their nature; otherwise the human domain would be invaded. They can very well grasp the notion of *one*, but never that of *unity*; the rudiments of numbering but never the idea of *number*; one, two, or a thousand triangles together or one after another but never the concept of *triangularity*. The constant association of certain ideas in our minds makes us confuse them, although they are essentially distinct. I see your two eyes and immediately I associate my perception of them with the idea of *duality*; in fact, however, the two notions are of a totally different order, and one does not lead to the other.

Since I am on the subject, I shall add that I shall never understand how the morality of intelligent beings, either the human species or any other *cognitive* species, can be separated from innate ideas. But let us go back to animals. My dog accompanies me to some public spectacle, an execution, perhaps: certainly it sees everything that I see: the crowd, the melancholy procession, the officers of justice, the soldiers, the scaffolds, the condemned man, the executioner, in a word everything: but what does it understand of all this?—what it should understand *in its quality as a dog*: it will be able to make me out in the crowd and find me again if by chance we are separated; it will contrive not to be trampled underfoot by the spectators; when the

executioner raises his arm, the animal, if it is nearby, will draw back
for fear that the blow is meant for him; if it sees blood, it might tremble, but it would do the same in a butcher's shop. Its understanding
stops there, and, no matter how much intelligent instruction it is given,
it will never progress beyond this point; the ideas of morality, sovereignty, crime, justice, authority, and so on, which are implicit in this
dismal spectacle, mean nothing to it. All the symbols of these ideas
surround it, touch it, press in on it, but all to no avail, for no symbol
can be meaningful unless the idea it represents is preexistent. It is one
of the most obvious laws of the temporal rule of Providence that every
active creature acts within a sphere laid down for it without being able
to escape from it. And no one of good sense could imagine otherwise!
Starting from this incontestable principle, who can deny that a vol-
cano, a whirlwind, or an earthquake is to me what the execution is to
my dog? Of these phenomena, I understand what I should understand, that is to say, everything that is in keeping with those innate
ideas appropriate to the human condition. The rest is a closed
book. . . .

As I have just said, animals are *surrounded, touched, pressed in*
by all the symbols of comprehension without being able to improve
the least of their acts: refine as much as you like by thought this
soul, this unknown principle, this *instinct*, this inner light which
has been given to them with so great a variety of direction and
intensity, yet you will find only an *asymptote* of reason, capable of
approaching it, if you will, but never of reaching it; otherwise the
province of creation would have been encroached upon, which is
obviously impossible.

For a very similar reason, no doubt we can ourselves be *surrounded,
touched, pressed in* by actions and agents of a superior order of
which we have no knowledge other than that appropriate to our
present situation. I am fully aware of the sublime uncertainty about
which you have just spoken: yes, *I know that I do not know*, perhaps
I know something more still; but it remains true that, by virtue of our
intelligence, we shall never be capable of achieving direct knowledge
on this point. I make great use, besides, of this uncertainty in all
my inquiries into *causes*. I have read thousand of witticisms about
the ignorance of the ancients *who saw gods everywhere*: it seems to
me that we, who see them nowhere, are much more foolish. We are
constantly told about *physical causes*, but what is a physical cause?

THE COUNT: It is a *natural cause*, if we want to confine ourselves to defining the word; but, in the modern usage, it is a *material cause*, that is to say, a cause which is not a cause, for *matter* and *cause* are mutually exclusive like *black* and *white* or *circle* and *square*. Matter has an effect only by movement: however, all movement being an effect, it follows that a *physical* cause is, strictly speaking, NON-SENSE and even a contradiction in terms. Thus there are and can be no *physical causes* properly speaking, because there is and can be no movement without an original mover, and because every original mover is outside matter; *everywhere, that which actuates comes before that which is actuated; that which leads comes before that which is led; that which commands comes before that which is commanded*: matter can be and even is nothing other than evidence of mind. If a hundred balls are placed in a line and each is moved successively by an impulse from the first, does this not presuppose a hand which impelled the first ball through an act of will? And when the disposition of things prevents me from seeing this hand, is it any the less obvious to my intelligence? Is not the mind of a clockmaker comprised within the drum of this clock, in which the mainspring is charged, so to speak, with the instructions of an intelligence? . . . The question is to know if there are nothing but material bodies in the world, and if these bodies can be moved by impulses of another kind. However, not only can they be so moved but originally they must have been so: for, since every movement can be conceived only as the result of another, it is necessary either to accept the idea of an infinite series of movements, that is to say, of effects without cause, or to agree that the principle of movement cannot be found in matter; and we carry in ourselves the proof that movement starts in the will. In a common and essential sense, it is quite legitimate to call *causes* effects that produce other effects: it is this sense that, in the line of balls I just referred to, every moving force is a *cause* except the first. But if we wish to speak with philosophic precision, we must use the word otherwise. It cannot be too often repeated that the ideas of *matter* and *cause* are mutually and rigorously exclusive.

On the question of the forces acting in the universe, Bacon developed a chimerical idea which has led to confusion in a host of thinkers: he supposed first of all material forces, then superimposed them indefinitely one on top of another; and the suspicion has often forced itself upon me that, in putting forward these genealogical trees in which everyone is a son except the first and everyone a father except the last, he made on these lines *a god of the ladder*, and that he arranged causes in the same way in his head; in his own way believing that one cause was the son of that which preceded, and that the generations, contracting as one goes back, would lead the true interpreter of nature to a common ancestor. Here are the ideas that this great jurist formed of nature and the science which must explain it: but nothing is more illusory.

I do not want to draw you into a long discussion. A single observation will suffice for the moment. It is that Bacon and his disciples have never and will never be able to quote to us a single example to support their theory. Let someone show us this alleged order of *general, more general, and most general* causes, as they are pleased to call them. Much has been argued and much discovered since Bacon: let someone give us an example of this wonderful genealogy, point out to us a single mystery of nature that has been explained, not necessarily by a cause, but even by a primary effect previously unknown, reached by working back from one to the other. Imagine the most common phenomenon, elasticity, for example, or any other you care to choose. Now, I shall not pose any difficulties; I do not ask for either the grandparents or the great-great-grandparents of the phenomenon, but will be content with its mother: alas, everyone remains silent; and always it is (I mean in the material order) *Proles sinè matre creata*. How can anyone be so blind as to seek causes in *nature* when nature itself is an effect? So long as the material sphere is looked at in isolation, no one man can progress more than any other in the investigation of causes: all are and must be checked at the first step.

The genius of discovery in the natural sciences consists solely in uncovering unknown facts or relating unexplained phenomena to already known primary effects that we take as causes. Thus, the discoverers of the circulation of the blood and of the sex of plants doubtless both advanced science; but the discovery of facts has nothing to do with the discovery of causes. For his part Newton immortalized himself by relating to gravity phenomena which no one had ever thought of attributing to it; but the great man's footman knew as much as he did about the cause of gravity. Certain disciples, for whom he would blush if he returned to the world, have ventured to say that gravitation is a *mechanical* law. Newton never blasphemed against common sense in such a way, and it is in vain that they have sought to give themselves so distinguished an accomplice. On the contrary, he said (and this certainly is quite a lot) *that he left to his readers the question of deciding if the agent which produces gravity is physical or spiritual.* Read, I pray you, his theological letters to Dr. Bentley: you will be equally enlightened and edified by them.

You can see, Senator, that I strongly approve of your way of envisaging this world and, unless I am absolutely mistaken, base it on very good arguments. For the rest, I repeat what you said, *I know that I do not know;* and this uncertainty fills me at once with joy and with gratitude, since I find united in it both the ineffaceable title deed to my grandeur and a salutary protection against all ridiculous or foolhardy speculation. In looking at nature from this point of view, in the greatest as in the least of its works, I always recall (and this is enough for me) the phrase of a Lacedaemonian thinking about what prevented a stiffened corpse from standing upright however it was positioned: *My God,* he said, *there must have been something inside.* Always and everywhere the same can be said, for without this *something* everything is a corpse and nothing can stand upright. The world, considered thus as a collection of appearances in which the least phenomenon hides a reality, is a true and wise system of ideal forms. In a very true sense, I can say that material objects are nothing like what I see; but what I see is real in relation to me, and it is sufficient for me to be so led to the existence of another order in which I believe firmly without seeing it. Resting on these principles, I understand perfectly not only that prayer is useful in general in warding off physical evil, but that it is the true antidote, the natural specific, for it and that in its essence it tends to destroy it. . . .

This digression on causes leads us to an equally just and fruitful idea: it is to look at prayer from the point of view of its effects simply as a secondary cause; for from this standpoint, it is nothing but that and should not be differentiated from any other secondary cause. If then a fashionable philosopher is surprised to see me use prayer to protect myself against lightning, for example, I shall say to him, *And why do you, sir, use lightning rods?* Or, to restrict myself to something more usual, *Why do you use fire engines in fires and medicines in illnesses? Are you not setting your face against eternal laws quite as much as I am?* "Oh, but that is very different," I shall be told, "for if it is a law, for example, that fire burns, it is also a law that water puts out fire." I shall reply, *That is exactly what I say for my part, for if it is a law that lightning produces a certain catastrophe, it is also a law that prayer, sprinkled in time on the* HEAVENLY FIRE, *extinguishes or diverts it.* And you can be sure, gentlemen, that there is no objection of this kind that I cannot counter to my advantage: there is no mid-point between a rigid, absolute, and universal fatalism and the widespread faith of men in the efficacy of prayer. . . .

How great has been the cost of natural sciences to man! It is entirely his own fault, for God had offered him sufficient safeguards; but pride has lent its ear to the serpent, and once again man has put his guilty hand to the tree of knowledge; he has lost his way, and unfortunately does not know it. Notice a fine decree of Providence; since the primitive ages (of which I shall not speak at this point), it has granted the experimental sciences only to Christians. The ancients certainly surpassed us in intellectual power, as is shown by the superiority of their languages, in a way which seems to silence all the sophistries of our pride; for the same reason, they surpassed us in everything that they undertook in common with us. On the other hand, their physical science was almost nothing; for not only did they not attach any value to physical experiments, they despised them, and even suspected them slightly of impiety, and this confused feeling came from further back. Once the whole of Europe was Christian, once priests were the universal teachers, once all the institutions of Europe were Christianized, once theology had taken its place at the head of teaching and all the other faculties had grouped themselves around it like ladies-in-waiting around their queen, humanity being prepared for them in this way, the natural sciences were given to it, *tantae molis erat* ROMANUM *condere gentem.* Ignorance of this great truth has misled very strong minds, and Bacon is no exception, and perhaps the misconception even started with him.

THE SENATOR: Since you have reminded me of him, I confess that I have more than once found him extremely amusing with his *desiderata.* He has the air of a man who frets beside a cradle, complaining that the infant who is being rocked is still not a professor of mathematics or an army commander.

THE COUNT: That is very well said, although I fancy one could quarrel with the exactness of your comparison, for science at the beginning of the seventeenth century was by no means an *infant in the cradle.* Leaving aside the illustrious monk of the same name three centuries earlier in England, whose teachings could still earn him from men of our time the title of *scholar*, Bacon was the contemporary of Kepler, Galileo, and Descartes, while Copernicus had preceded him: leaving aside a hundred other less well-known persons, these four giants alone deprive him of the right to talk with so much contempt of the state of the sciences, which already threw such a dazzling light in his own times and were at bottom as developed as they could then be. The sciences are not progressing as Bacon imagined: they germinate like everything that germinates; they grow like everything that grows; they are connected with the moral condition of man.

Although free and active, and in consequence capable of devoting himself to science and its perfection, as with everything that has been put within his reach, man is nevertheless left to his own devices in this field less perhaps than in any other; but Bacon took it into his head to abuse the knowledge of his age without ever being able to grasp it, and nothing is more curious in the history of the human mind than the imperturbable obstinacy with which this famous man continued to deny the existence of the light shining around him, because his eyes were not capable of seeing it, for there was never a man more ignorant of the natural sciences and the laws of the world.

Bacon has very justly been accused of having retarded the progress of chemistry by trying to make it mechanical, and I am intrigued that the charge has been leveled against him in his own country by one of the foremost chemists of our day.[15] He has done worse still by retarding the progress of that transcendental or *general* philosophy, of which he never stopped telling us, without ever having any idea of what it was about; he even invented words which are false and dangerous in the sense he gave to them, for example, *form* which he substituted for *nature* or *essence*, and to which modern gross ignorance has not failed to lay claim, by seriously proposing to inquire into the *form* of heat, expansiveness, and so on: and who knows if some day someone, following in his footsteps, will not come to teach us the *form of virtue?*

The force which seduced Bacon was not by any means yet fully developed at the time when he wrote, yet it can be seen even then fermenting in his writings, in which it boldly nurtured the seeds that we have seen blossom out in our own day. Full of an unconscious rancor, whose origin and nature he did not himself recognize, against all spiritual ideas, Bacon fastened the general attention with all his might upon the physical sciences in such a way as to turn men away from all

[15] J. Black, *Lectures on the Elements of Chemistry* (London, 1803), I, 261.

other branches of learning. He rejected all metaphysics, all psychology, all natural and positive theology, and locked them all up in the Church, forbidding them to come out; he relentlessly denigrated final causes, which he called the *limpets* on the ship of science: and he dared to hold openly that the inquiry into causes was harmful to true science, an error as gross as it was dangerous, and yet incredibly an infectious error, even for well-disposed minds, so much so that one of the closest and most distinguished followers of the English philosopher felt no compunction in warning us *to take great care not to allow ourselves to be carried away by the order we see in the universe.*

Bacon did not ignore any means to turn us away from Plato's philosophy, the human preface to the Scriptures, and praised, expounded, and propagated that of Democritus, that is to say, atomic philosophy, a desperate attempt of materialism pushed to extremes, which, being aware that matter escapes it and explains nothing, plunges into the infinitely small, seeking, so to speak, matter without matter and being completely happy even amid absurdities so long as it does not find intelligence.

In conformity with this system of philosophy, Bacon urges men to seek the cause of natural phenomena in the configuration of constituent atoms or molecules, the most false and gross idea ever to have stained the human understanding. And this is why the eighteenth century, which has always loved and praised men only for the evil they bear, made Bacon its god, while nevertheless refusing to give him justice for his good and even excellent qualities. It is quite wrong to believe that he forwarded the progress of science, for all the real scientific innovators preceded him or were ignorant of him. Bacon was a barometer who announced good weather, and because he announced it people believed that he had made it. Walpole, his contemporary, called him *the prophet of science,*[16] and this is all that can be granted to him. I have seen the design of a medal struck in his honor, of which the main part is a rising sun with the motto *Exortus uti aethereus sol.* Nothing is more obviously false; I would sooner accept a rising sun with the inscription *Nuntia solis,* and even this could be said to be exaggerated, for, when Bacon *arose,* it was at least ten o'clock in the morning. The immense respect paid to him in our own time is due, as I just before said, only to his reprehensible sides. Notice that he was

---

[16] See the preface to the small English edition of the *Works of Bacon*, published by Dr. Shaw, London 1802 [I, viii].

not translated into French until the end of the eighteenth century, and by a man who told us naïvely *that he had, against his own experience, a hundred thousand reasons for not believing in God.*

THE KNIGHT: Are you not afraid, Count, of being abused for such blasphemies against one of the *great gods* of our age?

THE COUNT: If it was my duty to be abused, I would have to bear it patiently, but I doubt if anyone is going to abuse me here. However, if it were a question of writing and publishing what I have said, I should not hesitate for a moment; I should not be very afraid of the storms, so convinced am I that the true intentions of a writer are always felt and that everyone renders justice to them. I am sure then that I would be believed if I protested that I think myself inferior in talent and knowledge to most of the writers now in the public eye, as much as I surpass them in the truth of the doctrines I profess. I am even pleased to confess their superiority in the first, which provides me with the subject of a charming reflection on the inestimable gift of the truth and on the sterility of talents which dare to divorce themselves from it.

There is a splendid book to be written, gentlemen, *about the harm inflicted on works of genius, and even on the characters of their authors, by the errors they have professed for three centuries.* What a subject if it were ably treated! The book would be the more useful as it would rest entirely on facts and so would lay itself open very little to pettifogging criticism. I can quote to you a striking example on this point, that of Newton, who comes to mind here as one of the most outstanding men in the realm of science. What did he lack to justify fully the beautiful tribute of an English poet, who called him

> ". . . pure intelligence, whom God
> To mortals lent, to trace his boundless works
> From laws sublimely simple."?[17]

He lacked the ability to rise above national prejudices, for surely if he had held more firmly to the truth, he would have written one book less. Exalt him as much as you like, and I shall agree fully, provided that he keeps to his place; but if he comes down from the heights of his genius to dabble in theology, I no longer owe him my respect. In error, there are not and cannot be great names or ranks or distinctions, NEWTON being the equal of *Villiers.*

[17] Thomson, *The Seasons,* "Summer."

After this profession of faith, which I am always ready to repeat, I am perfectly at peace with myself. I assure you I cannot accuse myself of anything, because I know what I owe to genius, but I know also what I owe to truth. Moreover, gentlemen, *the time is now ripe,* and all the old idols must now fall. Let us get back to the subject.

Do you find any difficulty at all in this idea that prayer is a secondary cause and that any objection to it could be made in the same way to medicine, for example? *This sick man is to die or he is not to die; thus it is useless to pray for him,* and for my part I say, *then it is useless to give him cures and there is no art of medicine.* Where, pray, is the difference? We do not want to hold that secondary causes form part of the higher scheme of things. *This sick man will die or will not die:* yes, undoubtedly he will die *if he does not take remedies,* and he will not die *if he does:* this condition is itself a part of the eternal order.

Without doubt God is the universal moving force, but each being is moved according to the nature that God has given it. What would you yourselves do, gentlemen, if you wanted to lead that horse we see in the meadow over there? You would mount it or lead it by the bridle, and the animal would obey you, *according to its nature,* although it is quite capable of resisting you and even of killing you with a blow of its hoof. But if you wanted that child we see playing in the garden to come to us, you would call him or, if you did not know his name, you would make some signal to him; the most understandable thing for him no doubt would be to show him this cake, and he would come *according to his nature.* If finally you had need of a book from my library, you would go to fetch it, and the book would be moved by your hand in a purely passive way *according to its nature.* This is quite a straightforward parallel to the action of God on his creatures. He directs angels, men, animals, brute matter, in sum all created things, but each *according to its nature,* and man having been created free, he is freely led. This rule is truly *the eternal law* and in it we must believe.

THE SENATOR: I agree with you with all my heart, yet it must be confessed that the agreement of the divine will with our free will and the acts that flow from it is one of those questions in which human reason, even when it is quite firm in its convictions, has not nevertheless the power to rid itself of a certain doubt that derives from fear and assails it in spite of itself. This is an abyss into which it is better not to look.

THE COUNT: My good friend, it is not entirely possible for us not to look into it; it is there before us, and, not to see it, we should have to be blind, which would be much worse than being afraid. Let us rather repeat that there is no philosophy without the art of ignoring objections, otherwise mathematics itself would be shaken. I must admit that, when one thinks of certain intellectual mysteries, one's head whirls a little. Yet it is possible to recover completely, and nature itself if wisely consulted leads us toward the truth. No doubt you have thought a thousand times about the relationship between movements. For example, if you run from east to west while the earth turns from west to east, what do you want to achieve? Let me suppose you want to travel a verst on foot from east to west in eight minutes: you have done it; you have achieved your end; you are weary and covered in sweat; you feel, in a word, all the symptoms of fatigue: but what did this superior power, this *prime moving force,* which is carrying you along with it, aim at? It wanted you to be carried back in space with an incredible speed, rather than moving forward from east to west; and this is what happened. It, like you, has thus achieved what it wanted. If you play at shuttlecock on a ship in sail, is there not in the movement which carries both you and the shuttlecock along something that interferes with your action? Suppose you hit the shuttlecock from the bows to the stern with a speed equal to that of the boat (which can be rigorously true): the two players are certainly doing *everything that they wanted,* but the prime moving force has also done *what it wanted.* One of the two believed he *hit* the shuttlecock, but only stopped it: the other player went to the shuttlecock rather than, as he thought, waiting for it and getting it on his racket.

Would you say perhaps that, since you have not done all you believed, you have not done all you wanted? In this case, you would be ignoring the fact that the same objection can apply to the superior moving force, about which it could be said that while it wished to carry the shuttlecock along, yet the shuttlecock remained where it was. Thus the argument could be used equally against God. Since the argument that divine power can be limited by human power has precisely the same force as the converse proposition, it follows that it is not applicable in either case and that the two powers act together without harming each other.

Many lessons can be learned from the relationship between moving forces which, whatever their number and direction, can act on the same body simultaneously and which all have their effect, so that the moving body at the end of a single movement produced by them will be at precisely the same point at which it would have stopped if they had all acted one after another. The only difference between the two dynamics is that in the case of bodies, the force moving them never belongs to them, while in the case of minds, the wills, which are in substance motions, themselves join, intersect, or collide, since they are nothing but motions. It can even come about that a created will cancels out, not perhaps the *exertion,* but the result of divine action; for in this sense, *God* himself has told us that God WISHES things which do not happen because man DOES NOT WISH THEM![18] Thus the rights of men are immense, and his greatest misfortune is to be unaware of them; but his real spiritual action is prayer by means of which, by putting himself in harmony with God, he so to speak exercises an omnipotent power by determining it.

Do you want to know what this power is and what its extent? Think what the human will can achieve in the sphere of evil; it can contradict God, as you have just seen: what then can this same will do when it acts in harmony with him? What are the limits of this power? Its nature is not to have any. The efficacy of the human will is dimly visible to us in social matters, and we often say that *man can do what he will*; but in the spiritual sphere, where effects are not so perceptible, ignorance on this point is only too general, and even in the material sphere we do not by far reflect sufficiently. For example, you can easily knock over this rosebush but you cannot overthrow an oak; why is this, I pray? The earth is full of foolish men who will hasten to reply, *Because your muscles are not strong enough*, thus mistaking completely the *limit* for the *means* of power.

Human power is limited by the nature of man's physical organs, and this is necessary in order that he can disturb the established order only up to a certain point; for you can imagine what would happen in this world if a man could unaided pull down a building or root up a forest. It is perfectly true that that same wisdom which made man perfectible has given him dynamics, that is to say, artificial means of augmenting his natural powers, but this gift is still accompanied by a striking sign of infinite foresight: for, wishing that every possible advance should be proportionate, not to the limitless desires of man,

[18] *O Jerusalem, Jerusalem . . . how often would I have gathered thy children together . . . and ye would not!* (Luke, 13:34).

which are immense and almost always ill directed, but only to his wise desires, based on his needs, this wisdom has determined that each of his powers is attended by a check which is born and grows with it, so that the power must necessarily destroy itself by the very effort it makes to expand.

For instance, the power of a lever cannot be increased without a proportional increase in the difficulties of working it, which must eventually render it useless; it can be said, moreover, that in general and in the very operations which are, properly speaking, far from mechanical, man cannot increase his natural powers without using proportionately more time, space, and material, which in the first place inconveniences him in a cumulative way and then prevents him from acting secretly, and this should be carefully observed. So, for instance, every man can blow up a house by means of dynamite, but the indispensable preparations are such that the public authorities will always have the time to ask him what he is doing. Optical instruments give another striking illustration of the same law, since it is impossible to perfect one of the qualities whose combination constitutes the perfection of these instruments without weakening another. Something similar could be said about firearms. In a word, there is no possible exception to a law the suspension of which would destroy human society. Thus, on all sides, in the natural as in the artificial order, limits are set. You will not bend the bush I was talking about before if you push it with a reed; but this would be because the reed, and not you, lacked the power; and this overweak instrument is to the rosebush what men's arms are to the oak. By its nature, the will would move mountains, but the muscles, nerves, and bones given to it as its means of acting in the material world give way to the oak as the reed gives way to the rosebush.

Imagine the suspension of the law that lays down that the human will can act materially in an immediate manner only on the body which it animates (a purely accidental law relative to our state of ignorance and corruption), and this will will be able to pull up a tree as easily as it lifts an arm. However one looks at the human will, one finds that its powers are extremely wide. But since prayer is the *dynamic* granted to men in the spiritual order, of which the material world is only an image and a kind of reflection, let us take great care not to deprive ourselves of it, for this would be like wanting to substitute our unaided strength for a winch or a fire engine.

The philosophy of the last century, which will appear to posterity as one of the most shameful phases of the human mind, ignored nothing in seeking to turn us away from prayer by considering *eternal and inevitable laws*. Its favorite, I almost said its *only*, object was to separate man from God: and what better means of success had it than by weakening prayer? In actual fact, this whole philosophy was nothing but a real system of practical atheism; I have given a name to this strange disease, calling it *theophobia*, which you can see in all the philosophic works of the eighteenth century, if you look closely. No one said openly, *There is no God*, an assertion that could have led to some physical inconvenience, but they said: *"God is not there.* He is not to be found in your ideas, which originate in the senses; he is not to be found in your thoughts, which are only *converted sensations*; he is not to be found in the scourges which afflict you, for these are physical phenomena like others that are explained by known laws. He does not think of you and has done nothing for you as an individual; the world is made for the insect as for you; he does not revenge himself on you for you are too insignificant and so on." In short, the name of God could not be mentioned to this philosophy without throwing it into consternation. Even those writers of the period who stood out above the crowd and were distinguished by excellent if partial views freely denied the creation. How could divine punishments be mentioned to these men without sending them into a rage? *No physical event can have a cause superior to man*: this was their dogma. Perhaps sometimes this philosophy does not dare to state this dogma in general, but when it is a question of detail, they constantly assert it, which comes to the same thing.

I can quote to you a remarkable example of this, which is in some ways amusing although in others it is saddening. Nothing shocked these writers so much as the Flood, the greatest and most terrible judgment God has ever imposed on man, yet nothing is better established by every kind of proof capable of establishing an important fact. What then were they to do? They started by obstinately refusing to us all the water necessary to the Flood, and I recall that in my salad days my young faith was unsettled by their reasoning; but, as the fantasy has since occurred to them that the world was created by precipitation and as water is absolutely necessary to them in this remarkable operation, the lack of water no longer troubles them, and they have gone as far as us by granting freely that there was an *envelope* eight miles high around the whole surface of the globe—which is very honest. Some have even thought of calling Moses to their aid and of forcing him by the strangest distortions to testify in favor of their cosmogenetic dreams. Of course, it is well understood by them that divine intervention does not enter at all into this venture, which has nothing extraordinary in it. Thus they have admitted the total submersion of the globe at the very time fixed by this great man, which seems to them sufficient seriously to declare themselves *defenders of Revelation*, but of *God*, of *crime*, and of *punishment*, not a word. We have even been given a gentle hint *that there were no men on the earth at the time of the great flood*, which is, as you can see, very *Mosaic*. The word *flood*, having something too *theological* about it to please them, it has been suppressed in favor of *catastrophe*: so they accept the *flood*, which they need for their futile theories, but they remove *God*, who tires them. Here, it seems to me, is a very clear symptom of *theophobia*.

I honor with all my heart the numerous exceptions which console the observer and, among the very writers who have been able to sadden the true faith, I gladly make the necessary distinctions; but the general character of this philosophy is nonetheless as I have described it, and it is this philosophy which, by working ceaselessly to separate man from God, has produced in the end the despicable generation which has done or allowed what we see before our eyes. . . .

Can I think, Knight, that you are now perfectly happy about eternal and inevitable laws? Nothing is necessary except God, and nothing is less necessary than pain. All pain is a punishment, and every punishment (except the last) is inflicted for love as much as for justice.

THE KNIGHT: I am happy that my petty quibbles have brought us reflections from which I will profit, but, I pray, what did you mean by the words, *Except the last*?

THE COUNT: Look around you and you will see the acts of human justice. What does it do when it condemns a man to a punishment less than the capital? It does two things in regard to the condemned; it chastises him, which is the work of justice, but it also wants to correct him, which is the work of love. If justice could not hope that punishment will make the condemned man examine his conscience, it would almost always punish by death; but when justice is finally persuaded, either by the repetition or the extent of the crimes, that a criminal is incorrigible, love withdraws and justice pronounces an eternal punishment, because every death is eternal, for a dead man cannot cease to be dead. Without doubt, both human and divine justice punish but to correct, and every punishment, *except the last,* is a remedy: but the last is *death.* . . .

We can then contemplate divine justice in our own, as in a mirror, dull in comparison with reality yet faithful, which can reflect no images other than those it has received. We see there that the only end of punishment is to root out evil, so that the greater and more deeply rooted is the evil, the longer and more painful is the operation. But if a man has surrendered completely to evil, how can it be cut away from him? And what room does he leave for love? All true teaching, so mingling fear with consolatory ideas, warns the free being not to advance to the limit beyond which there is no limit. . . .

SIXTH DIALOGUE

THE COUNT: If ever you are called on to make a strict examination of the *Essay concerning Human Understanding,* I recommend the chapter on liberty to you. La Harpe, forgetting what he had more than once said, *that he understood only literature,* went into ecstasies over Locke's definition of liberty. *Here,* he said majestically, *here is philosophy.* He would have done better to say, *Here is incapacity demonstrated,* for Locke makes liberty consist in the power to act, whereas this purely negative word signifies only *absence of obstacles,* so that liberty is and can be only the *unimpeded will,* that is to say, *the will.* Condillac, embellishing the mediocrity of his master, said in his turn *that liberty is only the power of doing what one has not done or of not doing what one has done.* This pretty antithesis can no doubt dazzle a mind unaccustomed to this kind of discussion, but it is obvious to every educated or experienced man that Condillac here takes the result or external sign of liberty, which is physical action, for liberty itself, which is entirely moral.

Liberty is the power to do. How is this? Has not the man who is in prison and laden with chains the power to make himself guilty of all crimes without acting? He has only to will them. . . . If then liberty is not the *power to do*, it can be only the *power to will*, but the power to will is the will itself, and to ask if *the will can will* is like asking *if perception has the power to perceive, if reason has the power of reasoning*, if a circle is a circle, a triangle a triangle, in a word *if a thing in itself is a thing in itself*. Now, if you consider that even God is unable to coerce the will, since a *coerced will* is a *contradiction in terms*, you will see that the will can be moved and led only by *sympathy*—an admirable word that all the philosophers together could not have invented. However, sympathy can have no effect on the will other than increasing its vigor by making it will still further, so that sympathy could no more detract from liberty or the will than teaching of any kind could harm the understanding. The curse that weighs on unfortunate human nature is the double sympathy.

Vim sentit geminam paretque incerta duobus.[19]

The philosopher who reflects on this terrible enigma will render justice to the Stoics, who at one time predicted a fundamental Christian dogma by declaring that *only the wise man is free*. Today this is no longer a paradox but an incontestable truth of the first order. *Where the spirit of God exists, there is to be found liberty*. Whoever has not grasped these truths will forever move around the principle, like Bernouilli's curve, without even reaching it. Now, would you like to see how far Locke was from the truth on this as on so many other subjects? I pray you, listen to his splendid nonsense. He claimed *that liberty, which is one faculty, has nothing in common with the will, which is another faculty, and that it is no less absurd to ask if the human will is free than it would be to ask if a man's sleep is rapid or his virtue squared*. What do you say to that?

THE SENATOR: This indeed is going a bit too far! But would your memory be good enough to recall the demonstration of this splendid theory, for doubtless it had one?

THE COUNT: It is of a kind that could never be forgotten. Listen and you will judge for yourself.

You are going across a bridge; it collapses; at the moment you feel it giving way under your feet, the exertion of your will, if it were free would no doubt carry you to the opposite bank; but its effort is useless: the sacred laws of gravitation must be carried out in the world, and

[19] Ovid, *Metamorphoses*, VIII, 472.

you must therefore fall and perish: THEREFORE *liberty has nothing in common with the will.*[20] I hope you are convinced. . . .

Locke is perhaps the only author known who has taken the trouble to refute his whole book or to declare it useless, from the beginning, by telling us *that all our ideas come from the senses or from reflection.* But who has ever denied that certain ideas come to us from the senses? What is it Locke wants to teach us? The number of simple perceptions being nothing compared to the innumerable combinations of thought, it remains clear, from the first chapter of the second book, that the immense majority of our ideas do not come from the senses. But where then do they come from? The question is embarrassing and, in consequence, his disciples, fearing the results, no longer talk of reflection, which is very prudent from their point of view.[21]

Since Locke started his book without reflection or any deep thought on his subject, it is not surprising that he constantly went off the tracks. He had first of all put forward the argument that all our ideas come to us from the senses or from reflection. Then, spurred on by his bishop pressing him hard and perhaps also by his conscience, he reached the point of agreeing that *general ideas* (which alone make up the intelligent being) came neither from the senses nor from reflection but were *inventions* and CREATURES *of the human mind.*[22] For, according to the doctrine of this great philosopher, man *makes* general ideas *with* simple ideas, just as he *makes* a boat *with* planks, so that the most abstract general ideas are only *collections* or, as Locke, seeking as always for the coarsest expression, says, *companies of simple ideas.* . . .[23]

Here I beg you to admire the illuminating course of Locke's argument: he establishes first that all our ideas come to us from the senses or from reflection and takes this opportunity to tell us *that he understands by reflection the knowledge that the mind gains of its different operations.*[24] Then, torturing the truth, he confesses *that general ideas come neither from the senses nor from reflection but are created or,* in his ridiculous phrase, *invented by the human mind.* Now, as reflection has just been expressly excluded by Locke, it follows that the human mind *invents* general ideas *without reflection,* that is to say, *without any knowledge or examination of its own operations.* But every idea

---

[20] *Essay,* Book II, Chap. xxi, Para. 9.
[21] Condillac, *Art de penser,* Chap. 1; *Logique,* Chap. vii.
[22] *Essay,* Book II, Chap. xxii, Para. 3.
[23] *Ibid.,* Book II, Chap. xxx, Para. 2.
[24] *Ibid.,* Book II, Chap. i, Para. 4.

that does not originate in either the interaction of the mind with external objects, or the consideration of itself by the mind, necessarily appertains to the substance of the mind. There are therefore innate ideas or ideas anterior to all experience; this, it seems to me, inevitably follows, but it is not a surprising conclusion.

All the writers who have set themselves against innate ideas have found themselves led by the force of truth alone to make admissions more or less favorable to this theory. I do not except even Condillac, although he was perhaps the eighteenth century philosopher the most on guard against his conscience. But I have no desire to compare these two men of very different character, the one foolish, the other brazen. Yet what reproaches cannot rightly be leveled against Locke and how can he be exonerated from having unsettled morality in order to overthrow the theory of innate ideas without knowing what he was attacking? At the bottom of his heart he himself felt that he was rendering himself guilty; *but*, he said, excusing himself by deceiving himself, *the truth must come first*,[25] which is to say that *the truth must come before the truth*.

Perhaps the most dangerous and the most culpable of these fatal writers who will not cease to damn the last century in the eyes of posterity, the one who has used the most talent with the most composure to produce the most evil, Hume, has also told us in one of his terrible *Essays, that the truth comes before everything else, that it is a somewhat ingenuous critic who reproaches certain philosophers for the harm that their opinions can do to morality and religion, and that such injustice can only hamper the discovery of truth.*[26] But no man, at least if he does not wish to fool himself, will be misled by this dangerous sophistry. No error can be useful, just as no truth can be harmful. What is misleading on this point is, in the first place, that the error is confused with some element of truth mingled in it, an element which is, according to its nature, beneficial in spite of its association with error; and, in the second place, that the *announcement* of truth is confused with the *acceptance* of truth. Doubtless it can be imprudent to expose the truth, but it is injurious only if it is rejected, whereas error, knowledge of which can be useful only like knowledge of poisons, begins to destroy the moment it has succeeded in ingratiating itself under the mask of its divine enemy. It is thus harmful *because people*

[25] *Ibid.*, Book I, Chap. iii, Para. 24.
[26] [*A Treatise of Human Nature*, Book II, Part iii, Sec. ii.]

accept it, whereas truth can be harmful only *because people combat it*: therefore everything that is harmful in itself is false, just as everything that is useful in itself is true. Nothing is clearer to the wise. . . .

In vain does Locke, as ever troubled in his mind, seek to deceive in another way by the explicit statement he makes, "That in denying an *innate law,* he does not at all mean to deny a *natural law,* that is to say, *a law prior to all positive law.*"[27] This is, as you can see, a new conflict between conscience and obligation. In fact, what is this natural law? And if it is neither positive nor innate, what is its base? Has he given us a single argument valid against innate law that is not equally valid against natural law? *The latter,* he tells us, *can be known by the light of reason alone, without the help of positive revelation.*[28] But what then is this *light of reason*? Does it come from men? Then it is positive. Does it come from God? Then it is innate.

If Locke had had more insight or diligence or good faith, instead of saying, *A certain idea is not present in the mind of such and such a people, therefore it is not innate,* he would on the contrary have said, *Thus it is innate for every man who possesses it,* for this shows that, if the idea did not preexist, the senses would never have given birth to it, since the nation which lacks it has five senses just as much as any other; and he would have inquired into how and why such an idea could have been destroyed or distorted in such a human group. But such a fruitful notion was very remote from a man who again went so far as to hold *that a single atheist* in the world was for him a sufficient justification for denying *that the idea of God is innate in man,*[29] or, to put this another way, that a single deformed child, born, for example, without eyes, would prove that sight is not natural to man. But nothing would stop Locke. Has he not told us that the voice of conscience is no proof of innate principles, *as the claims of conscience can differ from person to person?*[30]

It is very strange that it has never been possible to show to either this grand patriarch or his sorry followers the difference between ignorance of a law and admitted mistakes in applying this law. An Indian woman sacrifices her newborn infant to the goddess Gonza and they say, *Thus there is no innate morality*; but it should still be said, *Thus it is innate,* since the idea of duty is sufficiently strong in this

[27] *Essay,* Book II, Chap. ii, Para. 13.
[28] *Ibid.*
[29] *Ibid.,* Book I, Chap. iii, Para. 8.
[30] *Ibid.,* Book I, Chap. ii, Para. 8.

unfortunate mother to make her prepared to sacrifice to her duty the most tender and powerful feeling of the human heart. Abraham formerly showed his worth by determining on this same sacrifice which he rightly believed to be divinely ordained; he echoed the Indian woman, *God has spoken, and I must close my eyes and obey.* The one, bowing before divine authority which wished only to test him, obeyed a sacred and direct command; the other, blinded by a deplorable superstition, obeys an imaginary command; but, on both sides, the fundamental idea is the same, the idea of duty carried to its highest degree. *I ought to do it*—this is the innate idea whose nature is independent of every error of application. Do, by any chance, the errors men commit every day in their calculations prove that they have no idea of number? Now, if this idea was not innate, they could never have acquired it; they would never even have been able to be mistaken, since *to be mistaken* is to deviate from some anterior and known rule. The same is true of other ideas, and, I would add, what seems to me to be clear in itself, that, if this assumption is not accepted, it becomes impossible to conceive of *man,* that is to say, *the unity of mankind* or *the human species,* or consequently any coherence relative to a given class of rational beings.

It must also be admitted that Locke's critics are on a false track when they distinguish between ideas and take *innate* ideas to be only first-order moral beliefs, which seems to make the solution of the problem depend upon the rightness of these beliefs. I do not want to imply that they do not deserve particular attention, and I can come back to this subject; but for the philosopher who looks at this question in its most general terms, there is no distinction to be made here, because there is no idea that is not innate or foreign to the senses by virtue of the universality from which it takes its shape and of the intellectual act of thinking it.

Every rational belief is founded on antecedent knowledge, for man can learn nothing except because he knows. Since syllogism and induction always start from already known principles, it must be admitted that before reaching a particular truth we must already know it in part. Take, for example, a particular triangle; of course you were ignorant of it before seeing it, yet you already knew, if not this triangle, *the* triangle or *triangularity,* and this is how from different standpoints one can know and be ignorant of the same thing. If one rejects this theory, inevitably one falls into the insoluble dilemma of Plato's Meno, and is forced to agree either that men cannot learn anything or that everything they learn is only recollection. If one refuses to accept these innate ideas, no proof is any longer possible, for there are no longer any first principles from which it can be derived. Indeed, the essence of first principles is that they are anterior, evident, primary, undemonstrable, and *causal* in relation to the conclusion; otherwise they would themselves need to be proved, would in other words cease to be first principles, and it would be necessary to admit what the school calls *infinite regression*, which is impossible. Moreover, notice that these first principles on which proofs are founded must be not only *known*, but better known than the truths uncovered by their means, for *whatever or whoever imparts something must have a greater grasp of it than the subject who receives it*. For example, just as the man we love for love of another is always less loved than the latter, in the same way every acquired truth is less clear to us than the first principle which has made it visible to us. *The light* being by nature brighter than *the lit*, one must believe not only in science but also in the scientific principle, whose character is to be at once both necessary and necessarily believed. For proof has nothing in common with arbitrary and external assertion *which denies whatever it wishes*, but derives from that profounder voice that speaks in the heart of man and has no power to contradict truth. All the sciences communicate with one another by means of these common first principles; and I beg you to understand clearly that I mean by this word *common* not what these different sciences prove but that which they use in order to reach proofs—in other words, *the idea of the universal*, which is the root of every proof, which exists before any sensory perception or process, and which is so little the result of experience that without it each experience would always be unrelated and could be repeated to eternity without the gap being bridged between it and the universal. This puppy playing before you now played in the same way yesterday and the day before. Thus it has played and played and played, but from its point of view it has not played *three times*, as is apparent to you; for if you exclude the fundamental and consequently preexisting idea of *number* by which one experience can be related to another, *one* and *one* are nothing but *this* and *that*, never *two*.

You can see, gentlemen, how pitiful Locke is with his "experience," since the truth is nothing but *an equation between human thought and the object known*, so that if the former is not natural, preexistent, and immutable, the latter necessarily fluctuates and there is no truth.

Every idea therefore is innate in relation to the universal from which it derives its form, and is moreover totally foreign to the senses by reason of the intellectual act of affirmation; for, since thought or (what is the same thing) speech belongs only to the mind, or better since they are the mind, no distinction should be made in this respect between different classes of ideas. Once man says, THIS IS, he is necessarily talking by virtue of an internal and anterior knowledge, for the senses have nothing in common with truth, which the understanding alone can attain. Since what does not pertain to the senses is foreign to the material world, it follows that there is in man a nonmaterial principle in which knowledge resides; and since the sense can receive and transmit to the mind only impressions, not only is its function, which is essentially to judge, not helped by these impressions, but rather it is hindered and confused by them. We should therefore accept, as do the greatest men, that we have concepts naturally which have not come to us through the senses, the contrary opinion offending good sense as much as religion. . . .

The day will come, and perhaps it is not far off, when Locke will be universally placed among those writers who have perpetrated the most evil among men. Yet, despite all the charges I have brought against him, I have touched on only a part of his misdeeds, and perhaps the least part. Having laid the foundations of a philosophy as false as it is dangerous, his deadly mind turned toward politics with a no less deplorable effect. He spoke about the origin of laws as badly as about the origin of ideas, and on this point he again stated principles whose effects are now apparent. These fateful seeds would perhaps have withered in the coldness of his style, but nurtured in the hothouses of Paris, they have produced the revolutionary monster which has devastated Europe. . . .

THE KNIGHT: Today, Senator, I hope you will make good your promise to say something to us about war.

THE SENATOR: I am quite ready to do so, for this is a subject on which I have thought a great deal. Ever since I began to think, war has been in my mind; this terrible subject has engrossed my thoughts, yet I have never fully plumbed its depths.

The first charge I shall level against it will no doubt astonish you, but it is for me an incontestable truth: *"Given man with his reason, sentiments, and affections, there is no way of explaining how war is humanly possible."* That is my seriously considered opinion. Somewhere La Bruyère describes this huge human absurdity with all the power you know he commands. It was many years ago that I read this fragment, yet I can recall it perfectly. He insists strongly on the folly of war; yet the more foolish, the less explicable it is.

THE KNIGHT: Yet it seems to me that one could say at the outset *that rulers order you and you must obey.*

THE SENATOR: This is not at all the case, my dear Knight, I assure you. . . . Rulers can exact effective and durable obedience only when supported by opinion, which they cannot themselves determine. In every country there are much less repellent things than war that a sovereign would never dare to command. . . . Peter the First needed all the strength of his invincible personality to get beards shaved off and to alter the style of clothing: to lead countless legions on to the battlefield, even at the time *when he was vanquished to learn how to vanquish,* he needed, like every other ruler, only to say the word. Yet there is in man, in spite of his profound degradation, an element of love that draws him to other men: compassion is as natural to him as breathing. By what strange magic is he ever ready, at the first beat of the drum, to cast off his divine character in order to set out without resistance, often even with a certain gladness which has also its peculiar character, to hack to pieces on the battlefield a brother who has never offended him and who on his side comes to inflict the selfsame wounds if he can? I could still understand a truly national war, but how many such wars have there been? Perhaps one in a thousand years. As far as the others are concerned, especially those between civilized nations who can consider their actions and know what they are doing, I confess I am puzzled. It could be said, *Glory explains everything*, but, first, only the leaders gain the glory, and, second, this only pushes back the difficulty a stage, for I then ask precisely why this extraordinary prestige surrounds war.

I have often imagined a scene in which I want you to participate. I suppose that for some good reason a stranger to our planet comes here and talks to one of us about the condition of this world. Among the strange things that are recounted to him, he is told that corruption and vices, of which he has been fully informed, in certain circumstances necessitate men dying by the hand of men, and that we restrict the right of killing within the law to the executioner and the soldier. He will also be told: "The one brings death to convicted and condemned criminals, and fortunately his executions are so rare that one of these ministers of death is sufficient for each province. As far as soldiers are concerned, there are never enough of them, because they kill without restraint and their victims are always honest men. Of these two professional killers, the soldier and the executioner, one is highly honored and always has been by all the nations who have inhabited up to now this planet to which you have come; but the other has just as generally been regarded as vile. Try to guess on which the obloquy falls."

Surely this spirit from afar would not hesitate a moment; he would heap on the executioner all the praise which you did not feel able the other day to refuse him, Count, in spite of all our prejudices, when you talked of this *gentleman*, to use Voltaire's phrase. "He is a sublime being," he would say to us, "the cornerstone of society. Since crime is part of this world's order and since it can be checked only by punishment, once deprive the world of the executioner and all order will disappear with him. Moreover, what grandeur of soul, what noble disinterestedness must necessarily be assumed to exist in a man who devotes himself to services which are no doubt worthy of respect but which are so distressing and so contrary to human nature! For, since I have lived among you, I have noticed that it hurts you to kill a chicken in cold blood. I am therefore convinced that opinion must cover him with all the honor necessary and so rightly owing to him. As for the soldier, he is on the whole an agent of cruelty and injustice. How many obviously just wars have there been? How many obviously unjust! How many individual injustices, horrors, and useless atrocities! I imagine therefore that opinion among you has very properly poured as much shame on the head of the soldier as it has thrown glory over the impartial executor of the judgments of sovereign justice."

You know the truth, gentlemen, and the extent of the spirit's mistake. In fact, the soldier and the executioner stand at the two extremes of the social scale, but in quite the opposite extremes put forward by this splendid theory. Nothing is so noble as the first, nothing so abject as the second.... The soldier is so noble that he ennobles what public opinion regards as most ignoble, since he can act as an executioner without debasing himself, provided however that he kills only his fellow soldiers and that he uses only his weapons to kill them.

THE KNIGHT: Ah, but that is important, my dear friend! Wherever, and for whatever reason you like, a soldier is ordered to execute civilian criminals, in a twinkling of an eye and without apparent reason all the glory surrounding him fades. No doubt he will still be feared, for any man who carries a good and accurate rifle in the course of his day's work merits considerable attention: but the indefinable spell of honor has been irretrievably broken. The officer is no longer anything as an officer. If he has birth or virtues, he can still be well thought of, *in spite* rather than *because* of his military rank; he ennobles his commission rather than being ennobled by it, and, if his rank provides a large income, he can be wealthy but never noble. But you said, Senator, *"Provided, however, that the soldier does not kill anyone except his fellows and that he has only the weapons of his profession to kill them."* It should be added, *and provided that it is a question of a military crime*: once it is a question of a *low* crime, it is a matter for the executioner.

THE COUNT: In fact, this is the custom. Since the ordinary courts have jurisdiction over civil crimes, soldiers guilty of such offenses are sent to them. However, if it pleased the sovereign to order otherwise, I am very far from thinking it certain that the character of the soldier would be harmed by it. But we are all three agreed on the other two conditions, and do not doubt that this character would be stained indelibly if the soldier were forced to shoot an ordinary citizen or to kill his comrade by burning or hanging....

THE SENATOR: Although the military is in itself dangerous to the well-being and the liberties of every nation, because the motto of this profession will always be more or less that of Achilles, *Jura, nego mihi nata,* nevertheless those nations most jealous of their liberties have never disagreed with the rest of mankind on the preeminence of the military profession. Antiquity thought as we do on this subject; it is one of those on which men have always been and will always be in agreement. Here then is the problem I want to pose to you, *Explain why the right innocently to spill innocent blood is regarded as most honorable by the whole of humanity.* If you look at it more closely, you will see that there is something mysterious and inexplicable about the extraordinary value men have always placed on military glory, more especially as, if we consulted only theory and human reason, we should be led to directly opposite ideas. It is then not a question of explaining the possibility of war by the glory surrounding it, but first of all of explaining this glory itself, which is not easy.

I should like to tell you of another idea on the same subject. We have been told thousands of times that, since nations are in a state of nature in regard to one another, they can settle their differences only by war. But, as I am in a mood for questions today, I will put another one, *Why has every nation remained in a state of nature toward the others without making a single attempt to break out of it?* According to the foolish doctrines on which we were succored in our youth, there was a time when men did not live in society, and this imaginary state was ridiculously called *the state of nature.* They add that men, having judiciously balanced the advantages of these two states, decided on that which we know—

THE COUNT: Allow me to interrupt you for a moment to tell you of a thought that comes to my mind against this doctrine you have so rightly called foolish. The savage holds so strongly to his most brutal habits that nothing can tear him away from them. You have no doubt seen, at the head of the *Discourse on the Inequality of Conditions,* the engraving based on an anecdote, true or false, of the Hottentot who returns to his fellows. Rousseau little suspected that this frontispiece was a powerful argument against the book. The savage sees our arts, laws, sciences, wealth, taste, pleasures of every kind, and above all our superiority, from which he cannot hide yet which could arouse some ambition in those capable of it; but all this does not even tempt him, and continually *he returns to his fellows.* If then the savage of our own time, being aware of the two states and being able to compare them every day in certain countries, remains resolutely in his own, how can it be supposed that the primitive savage emerged from his state by means of deliberation and moved into another state of which he had no knowledge? Hence society is as old as man, and the savage is and can be nothing but a degraded and punished man. In truth, it seems to me that nothing is clearer to common sense unclouded by sophistry.

THE SENATOR: *You are preaching to the converted,* as the saying goes, but I thank you for your argument; one can never have too many weapons against error. But to return to what I was saying just now: If man passed *from the state of nature,* in the common usage of the term, into a civilized state either by deliberation or *by chance* (I am still speaking the language of the madmen), why have nations not had as much foresight or good fortune as individuals; and how is it that they have never agreed on an international society to end quarrels between nations, as they have agreed on a national sovereignty to end those between individuals? It is easy to ridicule *the impracticable peace of the Abbé de Saint-Pierre* (for I agree that it is impracticable), but I would ask why this is so, why nations have not been able to raise themselves to a social state like individuals; above all, how it is that an enlightened Europe has never attempted anything of this kind.

I would put a particular question to the faithful with still more confidence. How is it that God, the author of the society of individuals, allowed it to happen that man, his cherished creation with the divine attribute of perfectibility, has never even attempted to create a society of nations? Every possible argument to show that such a society is impossible militates in the same way against the society of individuals. The argument drawn primarily from the claim that such an extensive territory would be too comprehensive to be practical has no force, for it is not true that it would have to cover the whole world. Nations are already distinguished and divided by rivers, seas, mountains, creeds, and above all by more or less distinct languages. In practice it would be a great step in itself toward the good of humanity if only a certain number of nations agreed to move into *a state of civilization.* It might be said that the other nations will attack them. Well, what of it? They would still be more peaceful amongst themselves and stronger in regard to outsiders, which is enough. There is no need for absolute perfection; an approach to it would be a lot, and I cannot persuade myself that nothing of this kind would ever have been tried if it were not for a terrible and mysterious law demanding human blood.

THE COUNT: You look on it as an undeniable fact that this *civilization of nations* has never been attempted, yet in truth it has often and even stubbornly been tried—true, without it being known what was being attempted (which indeed was a factor working for its success), and in fact has come very close to succeeding, at least so far as the imperfection of our nature allows. But men made mistakes, mistaking one thing for another, and everything failed, apparently because of that mysterious and terrible law of which you spoke.

THE SENATOR: I would put several questions to you if I was not afraid of losing the thread of my ideas. I ask you then to look at a fact well worthy of your attention. It is that the profession of arms does not in the least tend to degrade or to make wild and hard at least those who follow it, as we might believe or fear if experience did not teach us: on the contrary, it tends to improve them. The most honest man is commonly the honest soldier, and, as I said not long ago, I have always for my own part had a particular respect for military good sense. I infinitely prefer it to the long circumlocutions of men of affairs. In ordinary human relationships, soldiers are often more pleasant, more relaxed and, it seems to me, often even more civil than other men. Amid political upheavals, they generally act as intrepid defenders of ancient beliefs, and the most dazzling sophistries are almost always wrecked on their uprightness. They willingly turn their attention to useful works and knowledge, political economy, for example. Perhaps the only work antiquity has left us on this subject is by a soldier, Xenophon, and the first recorded French work on the same subject is also by a soldier, Marshal de Vauban. In them religion combines with honor in a remarkable way; and even when religion reproaches them gravely for their conduct they will not refuse it their sword if it needs it. Much is said about *the licence of camps*; no doubt it is great, but usually the soldier does not find these vices in his camps; he carries them there. A moral and austere people always make excellent soldiers, frightening only on the battlefield. Virtue, even piety, easily allies itself with military courage, and, far from enfeebling the warrior, it exalts him. . . . Not only does the profession of arms generally ally itself very well with morality, but what is quite extraordinary is that it does not at all weaken those gentle virtues which seem the most opposed to military attitudes. The gentlest of men love war, desire war, and go to war with passion. At the first call, this likable young man here, brought up with a horror of violence and blood, rushes from his father's house, his weapons in his hand, to seek on the battlefield what he calls *the enemy* without yet knowing what an *enemy* is. Yesterday he would have fainted if he had accidentally killed his sister's canary; tomorrow you will see him climb a pile of corpses *in order to see further*, as Charron put it. The blood flowing on all sides serves only to inspire him to spill his own and that of others. He gradually inflames himself until he reaches *an enthusiasm for carnage*.

THE KNIGHT: You do not exaggerate. Before I was twenty-five, I had seen *the enthusiasm for carnage* three times. I have experienced it myself and I especially remember a terrible moment when I would have put an entire army to the sword if I had been able.

THE SENATOR: But if, at this moment, someone asked you to catch a white dove as cold-bloodedly as a cook, then—

THE KNIGHT: For shame, you make me sick at heart!

THE SENATOR: This is precisely what I was just talking about. The terrifying sight of carnage does not harden the warrior. Amid the blood he spills, he is humane, just as the wife is chaste in the transports of love. Once he has put back the sword into its scabbard, saintly humanity regains its sway, and perhaps the highest and most generous feelings are found among soldiers. . . .

In short, gentlemen, the functions of the soldier are terrible, but they must result from a great law of the spiritual world, and no one should be astonished that every nation in the world is united in seeing in this scourge something still more peculiarly divine than in others. You can well believe that there is a good and profound reason for the title LORD OF HOSTS being found on every page of the Holy Scriptures. Guilty, and unhappy because we are guilty, we ourselves make necessary all physical evils, but above all war. Usually and very naturally, men lay the blame on their rulers: Horace wrote playfully, "By the madness of kings nations are punished." But J. B. Rousseau said more seriously and philosophically:

> "The wrath of kings brings the earth to arms,
> The wrath of Heaven brings kings to arms."

Notice, moreover, that this law of war, terrible in itself, is yet only a clause in the general law that hangs over the world.

In the immense sphere of living things, the obvious rule is violence, a kind of inevitable frenzy which arms all things *in mutua funera*. Once you leave the world of insensible substances, you find the decree of violent death written on the very frontiers of life. Even in the vegetable kingdom, this law can be perceived: from the huge catalpa to the smallest of grasses, how many plants *die* and how many are *killed*! But once you enter the animal kingdom, the law suddenly becomes frighteningly obvious. A power at once hidden and palpable appears constantly occupied in bringing to light the principle of life by violent means. In each great division of the animal world, it has chosen a certain number of animals charged with devouring the others; so there are insects of prey, reptiles of prey, birds of prey, fish of prey, and quadrupeds of prey. There is not an instant of time when some living creature is not devoured by another.

Above all these numerous animal species is placed man, whose destructive hand spares no living thing; he kills to eat, he kills for clothing, he kills for adornment, he kills to attack, he kills to defend himself, he kills for instruction, he kills for amusement, he kills for killing's sake: a proud and terrible king, he needs everything, and nothing can withstand him. He knows how many barrels of oil he can get from the head of a shark or a whale; in his museums, he mounts with his sharp pins elegant butterflies he has caught in flight on the top of Mount Blanc or Chimborazo; he stuffs the crocodile and embalms the hummingbird; on his command, the rattlesnake dies in preserving fluids to keep it intact for a long line of observers. The horse carrying its master to the tiger hunt struts about covered by the skin of this same animal. At one and the same time, man takes from the lamb its entrails for harp strings, from the whale its bones to stiffen the corsets of the young girl, from the wolf its most murderous tooth to polish frivolous manufactures, from the elephant its tusks to make a child's toy: his dining table is covered with corpses. The philosopher can even discern how this permanent carnage is provided for and ordained in the whole scheme of things. But without doubt this law will not stop at man. Yet what being is to destroy him who destroys all else? Man! It is man himself who is charged with butchering man.

But how is he to accomplish this law who is a moral and merciful being, who is born to love, who cries for others as for himself, who finds pleasure in weeping to the extent of creating fictions to make himself weep, to whom finally it has been said that *whoever sheds blood unjustly will redeem it with the last drop of his own?*[31] It is war that accomplishes this decree. Do you not hear the earth itself demanding and crying out for blood? The blood of animals does not satisfy it, nor even that of criminals spilled by the sword of the law. If human justice struck them all, there would be no war; but it can catch up with only a small number of them, and often it even spares them without suspecting that this cruel humanity contributes to the necessity for war, especially if at the same time another no less stupid and dangerous blindness works to diminish atonement among men. The earth did not cry in vain: war breaks out. Man, seized suddenly by a divine fury foreign to both hatred and anger, goes to the battlefield without knowing what he intends or even what he is doing. How can this dreadful enigma be explained? Nothing could be more contrary to his nature, yet nothing is less repugnant to him: he undertakes with enthusiasm what he holds in horror. Have you never noticed that no one ever disobeys on the field of death? They might well slaughter a Nerva or a Henry IV, but they will never say, even to the most abominable tyrant or the most flagrant butcher of human flesh, *We no longer want to follow you.* A revolt on the battlefield, an agreement to unite to repudiate a tyrant is something I cannot remember. Nothing resists, nothing can resist the force that drags man into conflict; an innocent murderer, a passive instrument in a formidable hand, *he plunges unseeing into the abyss he himself has dug; he dies without suspecting that it is he himself who has brought about his death.*[32]

Thus is worked out, from maggots up to man, the universal law of the violent destruction of living beings. The whole earth, continually steeped in blood, is nothing but an immense altar on which every living thing must be sacrificed without end, without restraint, without respite until the consummation of the world, the extinction of evil, the death of death.[33]

But the curse must be aimed most directly and obviously at man: the avenging angel circles like the sun around this unhappy globe and lets one nation breathe only to strike at others. But when crimes, especially those of a particular kind, accumulate to a certain point, the angel relentlessly quickens his tireless flight. Like a rapidly turned torch, his immense speed allows him to be present at all points on his

[31] Genesis 9:6.
[32] Psalm 9:16.
[33] I Corinthians 15:26.

huge orbit at the same time. He strikes every nation on earth at the same moment. At other times, minister of an unerring and infallible vengeance, he turns against particular nations and bathes them in blood. Do not expect them to make any effort to escape or abridge their sentence. It is as if these sinful nations, enlightened by conscience, were asking for punishment and accepting it in order to find expiation in it. So long as they have blood left, they will come forward to offer it, and soon *golden youth* will grow used to telling of devastating wars caused by their fathers' crimes.

War is thus divine in itself, since it is a law of the world.

War is divine through its consequences of a supernatural nature which are as much general as particular, consequences little known because they are little sought but which are nonetheless indisputable. Who could doubt the benefits that death in war brings? And who could believe that the victims of this dreadful judgment have shed their blood in vain? But this is not the time to insist on this kind of question; our age is not yet ready to concern itself with it. Let us leave it to its physics and for our own part keep our eyes fixed firmly to that invisible world which will explain everything.

War is divine in the mysterious glory that surrounds it and in the no less inexplicable attraction that draws us to it.

War is divine in the protection granted to the great leaders, even the most daring, who are rarely struck down in battle, and only when their renown can no longer be increased and when their mission is completed.

War is divine by the manner in which it breaks out. I do not want to excuse anyone inopportunely, but how many of those who are regarded as the immediate authors of wars are themselves carried along by circumstances! At the exact moment brought about by men and prescribed by justice, God comes forward to exact vengeance for the iniquity committed by the inhabitants of this world against him....

War is divine in its results which cannot be predicted by human reason, for they can be quite different for two different nations, although the war seems to have affected both equally. There are wars that degrade nations, and degrade them for centuries; others exalt them, improve them in all kinds of ways and, what is more extraordinary, very quickly replace momentary losses by a rapid increase in population. History often shows us the sight of a population growing in wealth and numbers during the most murderous conflicts; but there are vicious wars, accursed wars, more easily recognized by conscience than by reason: nations are mortally wounded by them, both in their power and in their character; then you can see the victor himself degraded, impoverished, and miserable among his victory laurels, whereas you will find that in the vanquished land, in a very short time, there is not an unused workshop or plow.

War is divine through the indefinable power that determines success in it. Surely you were not thinking, my dear Knight, when you repeated the other day the well-known saying that *God is always on the side of the big battalions.* I will never believe that it was really said by the great man to whom it is attributed;[34] perhaps he put forward this maxim as a jest, or seriously in a limited and very true sense, for God in his providential temporal government does not depart (except in the case of miracles) from the general laws he has laid down for all time. Thus, as two men are stronger than one, so a hundred thousand must be more powerful and effective than fifty thousand. When we ask God for victory, it would be foolish to be asking him to depart from the general laws of the world, but these laws combine in a thousand different ways and can bring victory in a manner which cannot be foreseen. Doubtless three men are stronger than one: the general proposition cannot be contested; but one clever man can profit from certain circumstances, and one Horatius will kill three Curiatii. *A body with the greater mass has the greater momentum*: this is true if speeds are equal, but three parts of mass and two of speed are equivalent to three of speed and two of mass. In the same way, an army of forty thousand men is physically inferior to another of sixty thousand, but, if the former has more courage, experience, and discipline, it can beat the latter, for it is more effective with fewer numbers. This we can witness on every page of history. Wars, moreover, always suppose a certain equality, otherwise there would be no wars. I have never read of the Republic of Ragusa declaring war on the sultans, nor that of Geneva on the kings of France. There is always a certain balance in the political world and (if certain rare, precise, and limited cases are excepted) man cannot upset it at will. This is why coalitions are so difficult. If they were not, since politics is little governed by justice, there would be continual combinations to destroy a particular power; but such projects seldom succeed, and history shows even the weakest power escaping from them with an astonishing ease.

[34] Turenne.

When an overdominant power frightens the world, men are angry that no means have been found of checking it, and bitter reproaches are leveled against the selfishness and immorality of the rulers who are preventing an alliance to ward off the common danger. This was the cry heard at the height of Louis XIV's power. But at bottom these complaints are not valid. A coalition between several powers, based on a pure and disinterested morality, would be a miracle. God, who is not obliged to do miracles and never does one needlessly, uses two very simple means to restore the balance: sometimes the giant kills itself; sometimes a much weaker power throws in its path some small obstacle, which yet then grows in some unaccountable way and becomes insurmountable, just as a small branch, stuck in the current of a river, can in the end cause a blockage which diverts its course.

Starting, then, from this hypothesis of a balance, ever present at least in a rough form either because the belligerent powers are equal or because the weakest have allies, how many unforeseen circumstances can disrupt the balance and bring frustration or success to the greatest plans in spite of every prudential calculation! . . . Moreover, if you take a more general look at the role played by moral power in war, you will agree that nowhere does the divine hand make itself felt more acutely to man. It might be said that this is a *department*, if you will allow me the phrase, whose direction Providence has reserved to itself and in which it has left to man the ability to act only in a well-nigh mechanical manner, since success here depends almost entirely on something he can least control. At no time other than in war is he warned more often and more sharply of his own feebleness and of the inexorable power ruling all things. It is opinion that loses and wins battles. *The fearless Spartan used to sacrifice from fear* (Rousseau somewhere expresses astonishment at this, I don't know why); Alexander also sacrificed from fear before the Battle of Arbela. Certainly these people were quite right and, to correct this sensible devotion, it is enough to pray *to God that he deigns not to send fear to us.* Fear! Charles V made great fun of that epitaph he read in passing, *Here lies one who never felt fear.* And what man never has felt fear in his life? Who has never had occasion to realize, both in himself, in those around him and in history, the way in which men can be overcome by this passion, which often seems to have the more sway over us the fewer the reasonable causes for it. *Let us then pray*, Knight, *for it is to you that I should like to address this discourse,* since you have called up these reflections; let us pray to God that he keeps us and our friends from fear, which is within his power and which can ruin in an instant the most splendid military ventures.

And do not be frightened by this word *fear*, for if you take it in its strictest sense you can say that the experience it expresses is rare and that it is shameful to be afraid of it. There is a womanish fear reflected in panicky flight, and this it is proper, even necessary, to dismiss entirely, although it is not a completely unknown sight. But there is another very much more terrible fear that descends on the most masculine heart, freezes it, and persuades it that it is beaten. This is the appalling scourge constantly hanging over armies. I put this question one day to a soldier of the highest rank whom you both know. *Tell me, General, what is a lost battle? I have never been able to understand this.* After a moment's silence, he answered, *I do not know.* After another pause he added, *It is a battle one thinks one has lost.* Nothing could be truer. One man fighting with another is beaten when he is killed or overthrown while the other is standing. It is not so with two armies; the one cannot be killed while the other remains on its feet. The balance of strength swings one way, then the other, as does the number of deaths, and, especially since the invention of gunpowder gave more equality in the means of destruction, a battle is no longer lost materially, that is to say, because there are more dead on one side than on the other. It was Frederick II, no mean thinker on this question, who said, *To win is to advance.* But who is the person who advances? It is he whose conscience and bearing make the other fall back. Do you recall, Count, that young soldier of your own acquaintance who one day portrayed to you in one of his letters *that solemn moment when, without knowing why, an army feels itself carried forward, as if it was sliding down an inclined plane.* I remember that you were struck by this phrase which indeed describes exactly the crucial moment; but this moment is far from a matter of reflection. Notice particularly that it is by no means a question of numbers. Has the soldier *who slides forward* counted the dead? Opinion is so powerful in war that it can alter the nature of the same event and give it two different names, for no reason other than its own whim. A general throws his men between two enemy armies and he writes to his king, *I have split him, he has lost.* His opponent writes to his king, *He has put himself between two fires, he is lost.* Which of the two is mistaken? Whoever is seized by *the cold goddess.* Assuming that all things, especially size, are at least approximately equal, the only difference between the two positions is a purely moral one. . . . It is imagination that loses battles.

It is not even by any means always on the day they are fought that it is known whether they have been lost or won; it is on the next day, even two or three days afterward. Men talk a great deal about battles in ignorance of what they are. There is an especial tendency to consider them as happening on a particular spot, whereas they stretch over five or six miles. One is asked seriously, *How is it that you do not know what happened in this battle when you were there?* Whereas precisely the opposite could very often be said. Does the man on the right flank know what is happening on the left? Does he even know what is happening two paces from him?

I can very well imagine one of these frightful scenes. On a vast field covered with all the apparatus of carnage and seeming to shudder beneath the feet of men and horses, amid the fire and the whirling smoke, dazed and befuddled by the din of firearms and cannons, by voices that command, howl, or die away, surrounded by dead, dying, and mutilated corpses, possessed in turn by fear, hope, anger, by five or six different passions, what happens to a man? What does he see? What does he know after a few hours? What can he know about himself and others? Among this host of fighting men who have battled the whole day, there is often not a single one, not even the general, who knows who the victor is. I need only cite modern battles to you, famous battles whose memory will never fade, battles which have changed the face of Europe, and which have been lost only because such and such a man has believed they were lost; whereas, in the same circumstances and with the same losses, another general would have had the *Te Deum* sung in his country and forced history to say quite the opposite of what it will say. But, I ask you, what age has seen moral power play a more astonishing role in war than our own? Is not what we have seen for the last twenty years truly magical? Without doubt it behoves men of this epoch to cry out:

"And what age has ever been more fertile in miracles?" . . .

EIGHTH DIALOGUE

THE KNIGHT: Our conversations started by an examination of the great and eternal complaint constantly being raised against the success of crime and the misfortune of virtue; and we have been wholly convinced that nothing in the world has less justification than this complaint and that, even for those who do not believe in another life, the path of virtue is the best way of securing the highest chance of temporal happiness. What has been said about punishment, illness, and remorse does not leave the slightest doubt on this point. I have paid particular attention to two fundamental axioms; namely, in the first place, *that no man is punished because he is just, but always because he is a man,* so that it is false that virtue suffers in this world; it is human nature that suffers and it always deserves it: and, second, *that the greatest temporal happiness is not and cannot be promised to the virtuous man but to virtue.* In fact it is enough to make the dispensation visible and irreproachable even in this world that the greatest volume of happiness goes to the greatest volume of virtues in general; and, given man as he is, our reason cannot even envisage another order of things which would have any appearance of rationality and justice. But, as there is no such thing as a just man, there is no one who has the right to refuse to accept readily his share of human miseries, since he is necessarily guilty or has guilty blood; which led us to a full examination of the whole theory of *original sin,* which is unhappily that of human nature. We have seen in savage tribes a pale image of the original crime; and, since man is only a talking animal, the degradation of language appears to us, not as the sign of human degradation, but as this degradation itself; which gave rise to several reflections on languages and on the origins of speech and ideas. These points cleared up, prayer naturally presented itself to us as a supplement to everything that had been said, since it is a remedy given to man to restrict the ravages of evil by perfecting himself, and since he should lay the blame only on his own defects if he refuses to make use of this remedy.

We have considered the great objection raised against this word *prayer* by a foolish or guilty philosophy which, seeing physical pain as nothing but the inevitable result of the eternal laws of nature, persists in maintaining that for that very reason it could not be affected in the least by prayer. This fatal piece of sophistry has been discussed and countered in the greatest detail. The scourges which strike us, and which are very rightly called *scourges of Heaven,* seemed to us *laws of nature* in precisely the same way as punishments are *laws of society,* and are consequently only secondarily necessary, which should stimulate rather than discourage our prayer. Doubtless in this connection we could have contented ourselves with general ideas and lumped all these kinds of calamity together; however, we allowed the conversation to roam a little over this sad field, and war in particular occupied our attention. I assure you that, of all our digressions, this is the one that has held me most, for you have made me see the scourge of war from a point of view totally new to me, and I expect to think again on this matter with all my might—

THE SENATOR: Excuse me if I interrupt, Knight, but before leaving the interesting discussion on the sufferings of the just completely, I should like just to put to you one or two ideas which I believe to be well founded and which, to my mind, can make the temporal afflictions of this life appear as one of the greatest and most natural answers to all the objections raised on this point to divine justice. The just man, as a man, is subject to all the ills that threaten humanity and, precisely because he is submitted to them only as a man, he has no rightful grievance; you have observed this and nothing is clearer. But you have also observed, what unfortunately has no need of proof, that there is no such thing as a *just man* in the full rigor of the term; and it follows that every man has something to expiate. Now, if the just man (so far as he is possible) accepts the sufferings due to his being a man, and if divine justice in its turn accepts his acceptance, I think nothing could be more fortunate for him, nor so evidently just.

Moreover, I believe, in my soul and conscience, that if man could live in this world free from every kind of misfortune, he would end by degenerating to the point of forgetting completely all spiritual matters and God himself. In such a situation, how could he be interested in a superior order, seeing that, even in the world we actually inhabit, the miseries overwhelming us cannot disenchant us with the deceptive charms of this unhappy life?

THE KNIGHT: Perhaps I am wrong, but it seems to me that nothing could be more unfortunate than a man who had never experienced misfortune, for such a man could never be sure of himself or know his own worth. For the virtuous man, sufferings are what battles are for the soldier; they improve him and add to his worth. Does the brave soldier ever complain at being chosen always for the most hazardous expeditions? On the contrary, he seeks them out and glories in them; for him, sufferings are a job and death an adventure. Let the poltroon spend his life in frivolity as much as he likes, but let him not bemuse us with his impertinences about the unhappiness of those who do not resemble him. The comparison seems to me perfectly fair. If the brave man thanks the general who sends him to the assault, why should he not thank the God who imposes sufferings on him in the same way? I do not know how it comes about, but it is nevertheless certain that man gains in stature by voluntary suffering and that general opinion itself thinks the more of him for it. I have often noticed in regard to religious asceticism that the very vice that makes game of it cannot prevent itself from rendering homage to it. Has any libertine ever discovered a rich courtesan, who sleeps on feathers at midnight, happier than the austere Carmelite, who rises and prays for us at the same hour? But always I return to what you have so rightly observed, *that there is no such thing as a just man.* Thus it is by a special act of mercy that God punishes in this world rather than punishing much more severely in the next.

You should know, gentlemen, that there is nothing in which I believe more firmly than in purgatory. Why are sufferings not always proportionate to crimes? It strikes me especially that the new reasoners who have denied everlasting punishment make a strange blunder if they do not expressly admit purgatory, for, I ask you, whom can these people persuade that Robespierre's soul goes from the scaffold to God's arms like that of Louis XVI? Yet this view is not so uncommon as one might think. I have spent several years since my hegira in different parts of Germany where the doctors of law no longer want either hell or purgatory. Nothing could be more absurd. Whoever thought of having a soldier shot because he had stolen a clay pipe from a barrack room? Yet this pipe must not be stolen with impunity; the thief must be *purged* of his theft before he can take his place in line with his honest fellows. . . . Now, I claim that purgatory is a dogma of good sense; as every sin must be expiated in this world or the next, it follows that the afflictions visited by divine justice on men are a real benefit, since these punishments, when we have the wisdom to accept them, are, so to speak, *deducted* from those of the future. I should add that they are a manifest sign of love, for this anticipation or commutation of the punishment obviously excludes an eternal penalty. Whoever has not suffered in this world cannot be certain of anything, and the less he has suffered, the less sure he is. But I do not see what he can fear or, to put it more precisely, what he can *allow himself to fear* who has suffered without complaint.

THE COUNT: You have argued very soundly, Knight. . . . But I beg you to be on your guard against a slight confusion of ideas. There is no problem about the glory attached to the virtue that bears dangers, privations, and suffering tranquilly, for everyone is in agreement about this: the question is to know why it has pleased God to make this excellence necessary. You will find blasphemous and even simply facile men inclined to tell you *that God would have done much better to exempt virtue from this sort of glory.* . . . Even while putting this consideration to one side, you, Senator, have very properly recalled that every man suffers because he is a man, because he would be God if he did not suffer, and, because those who ask for a man beyond grief ask for another world. You added something no less indisputable when you said that, as no man is wholly righteous, that is to say, free from present sin (if saints, properly understood, are excepted, and they are very rare), God is really merciful to the guilty by punishing them in this world. . . .

The righteous, in suffering voluntarily, make amends not only for themselves but for sinners by way of substitution.

This is one of the greatest and most important truths of the spiritual order, but, to treat it fully, I should need more time than remains to me today. Let me then postpone the discussion until tomorrow and let me devote the remaining time this evening to developing one or two ideas that have struck me on this same subject.

It is said that *reason alone cannot explain the success of the wicked and the sufferings of the righteous in this world.* Which doubtless means *that there is in the temporal order an injustice which violates the justice of God,* otherwise the objection would have no sense. Now, as this objection can be heard from an atheist or a theist, I shall take to begin with the case of the atheist to avoid all confusion. You can see the intention of this on the part of one of these atheists by faith and profession.

I do not know if the unfortunate Hume himself knew what he was saying when he remarked so criminally, and even, with all his genius, so foolishly, *that it is impossible to justify the character of the Divinity.* To justify the character of an unknown being!

Again, what is the meaning of this? It seems to me that it all boils down to this reasoning—God is unjust; therefore he does not exist. How curious! This is as good as the Spinoza of Voltaire who said to God, *Just between ourselves I believe that you do not exist.* The unbeliever must therefore turn round and say *that the existence of evil is an argument against the existence of God, for, if God existed, this evil, which is an injustice, would not exist.* But then these gentlemen know that the God who does not exist *is just by nature!* They know the attributes of a chimerical being, and are ready to tell us to the last detail how God would be made if by chance there was one. In truth, there could be no more well-seasoned folly. If one could laugh on such a sad subject, who could refrain on hearing men, who have surely a head on their shoulders like us, argue against God using the very idea he has given to them of himself, without their thinking that this idea alone proves the existence of God, since one cannot have an idea of something that does not exist? . . . Man can conceive only what is; thus the atheist, to deny God, assumes him.

Moreover, gentlemen, all this is only a kind of preface to a favorite idea I should like to impart to you. Let me admit the foolish supposition of a hypothetical God, and admit further that the laws of the universe can be unjust or cruel in respect to us without their having a cogitative author: all this is the height of nonsense, but what follows from it against the existence of God? Nothing at all. A mind can prove itself to the mind only by means of proportionality. All other considerations can relate only to certain properties or qualities of the thinking subject, which have nothing in common with the basic question of existence.

Proportionality, gentlemen, *proportionality!* Or order and symmetry, for order is nothing but *deliberate proportionality,* and symmetry nothing but *recognized and compared order.*

I pray you, tell me if, when Nero formerly lighted his gardens with torches each of which enclosed and burned a living man, the alignment of these horrible torches did not prove to the onlooker an ordering intelligence just as much as the peaceable illuminations put on yesterday for the Queen Mother's name day? If the plague recurred each year during July, this pretty cycle would be just as regular as the return of harvest time. Let us start, then, by seeing if there is *proportionality* in the world, only then to seek *if* and *why* man is treated well or badly in this same world; this is a different question that can be looked at some other time and that has nothing to do with the first.

Proportionality is the obvious barrier between brute beasts and ourselves; in the spiritual as in the physical order, the use of fire distinguishes us from them in a sharp and unmistakable manner. God has given us proportionality, and it is by proportionality that he proves himself to us, as it is by proportionality that man proves himself to his fellows. Remove proportionality and you remove the arts, sciences, speech, and in consequence intelligence. Bring it back and with it reappear those two graces, harmony and beauty; *cries* become *songs*, noise receives *rhythm*, movements are *dances*, blind force is called *dynamics*, and doodles are *shapes*. A clear proof of this truth is that in languages (at least in those I know, and I believe the same is true in those I do not) the same words express the ideas of proportionality and of thought. . . .

Like beauty, intelligence takes pleasure in contemplating itself: the mirror of intelligence is proportionality. From this arises the liking we all have for symmetry, for every intelligent being likes on every side to recognize and find a place for its manifestation, which is *order*. Why are soldiers more pleasing to the eye in uniform than in mufti? Why would we rather see them marching in line than straggling? Why must the trees in our gardens, the dishes on our tables, the furniture in our houses be placed symmetrically to please us? Why do rhymes, meters, refrains, time, and rhythm delight us in music and poetry? Can it ever be imagined that there is, for example, any intrinsic beauty in rhyming couplets? This form and so many others can please us only because the intelligence takes pleasure in everything that proves intelligence and because its principal manifestation is proportionality. Thus it rejoices wherever it recognizes itself, and the pleasure symmetry gives us cannot have any other cause. But let us disregard this pleasure and examine only the thing in itself. Just as the words I am now speaking prove to you the existence of the speaker, and if they were written, would in the same way prove it to all those who read these words arranged according to the laws of syntax, so all created beings prove by their *syntax* the existence of a supreme writer who communicates with us by these symbols. Indeed, all these beings are letters whose combination forms a discourse proving God, that is to say, the intelligence that gives it: for there can be no discourse without *a talking soul*, or writing without a writer, unless one wants to hold that the rough curve I draw on paper with compasses adequately proves an intelligence that has drawn it while a similar curve described by a planet proves nothing, or that an achromatic telescope fully proves the existence of *Dollond* and of *Ramsden* while the eye, of which this wonderful instrument is only a gross imitation, does not prove in any way the existence of a supreme artist or an intention to prevent optical aberration! . . . Perhaps it will be said that *this is chance*: what nonsense! Some desperate madmen go about it in another way: they say, and I have heard this, *that it is a law of nature*. But what is a law? Is it the will of a legislator? In this case they are saying the same as we are. Is it the purely mechanical result of certain elements set going in a certain way? Then, as these elements must be set in order and work in some unvarying manner to produce a general and invariable order, the question comes up again, and it is found that, in place of one proof of order and the intelligence that has produced it, there are two; as if several dice thrown a great number of times all always show sixes, intelligence is proved by unvarying proportionality which is the effect, and the internal travail of the creator, which is the cause.

In a certain town excited by philosophic ferment, I have had reason to notice a curious fact: it is that the sight of order, of symmetry, and in consequence of proportionality and intelligence struck certain men, whom I remember clearly, too sharply for them to escape pangs of conscience, and they invented an ingenious subterfuge of which they made the greatest use. They began to maintain that it is impossible to recognize *intention* unless one knows *the purpose of the intention*. You cannot imagine how strongly they held to this idea, so attractive to them since it freed them from the common sense tormenting them. They made the study of intentions into a matter of the first importance, a kind of *arcanum* involving, according to them, profound knowledge and immense labors. I have heard them say, in talking of a great scientist who had said something of this sort, *He dares to inquire even into final causes* (this is what they call intentions). What a splendid effort! Another time they warned us *to take great care not to mistake an effect for an intention,* which would indeed be very dangerous as you can see, for if you come to the conclusion that God interferes in an automatic process, or that he has a certain intention whereas he formerly had another, what serious consequences would follow from such an error! . . . But, sooner or later, every argument comes back to their great maxim, that the *intention* cannot be proved so long as the *purpose of the intention* has not been proved. Yet I can imagine no grosser sophistry. How is it not seen that there can be no symmetry without purpose, since the symmetry itself is a *purpose* of the maker of symmetry? . . . Thus having no need of *a purpose* to support our conclusion, we need not reply to the sophist who asks us, *What purpose?* I have a canal cut around my country house: someone says, *It is to preserve fish;* someone else, *It is as a protection against thieves*; finally a third, *It is to drain and reclaim the land.* All of them could be mistaken, but he would certainly be right who restricted himself to saying, *He has had it cut for ends known to himself.* . . .

These philosophers talk of *disorder* in the world; but what is *disorder?* It is obviously a departure from *order.* Thus one cannot object to *disorder* without admitting a previous *order* and consequently intelligence. . . .

You see now the essence of the well-known argument, *Either God could prevent the evil we see and was deficient in kindness; or, wishing to prevent it, he could not and was deficient in power.* My God, what does this mean? It is not a question of either omnipotence or omnibenevolence, but only of *existence* and *power.* I well realize that God cannot change the natures of things, but I know only an infinitesimal part of their natures, so that I am ignorant of an infinitely large number of things that God cannot do, without ceasing because of that to be omnipotent. I do not know what is possible or what is impossible. In my lifetime, I have studied only proportionality; I believe only in proportionality; it is the mark, the voice, the speech of intelligence, and, since it is everywhere, I see it everywhere.

But let us leave the atheists, who fortunately are very few in number in the world, and take issue again with theism. I want to show myself just as obliging to the theist as I have been to the atheist, so he will not take it amiss if I start by asking him what an injustice is. If he does not concede to me that *it is an act that violates a law,* the word no longer has any meaning; and if he does not concede to me that *law is the will of a legislator, manifested to his subjects to be their rule of conduct*, I will understand the word *law* no better than the word *injustice*. Now I can understand how a human law can be *unjust* when it violates a divine or revealed or innate law. But the legislator of the universe is God. What, then, is an injustice of God in regard to men? Is there by any chance some common legislator above God who prescribes to him the way in which he should act toward men? And who will be the judge between this being and ourselves? If the theist believes that the idea of God does not involve the notion of a justice similar to ours, what is his complaint? He does not know what he is saying. But if, on the contrary, he believes God to be just according to our lights, while still complaining of the injustices he sees in our situation, he makes, without knowing it, a shocking contradiction, that is to say, *the injustice of a just God. A certain order of things is unjust; therefore it cannot take place under the rule of a just God*: this argument is only an error in the mouth of an atheist, but from a theist it is an absurdity. Once God is admitted, and once his justice is admitted as a necessary attribute of divinity, the theist cannot retrace his steps without talking nonsense, and he must say on the contrary, *A certain order of things takes place under the rule of an essentially just God: thus this order of things is just for reasons of which we are ignorant*, explaining the order of things by the attributes instead of foolishly condemning the attributes because of the order of things.

But I shall even accept from this imaginary theist the no less culpable and foolish proposition *that there is no way of justifying the character of the Divinity.*

What practical conclusion are we to draw from this? For this is the most important question. Allow me, I pray you, to set up this impressive argument: *God is unjust, cruel, pitiless; God takes pleasure in the unhappiness of his creatures; therefore*—here I pay attention to the grumblers—*therefore* apparently *there is no need to pray to him.* On the contrary, gentlemen, and nothing is more obvious, *therefore it is necessary to pray to him and serve him with much more zeal and care* than if his mercy was without bounds, as we think is the case. I should like to put a question to you. If you had lived under the rule of a prince, not, you will note, wicked, but only severe, touchy, never easy in his authority, and seeking to supervise every movement of his subjects, I am curious to know if you would have thought yourself able to take the same liberties as under the rule of another prince of a wholly opposite character, content with general liberty, always tender of individual freedom, and always fearing his own power so that no one else should fear it? Certainly not. Well, the comparison leaps to the eye and admits no reply. The more terrible God seems to us, the more we must increase our religious fear of him, the more ardent and indefatigable must be our prayers, for there is no reason for us to think that his goodness will make up for our ignoring them. Since the proof of the existence of God precedes that of his attributes, we know *that he is* before knowing *what he is*; it is even that we can never know fully *what he is*. Here we are then placed under an empire whose sovereign has proclaimed once for all the laws which regulate all things. These laws in general bear the stamp of a remarkable wisdom and even kindness: nevertheless some (I assume for the moment) seem hard, even *unjust*, if you like. That being the case, I ask all the discontented, what are we to do? To leave the empire, perhaps? Impossible; it is everywhere and all-embracing. Complain, take offense, write against the sovereign? This will result in chastisement or being put to death. There is no better course to take than that of resignation and respect, I might even say of *love*, for, as we start from the assumption that the master exists and that it is absolutely necessary to serve him, is it not better (whatever he is) to serve him with love than without?

I shall not go back over the arguments with which we have in our previous conversations refuted the complaints that the foolhardy have raised against Providence, but I think I should add that in these complaints there is something false and even foolish, or, as the English say, a certain *non-sense* that hits the eye. In fact what meaning have these sterile or culpable complaints, which do not provide man with any practical consequences, any guide capable of enlightening and improving him, complaints which on the contrary can only harm him, are useless even to the atheist since they do not touch on the basic truth and even argue against it, which are finally at once ridiculous and dangerous in the mouth of a theist, since they can end only by depriving him of love while leaving him with fear? For my own part, I do not know anything so contrary to the most elementary lessons of common sense.

But do you realize, gentlemen, the source of this flood of insolent doctrines which unceremoniously judge God and call him to account for his orders? They come to us from that great phalanx we call *intel-*

lectuals and whom we have not been able in this age to keep in their place, which is a secondary one. At other times, there were very few intellectuals, and a very small minority of this very small minority were ungodly; today one sees nothing but *intellectuals*; it is a profession, a crowd, a nation; and among them the already unfortunate exception has become the rule. On every side they have usurped a limitless influence, and yet if there is one thing certain in this world, it is to my mind that it is not for science to guide men. Nothing necessary for this is entrusted to science. One would have to be out of one's mind to believe that God has charged the academies with teaching us what he is and what we owe to him. It rests with the prelates, the nobles, the great officers of state to be the depositaries and guardians of the saving truths, to teach nations what is bad and what good, what true and what false in the moral and spiritual order: others have no right to reason on this kind of matter. They have the natural sciences to amuse them, what are they complaining about? As for those who talk or write to deprive a people of a national belief, they should be hung like housebreakers. Rousseau himself agreed with this without dreaming of what he was demanding for himself.[35] What folly it was to grant everyone freedom of speech! This is what has ruined us. The so-called philosophers have all a certain fierce and rebellious pride which does not compromise with anything; they detest without exception every distinction they themselves do not enjoy; they find fault in every authority; they hate anything above them. If they are allowed, they will attack everything, even God, because he is master. See if it is not the same men who have attacked both kings and the God who established them. . . .

NINTH DIALOGUE

THE SENATOR: Well, Count, are you ready to take up the question you were talking about yesterday?

[35] *Social Contract* [Book iv, Chap. viii].

THE COUNT: I shall leave no stone unturned, gentlemen, to meet your wishes, according to my power; but allow me first of all to point out to you that all sciences have their mysteries and show at certain points a contradiction between the apparently most obvious theory and experience. Politics, for instance, gives a number of illustrations of this truth. Is there anything more absurd in theory than hereditary monarchy? We judge it by experience, but if government had never been heard of and it was necessary to set one up, whoever hesitated between hereditary and elective monarchy would be regarded as a madman. Yet we know from experience that, everything considered, the first is the best imaginable and the second the worst. How many arguments there are for showing that sovereignty derives from the people! Yet it is nothing of the sort. Sovereignty is always *taken,* never *given*; and a second, more profound theory then brings out that this must be so. Who would not say that the best political constitution is that which has been debated and written by statesmen thoroughly acquainted with the national character, who have foreseen all circumstances? Nevertheless nothing could be falser. The best-constituted people are those which have the fewest written constitutional laws; and every written constitution is sterile. . . .

We should not then be astonished if, in other branches of knowledge, particularly in metaphysics and natural history, we come across propositions which offend our reason deeply and yet which are then demonstrated by the most solid arguments.

Among the most important of these propositions must be ranged one that I was happy to put yesterday, *that the righteous, suffering willingly, make amends not only for themselves but also for the culpable who, of themselves, could not expiate themselves.* . . .

Men have never doubted that innocence can make amends for transgression and have believed, moreover, that there is an expiatory power in blood; so that *life*, which is blood, can atone for another *life*.

Look at this belief closely and you will see that if God himself had not put it into the human mind, it could never have been thought of. The big words *superstition* and *prejudice* explain nothing, for no error has ever been universal and constant. If a false opinion holds sway over a people, you will not find it among its neighbor; or if sometimes it seems to stretch, perhaps not over the whole world, but over a great number of nations, the passing of time will efface it.

But the belief I am talking about has been held at all times and in all places. Ancient and modern nations, civilized or barbaric nations, advanced or backward ages, true or false religions, there has not been one voice of disagreement in the world.

Finally, the idea of *sin* and that of *sacrifice for sin* were so closely identified in the minds of men of antiquity that the holy language expressed both by the same word. Hence that well-known Hebrew phrase, used by Saint Paul, that God made the Saviour *to be sin for us*[36]. . . .

Humanity professed these dogmas from the time of its fall, until the greatest of victims, *raised to draw all to him,* cried,

ALL THINGS ARE ACCOMPLISHED.

Then *the veil of the Temple was rent in twain,* the great secret of the sanctuary was known, so far as it can be known in the order of things of which we form part. We understood why men had always believed that one soul could be saved by another and why they had always sought regeneration in blood.

Without Christianity man does not know what he is because he is alone in the universe and cannot compare himself with anything; the prime service this religion renders to him is to show him his value by showing him what he has cost.

BEHOLD IT IS A GOD WHO HAS A GOD KILLED.[37]

Yes, let us behold it attentively, my friends, and we shall see everything in this sacrifice: the enormity of the crime that called for such an expiation, the incredible grandeur of the being capable of committing it, the boundless value of the victim who said, *Lo, I come.*[38]

Now, it can be seen that, on the one side, this whole doctrine of antiquity was only the prophetic cry of humanity heralding salvation by blood, and that, on the other, Christianity came to justify this prophecy, substituting reality for myth, so that an innate and basic dogma continually foretold the great sacrifice which is the basis of the new revelation, and this new revelation, glittering with all the brightness of truth, proves in its turn the divine origin of the dogma which we see constantly like an oasis of light among the shadows of paganism. This agreement is one of the most stirring proofs it is possible to imagine.

[36] 2 Corinthians 5:21.
[37] Aeschylus, *Prometheus Bound,* 92.
[38] Psalm 40:7; Hebrews 10:7.

But these truths are not proved by calculation or by mechanical laws. The man who has lived his life without ever tasting the divine fruits, who has narrowed his mind and dried up his heart with sterile speculations incapable either of making him better in this life or of preparing him for the next; such a man, I say, will reject this kind of proof and will not even understand it. There are truths that men can grasp only with *the imagination of their hearts*.[39] Often the upright man is shaken by seeing men whose minds he admires reject proofs which seem to him to be clear: this is a pure illusion. These men lack a sense, that is all. If the cleverest man has not the religious sense, not only can we not beat him in argument, but we lack even any means to make ourselves understood to him, which proves nothing except his misfortune. . . .

I should have to go into much greater detail to plumb the depths of the fascinating subject of sacrifices, but I should abuse your patience, and be afraid of going astray. It is one of those questions that require all the calm of a written discussion to be treated in depth.[40] I think, my good friends, that we have at least learned sufficient about it to deal with the sufferings of the just. This world is an army, an eternal battle. All those who have fought courageously in a battle are doubtless worthy of praise, but doubtless also the greatest glory belongs to those who return from it wounded. . . . As we have so often said, there are no wholly righteous men; but, if there was a man *sufficiently righteous* to merit the approval of his Creator, who could be astonished if God, ATTENTIVE TO HIS OWN WORK, takes pleasure in improving him? The father of a family can laugh at a coarse servant who curses or lies, but his tenderly severe hand punishes rigorously these same faults in an only son for whom he would freely lay down his life. If tenderness forgives nothing, it is because there is no longer anything to forgive. In visiting misfortune on the righteous man, God purifies him of his past faults, puts him on guard against future faults, and prepares him for Heaven. Without doubt *he takes pleasure* in seeing him escape the inevitable justice awaiting him in another world. Is there a greater joy for love than the submission that disarms it? And when one thinks, moreover, that these sufferings are not only useful to the righteous but also that they can, by a holy agreement, profit the guilty, and that in suffering thus they really *sacrifice* themselves for all men, one will

[39] Luke 1:51.
[40] See *Enlightenment on Sacrifices*.

agree that it is in fact impossible to imagine a sight more worthy of the Divinity.

One more word on the sufferings of the *righteous*. Do you by any chance believe that the viper is venomous only at the moment it bites and that the man afflicted with epilepsy is truly epileptic only when he is having a fit?

THE SENATOR: What is your point, my worthy friend?

THE COUNT: I am not going a long way round, as you will see. The man who knows men only by their actions calls them *wicked* only when he sees them commit a crime. Yet we might as well believe that the viper's venom is engendered at the moment of the bite. The event does not create wickedness; it manifests it. But God who sees all things, God who knows our most intimate inclinations and thoughts much better than men know one another through the senses, uses punishment prophylactically and strikes the man who seems to us healthy to extirpate the disease before the seizure. Often in our blind impatience we complain of the delays of Providence in punishing crimes; and, by a curious contradiction, we still blame it when with salutary speed it represses vicious inclinations before they have given rise to transgressions.

Sometimes God spares a known sinner, since punishment would be useless, whereas he chastises the hidden sinner since this chastisement will save a man. Thus the wise doctor avoids tiring an incurable patient by useless remedies and operations. *"Leave him,"* he advises, *"keep him amused; give him everything he asks for."* But if the nature of things allowed him to see clearly in the body of an apparently healthy man the germ of an illness which will kill him tomorrow or in ten years, would he not advise him to submit to the most distasteful remedies and the most painful operations in order to escape death? And if a coward preferred death to pain, would not the doctor, whose eye and hand we suppose to be equally infallible, advise his friends to tie him down and save him in spite of himself for his family? Those surgical instruments whose sight sickens us—the saw, the trepan, the forceps, the cystotome—have presumably not been invented by some evil genius of humanity. Well, these instruments are in man's hand, for the cure of physical ills, what physical ills are in God's hand, for the extirpation of true ills. Can a dislocated or fractured limb be restored without pain? Can a hemorrhage or an internal complaint be cured without abstinence, without privations of all kinds, without a more or

less tedious regimen? In the whole of pharmacology, how many remedies are there that do not revolt our senses? Are sufferings, even those
caused immediately by illnesses, anything other than the effort of life
to preserve itself? In the sensory as in the higher order, the law is the
same and is as old as evil: THE REMEDY FOR DISORDER WILL BE PAIN. . . .

TENTH DIALOGUE

THE SENATOR: It seems to me, Count, that you have put the principle of sacrifices beyond any attack and have drawn from it a host of
useful conclusions. I believe, moreover, that the theory of *substitution*
is so natural to man that it can be regarded as an *innate* truth in the
full meaning of the term, since it is absolutely impossible that we have
learned it. But do you think that it is equally impossible to *discover* or
at least to *catch a glimpse* of the reason for this universal belief?

The more one looks at the world, the more one feels oneself led to
believe that evil derives from some kind of inexplicable discord and
that the return to good depends on an opposite force which constantly
impels us toward some kind of unity just as inexplicable. This community of deserts, this substitution that you have so well proved, can
come only from this unity beyond our comprehension. Reflecting on
the general beliefs and natural instincts of men, one is struck by the
tendency they have to unite things that nature seems to have totally
separated. For example, they are very much inclined to regard a people, a town, a corporation, and above all a family as a single moral
being, having good and bad qualities, open to praise or blame and
consequently open to reward and punishment. From this stems the
prejudice or, more exactly, the *dogma* of nobility, so generally held
and deeply rooted amongst men. If you submit this to the bar of reason, it will not pass the test, for, if we consult nothing but reason, there
is no distinction more foreign to us than that which we owe to our
ancestors: yet there is none more esteemed or even more willingly

recognized except in factious times, and even then the attacks made on it are still an indirect homage and a formal recognition by those who would like to destroy it.

If glory is hereditary in the eyes of all men, so too is blame, and for the same reason. It is sometimes unthinkingly asked why the shame of a crime or a punishment should fall on the descendants of the criminal; yet those who put this question then brag about the merits of their ancestors: it is an obvious contradiction. . . .

Could not this same theory throw some light on the dark mystery of the punishment of sons for the crimes of their fathers? At first sight nothing is so shocking as a hereditary malediction; yet why not, since benediction is also hereditary? And notice that these ideas do not come only from the Bible, as is often imagined. This fortunate or unfortunate heredity belongs to all times and all countries: it belongs to paganism as well as to Judaism or Christianity, to the infancy as well as the old age of nations; the idea is found in theologians, philosophers, poets, in the theater and in the Church. . . .

The family is no doubt composed of individuals who, according to reason, have nothing in common, but, according to instinct and general persuasion, every family is *one*.

This unity is especially conspicuous in reigning families: the sovereign changes his name and face, but he is always, as they say in Spain, THE KING HIMSELF. You Frenchmen, Knight, have two acute maxims, truer perhaps than you think; one of civil law, *The dead distrain the living;* the other of constitutional law, *The king does not die.* Therefore a king should not be treated as a separate entity when the time comes to judge him.

People are sometimes astonished at seeing an innocent monarch perish miserably in one of those political upheavals so frequent in the world. You can well believe that I have no wish to stifle compassion in men's hearts, and you know how much recent crimes have wrung my own; nevertheless, if I stick to strict logic, what can be said? Every culprit can be *innocent* and even *saintly* on the day of his punishment. There are crimes which become obvious and are consummated only after a long interval: there are others which consist in many acts more or less excusable taken separately, but whose repetition in the end becomes highly criminal. In this sort of case, it is obvious that the penalty cannot precede the completion of the crime.

Even in instantaneous crimes, punishments are always suspended, and this must be the case. This is again one of those instances when human justice serves as an interpreter of that justice of which it is simply an image and a branch.

A thoughtless or frivolous act, a breach of some bylaw, can be countered at once, but in questions of crime properly speaking the culprit is never punished the moment he becomes one. Under the rule of Muslim law, authority punishes, even with death, the man it thinks deserves it at the very moment and place it seizes him; this brusque enforcement of the law, which has not lacked blind admirers, is nevertheless one of the many proofs of the brutalization and divine censure of these peoples. Among us, things are quite different. The culprit must be arrested, he must be charged, he must defend himself, he must above all settle his conscience and his worldly affairs, practical arrangements for his punishment must be made; finally, to take everything into account, a certain time must be left to take him to the appointed place of punishment. The scaffold is an *altar*: it cannot therefore be either set up in a certain place or moved except by authority. These delays, praiseworthy in their very excessiveness yet still not lacking their blind detractors, are no less a proof of our superiority.

If then it happens that, during the inevitable interval between the crime and its punishment, sovereignty changes hands, what does this matter to justice? It must take its ordinary course. Even disregarding the unity I am reflecting upon at the moment, nothing is more humanly just, for nowhere can the rightful heir avoid paying the debts of his inheritance, unless he *renounces* it. The sovereign is responsible for all the acts of sovereignty. All its debts, all its treaties, all its crimes bind him. If, by some dissolute act, he sows a bad seed today whose natural growth will bring about a catastrophe in a hundred years' time, the blow will fall with justice on the crown *in a hundred years' time*. To escape the penalty, the king would have to refuse the crown. It is not THIS king, it is THE king who is innocent or guilty. . . .

Having looked at man, let us look at his most wonderful characteristic, speech. Again we find the same mystery, that is to say, an inexplicable division and just as inexplicable a tendency toward some kind of unity. The two greatest dates in the spiritual calendar are without doubt that of *Babel*, when languages split up, and that of *Pentecost*, when they made a prodigious attempt to unite: on this it can be remarked in passing that the two most extraordinary wonders of which mention is made in human history are at the same time the most certain facts we possess. Anyone who contests them must lack both reason and integrity. . . .

Our mutual unity results from our unity in God praised by philosophy itself. Malebranche's theory of *vision in God* is only a superb commentary on the well-known words of Saint Paul, *For in him we live, and move, and have our being.*[41] The pantheism of the Stoics and that of Spinoza is a corruption of this great idea, but it is still the same principle, it is still this tendency toward unity. The first time I read in the work of the worthy Malebranche, so neglected by his unjust and blind country, *that God is the locus of souls as space is the locus of bodies,* I was dazzled by this flash of genius and ready to prostrate myself before it. Few sayings are as beautiful. . . .

Sometimes I should like to leap beyond the narrow limits of this world, to anticipate the day of revelations and lose myself in infinity. When the twofold law of human nature is annulled and man's two poles are merged, he will be ONE, for, being no longer torn by inner conflict, how could the idea of duality occur to him? But, if we consider men in their relations with one another, what will they be like when evil is destroyed and with it passion and personal interests? What will become of the EGO when all thoughts, like all desires, are common, when every mind will see itself as others see it. Who can comprehend, who can imagine this heavenly Jerusalem all of whose inhabitants, filled with the selfsame spirit, will fuse together and reflect happiness on one another? A countless number of shining specters of the same size, coming together on exactly the same spot, are no longer a countless number; they become a single, intensely shining specter. However, I am taking good care not to deal with *individuality,* without which immortality is nothing; but I cannot avoid being struck by the fact that everything leads us back to this mysterious unity.

Saint Paul invented a word that has passed into every Christian language; it is *to edify,* a word which is at first sight very surprising, for what is there in common between the construction of an edifice and good advice given to one's fellow creature.

But the root of this expression is soon unearthed. Vice separates men, just as virtue unites them. There is no act against order that is not born of an individual interest contrary to the general order; there is no pure act that does not sacrifice an individual interest to the general interest, that is to say, that does not tend to create one indivisible

---

[41] [*Acts* 17, 28.]

and steady will in place of a multitude of divergent and culpable wills. Saint Paul then started from the fundamental idea that we are all *God's edifice, and that this edifice we must build is the body of the Saviour*.[42] He turned this idea to many uses. He wanted us to *edify* one another; that is, he wanted each man freely to take his place as a stone in the spiritual edifice and to strive with all his might to call others to the same task, so that every man *edifies and is edified*. Above all, he gave us the well-known saying, *Knowledge puffs up but charity edifies*,[43] an admirable and strikingly true phrase, for knowledge left to itself divides rather than unites and all its works are only appearances, while virtue truly *edifies* and indeed cannot act without *edifying*. Saint Paul had read in the sublime testament of his master that men are one and many like God,[44] so that all *are brought to fulfillment and perfected in unity*,[45] for until then the work is unfinished. And how could there not be some kind of unity (let it be and be called what you will) between us, since *a single man ruined us by a single act*? I am not here arguing in a circle, proving unity by the origin of sin and the origin of sin by unity: not at all, sin is only too well proved by its existence, being everywhere and especially in ourselves. But of all possible theories explaining its origin, none satisfies good sense, the enemy of quibbling, so much as the belief that sees it as the hereditary result of an original transgression and that has the weight of every human tradition in its support.

The fall of man can thus be numbered among the proofs of human unity and can help us to understand how, by the law of analogy that rules all divine things, *salvation likewise came* from a single man. . . .[46]

Following this train of thought, Count, do you think it completely impossible to form some idea of this joint responsibility between men (if you will allow this legal term), from which flows the reversibility of deserts that explains everything?

THE COUNT: It would be impossible, my good friend, to tell you, however imperfectly, how much pleasure your discourse has given me, but I confess with a frankness your worth demands that this pleasure is mixed with a certain fear. The path you have taken can only too easily lead you astray, more especially as you have not, like me, a

[42] 1 Corinthians 3:9–11.
[43] 1 Corinthians 8:1.
[44] John 17:11, 21, 22.
[45] *Ibid.*, 17:23.
[46] Romans 5:17.

light to guide you at all times and over any distance. Is it not foolhardy to want to understand things so far above us? Men have always
been attracted to unusual ideas that flatter the pride: it is so pleasant
to walk along out-of-the-way paths previously untrodden by human
feet! But what is the point? Does man become better by it?—For that
is the important question. Why should we place our trust in these
beautiful theories if they cannot lead us very far or in the right direction? I admit that there were some very profound insights in everything you have just said, but, to repeat myself, are we not running two
grave risks—of going astray in a fatal manner and of losing in vain
speculation precious time that could be better spent in useful study
and perhaps even discoveries?

THE SENATOR: Precisely the opposite is true, my dear Count. No
studies are more useful than those that have the intellectual world for
their subject, and they form the best road to discoveries. Everything
that can be known in theoretical philosophy is to be found in a passage of Saint Paul; this is it:

THIS WORLD IS A SYSTEM OF INVISIBLE THINGS VISIBLY MANIFESTED. . . .

If you consider that everything has been made *by* and *for* intelligence; that all motion is an effect, so that properly speaking the *cause*
of a movement cannot be a movement; that the words *cause* and *matter* are as mutually exclusive as *circle* and *triangle*; and that everything
in this world we see is related to another world we do not see; then
you will accept easily that we do indeed live *in a system of invisible
things visibly manifested.* Run your eye over the sciences and you will
see that they all start from a mystery. . . .

There is therefore no law of the natural world that has not *behind
it* (if you will allow this ridiculous phrase) a spiritual law of which the
former is only a visible expression; and this is why no explanation of
cause in material terms will ever satisfy a good mind. Once you leave
the sphere of material and sensory experience to enter that of pure
philosophy, you must leave matter and explain everything metaphysi-
cally. I mean here the true metaphysics, and not that which has been
cultivated so ardently for the last century by men who are seriously
called *metaphysicians*. Splendid metaphysicians, who have spent their
lives proving that there is no such thing as metaphysics, famous ruf-
fians in whom genius was *brutalized*!

Thus, my worthy friend, it is absolutely certain that one cannot succeed except by those *out-of-the-way paths* you fear so much. But if I am not successful, either because I lack the ability or because authority has raised barriers along my route, is not the knowledge that I am on the right road an important point in itself? Every inventor, every man of originality has been religious and even fanatically so. Perverted by irreligious skepticism, the human mind is like waste land that produces nothing or is covered with weeds useless to man. At such a time even its natural fertility is an evil, for these weeds harden the soil by tangling and intertwining their roots and moreover create a barrier between the sky and the earth. Break up these accursed clods; destroy these fatally hardy weeds; call on every human aid; drive in the plow; dig deep to bring into contact the powers of the earth and the powers of the sky.

Here, gentlemen, is the natural analogy to the human intelligence opened or closed to divine knowledge.

The natural sciences themselves are subject to the general law. Genius does not rely much on the slow crawl of logic. Its gait is free, its manner derives from inspiration; one can see its success, but no one has seen its progress. . . . Let no one appeal to *enlightenment* and to *mysticism*. These words mean nothing, and yet it is with this nothing that genius is intimidated and its way to discoveries barred. Certain philosophers in this age have taken it into their heads to talk of *causes*, but when will it be understood that there cannot be *causes* in the material order, for they must all be sought in another sphere?

Now, if this is the rule, even in the natural sciences, why, in sciences of a preternatural kind, should we not devote ourselves to researches that we can also call *preternatural*? I am surprised, Count, to find prejudices in you from which the independence of your mind should have been able to escape easily.

THE COUNT: I assure you, my dear friend, that there might well have been a misunderstanding between us, as happens in most discussions. God preserve me from ever intending to deny that religion is the mother of knowledge. Theory and experience join forces to announce this truth. The scepter of science belongs to Europe only because it is Christian. It has reached this high point of civilization and knowledge only because it has started from theology, because its universities were in the beginning nothing but theological schools, and because all the sciences, grafted onto this divine subject, have shown their divine sap by their long vegetation. The indispensable necessity for this lengthy development of the European genius is a basic truth that has totally escaped modern thinkers. Bacon himself, whom you have rightly criticized, was as mistaken about this as lesser men. His treatment of the subject is extremely amusing, especially when he flares up about scholasticism and theology. It must be agreed that this famous man appeared completely to disregard the preparations necessary if science is not to be a great evil. Teach young people physics and chemistry before having steeped them in religion and morality, or send scientists before missionaries to a new nation, and you will see the result. I believe it can even be proved conclusively that there is in science, if it is not entirely subordinated to the national creed, some hidden element that tends to degrade man and above all to make him a useless or bad citizen. Properly worked out, this principle would provide a clear and decisive solution to the difficult problem of the utility of the sciences, a problem that Rousseau greatly confused in the middle of the last century by his treacherous mind and his half-knowledge.

Why are intellectuals almost always bad statesmen and in general inept in administration?

What is the reason that, on the contrary, priests (I repeat PRIESTS) are statesmen by nature? In other words, why does the sacerdotal order produce more of them in proportion than all the other orders of society? Why especially does it produce more of those *natural* statesmen, if I can use the phrase, who throw themselves into government and succeed without preparation, such as for instance those whom Charles V and his son employed a great deal and who played such a striking role in history?

Why has the noblest, strongest, and most powerful of monarchies been literally *made* by BISHOPS (this is Gibbon's confession) *as a hive is made by bees?*

I could go on endlessly about this great subject; but, my dear Senator, for the very benefit of this religion and the respect due to it, let us remember that it commends nothing to us so strongly as simplicity and obedience. Who knows our clay better than God? I dare say that what we ought to be ignorant of is more important for us than what we ought to know. If he has put certain subjects outside our range of vision, it is doubtless because it would be dangerous for us to perceive them clearly. I wholeheartedly accept and admire your simile of the earth open or closed to the influences of the sky; yet take care not to draw a false conclusion from an obvious principle. That religion and even piety are the best preparations for the human mind, that they incline it, as far as individual capacity allows, to every kind of knowledge, and that they set the mind on the road to discoveries, these are matters beyond dispute for every man who has even moistened his lips on the cup of true philosophy. But what conclusion should we draw from these truths? *That we must make every effort to penetrate the mysteries of this religion?* Not at all; allow me to say that this is sheer sophistry. The legitimate conclusion is that we must subordinate our learning to religion, hold firmly that we study by praying, and above all, when we are concerned with pure philosophy, never forget that every metaphysical proposition that does not issue from a Christian dogma is and can be nothing but a culpable extravagance. This is sufficient for our practical life, and what does all the rest matter?

I have followed with keen interest everything you have told us about this incomprehensible unity, the necessary basis for *substitution* which would explain all things if they could be explained. I applaud your learning and the way in which you are able to draw it together: yet what advantage does it give you over me? I believe in substitution just like you, as I believe in Peking just as much as the missionary we dined with the other day who has returned from there. When you penetrate the reason for this dogma, you will lose the merit of faith, not only without profit but also with very grave danger to yourself, for, in this event, you will not be able to answer for the direction of your thoughts. Do you remember what we read together some time ago in a book of Saint-Martin? *That the rash chemist runs the risk of adoring his own work.* This is not an idle phrase: did not Malebranche say that *a false belief about the efficacy of secondary causes could lead to idolatry?* It is the same idea. . . . We often talk with an inane surprise about the absurdity of idolatry, but I can well assure you that, if we had the learning which misled the first idolaters, we would all be idolaters or at least God could mark down for himself barely *twelve thousand men in each tribe.* We always start from the banal hypothesis that man has gradually raised himself from barbarism to science and civilization. This is the favorite dream, the root error, and as the school has it, the *protopseudodox* of our time. But if the philosophers of this unhappy age, with the horrible perversity that marks them and the obstinacy that they still persist in despite the warnings they have had, had possessed in addition some of the acquirements which the first men must have had, woe betide the world! They would have brought on humanity some catastrophe of a supernatural order. Just look at what they have achieved and have drawn on us in spite of their profound ignorance of the spiritual sciences.

I am therefore completely opposed to all inquisitive research that moves outside man's temporal sphere. *Religion is the spice that prevents science becoming tainted*: Bacon put this excellently and, for once, I have no wish to criticize him. I am just a little tempted to think that he did not himself take sufficient heed of his own maxim, since he worked expressly to divide the *spice* from science.

Again notice that religion is the greatest vehicle of science. No doubt it cannot create talent which does not exist, but it exalts it without stint wherever it finds it, especially the talent for discoveries, whereas irreligion always restrains and often stifles it. What more do we want? We are not allowed to fathom the secrets of this instrument that has been given to us to fathom secrets. It is too easy to break it or, what is worse perhaps, to make it false. I thank God for my ignorance still more than for my knowledge; for my knowledge is mine, at least in part, and in consequence I cannot be sure that it is good, but my ignorance, at least that of which I am speaking, is his, therefore I trust it fully. I shall not go and try to scale the necessary wall with which the divine wisdom has surrounded us; on this side, I am certain to stand on the grounds of truth, but who can vouch that on the other (to put it in its best light) I shall not find myself in the field of superstition?

THE KNIGHT: Between two superior combatant powers, a third, although very weak, can well come forward as a mediator, provided that it is acceptable to them and acts in good faith.

It seems to me first of all, Senator, that you have been a little too indulgent to your religious ideas. You say the explanation of causes must always be sought outside the material world, and you cite Kepler who reached his famous discoveries by some system or another of celestial harmony, about which I am wholly ignorant; but I do not see in all this a shadow of religion. It is quite possible to be a composer and work out chords without being pious. It seems to me that Kepler could very well have discovered his laws without believing in God.

THE SENATOR: You have replied to yourself, Knight, by saying *outside the material world*. I did not say that each discovery must issue from a dogma as the chicken comes from the egg: I said that there are no causes in matter and that consequently they should not be sought in matter. Now, my dear friend, only religious men want to or can go outside it. The others believe only in the material world and get angry if one so much as talks to them of another order of things. Our age must have a mechanistic astronomy, a mechanistic chemistry, a mechanistic gravity, a mechanistic morality, a mechanistic language, mechanistic remedies to cure mechanistic illnesses, and goodness knows what else besides—is not everything mechanistic? Now, only the religious spirit can cure this disease. We talked of Kepler, but Kepler would never have taken such a fruitful path if he had not been eminently religious. . . .

THE KNIGHT: All right, I am no match for you in argument, but there is one point on which I should still like to quarrel with you. Our friend has said that your taste for out-of-the-way explanations could perhaps lead you and others into very grave dangers and that moreover they have the serious disadvantage of being prejudicial to useful studies. To this you replied that precisely the opposite was true and that nothing favors the advancement of the sciences and of discoveries of every kind so much as the cast of mind that carries us continually outside the material world. Again this is a point on which I do not think myself capable of arguing with you, but what seems to me to be clear is that you have left on one side the other objection, and yet it is a serious one. I agree that mystical and extraordinary ideas can sometimes lead to important discoveries, but the drawbacks that can result from them must be put into the opposite side of the balance. Let us agree, for example, that they can inspire a Kepler; if nevertheless they necessarily produce ten thousand fools who disturb and even corrupt the world, I feel very inclined to sacrifice the great man.

Thus, if you will forgive my impertinence, I think that you have gone a little too far and that it would not be a bad thing for you to be a little more suspicious of your *spiritual impulses*: at least, I would never have said so much, as far as I can judge. But, as the duty of a mediator is to deny and to concede something to both parties, I must also tell you, Count, that you seem to me to push timidity to excess. I congratulate you on your religious obedience. I have seen much of the world, and, truly, I have found nothing more impressive, but I cannot easily understand how faith leads you to fear superstition. Quite the opposite should happen, it seems to me; I am more surprised that you bear so much ill-will toward this superstition which does not seem to me such a bad thing. What is superstition at bottom? ... It is neither *error* nor *fanaticism*, nor any other monster of this kind under another name. I repeat, what is then superstition? Does not *super* mean *beyond*? Superstition will therefore be something which goes *beyond* a sufficient belief. Really, there is nothing in this to raise a hue and cry. I have often noticed that in this world *what suffices is not sufficient*; do not take this as a play on words, for he who wants to do just what is permissible will soon do what is not. We are never sure of our moral qualities except when we have been able to exalt them a little. In the political world, the constitutional powers established in free nations scarcely exist except by coming into conflict. If someone comes to knock you over, it is not enough to stand your ground; you must hit him yourself and make him retreat if you can. To jump a ditch, you must always fix your eyes well beyond the bank if you do not want to fall in. Indeed, this is a general rule; it would be very peculiar if religion was an exception to it. I do not think that a man, and still less a nation, can believe just what he should. He will always fall a little above or a little below the mark. I imagine, my good friends, that honor cannot fail to please you. Yet what is honor? It is *the superstition* of valor or it is nothing. In love, friendship, loyalty, sincerity, and so on, superstition is pleasing, even valuable and often necessary; why should not the same be true of piety? I am inclined to believe that the outcries against *the excesses of a thing* start from the enemies of the thing. Reason is no doubt good, but it is very far from the case that everything ought to be settled by reason. ...

I believe that superstition is an *advanced fortification* of religion which must not be destroyed, for it would not be safe to allow men to come unimpeded to the foot of the wall to measure its height and set up ladders. You will use errors as an argument against me; but first, do you not think that mistakes about something divine have certain natural limits in the very nature of the case and that the disadvantages of these mistakes could never outweigh the danger of unsettling belief? To follow my metaphor, I shall add that, if an advanced fortification is too far forward, this is also a great error, for it is useful only to the enemy who will make use of it to take cover and to attack the town: is it necessary then not to set up advanced fortifications at all? With such an exaggerated fear of *mistakes*, one would end by no longer daring to move. ...

THE COUNT: I should like to put to you an idea that might well, it seems to me, serve as a peace treaty between us. It has always appeared to me that, in higher metaphysics, there are rules of *trial and error* as there were formerly in arithmetic. This is how I regard all opinions which depart from express revelation and which are employed to explain in a more or less plausible way such and such a point in this same revelation. If you like, let us take as an example the idea of the preexistence of souls which has been used to explain original sin. You can see at once all that can be said against the successive creation of souls and the use that can be made of preexistence to provide a host of interesting explanations. Nevertheless I can tell you without demur that I do not claim to adopt this system as a truth, but I say (and here is my rule of *trial and error*), "If I, a puny mortal, have been able to find a by no means absurd solution that accounts reasonably well for a puzzling problem, how can I doubt that, if this theory is untrue, there is another solution of which I know nothing and which God has thought advisable to hide from our curiosity?" I say as much of the ingenious hypothesis that the renowned Leibnitz based on the crime of Tarquin and developed with so much wisdom in his *Théodicée*; I say as much of a hundred other theories and of yours in particular, my worthy friend. So long as they are not regarded as proved, are put forward modestly, are propounded to set the mind at rest, as I have just told you, and above all do not lead to pride or contempt for authority, it seems to me that criticism should keep silent in view of these precautions. Progress is slow and cautious in all the sciences; why should metaphysics, the most obscure of all, be excepted? I always come back to the point that, however little you indulge in this kind of transcendental inquiry, you show at least a certain disquiet that clearly displays the merit of faith and docility. Have we not already spent some considerable time in the clouds? And have we been improved by it? I doubt it a little. It is time to come down to earth. I must confess I am very fond of practical ideas and especially of those striking analogies that exist between Christian doctrines and the universal beliefs humanity has always held without it being possible to trace any human origin for them. . . .

ELEVENTH DIALOGUE

THE KNIGHT: Although you do not like excursions in the clouds much, my dear Count, I should nevertheless like to take you there again. . . . In our own day, men seem no longer able to live within the old sphere of the human faculties. They wish to pass beyond it; they grow restless like an eagle angry with the bars of his cage. See what they are attempting in the natural sciences! See, too, the new alliance that they have created and that they promote with so much success between physical theories and the arts. As it works wonders in the cause of science, how can this general spirit of the age not stretch itself to questions of the spiritual order? And why should it not be allowed to direct its attentions toward the subject that is most important to men, provided that it can restrain itself within the limits of a prudent and respectful moderation?

THE COUNT: First, Knight, I do not think I would be demanding too much if I asked that the human mind, free on every other subject with this one exception, should refrain from all rash inquiry into this. In the second place, this moderation of which you speak and which is so splendid in theory, is actually impossible in practice; at least, it is so rare that it must pass for impossible. Now, you will allow that when a certain inquiry is not necessary and is capable of producing countless evils, it is a duty to abstain from it. This is what has always made all these spiritual impulses of the *illuminés* suspect and even, I confess, odious to me.

THE SENATOR: You are certainly afraid of the *illuminés*, my dear friend! But I do not think I am asking too much on my part if I put the humble request that words be defined, and in short that someone be kind enough to tell us what an *illuminé* is, so that we know who and what we are talking about. This name, *illuminés*, is given to those disgraceful men who have dared in our own time to conceive and even to organize in Germany, by the most criminal association, the frightful project of killing off Christianity and sovereignty in Europe. The same name is given to the virtuous followers of Saint-Martin, who not only profess Christianity but who work only to raise themselves to the most sublime heights of this divine law. You must admit, gentlemen, that never have men fallen into a greater confusion of ideas. I confess even that I am unable to listen calmly in society to the fools of both sexes crying out against *illuminism*, at the least word that passes their understanding, with a frivolity and ignorance which pushes to the limit the most practiced patience. But you, my dear *Roman* friend, you, who are such a strong defender of authority, speak to me candidly. Can you read the Holy Scripture without being forced to acknowledge a host of passages which oppress your mind and tempt it to devote itself to attempting a discreet *exegesis*? Have not you like others been told, *Search the Scriptures*? In conscience tell me, I pray, do you understand the first chapter of Genesis? Do you understand the Apocalypse and the Song of Songs? Does Ecclesiastes not give you any difficulty? When you read in Genesis that the moment our first ancestors became aware of their nakedness *God made them coats of skins*, do you take this literally? Do you think the All-powerful spent his time killing animals, skinning them, curing their pelts, finally creating needles and thread to finish off these new costumes? Do you believe that the guilty rebels of Babel really undertook, to put their minds at rest, to build a tower whose weathercock merely reached the moon (I am not saying much, as you see!); and *when the stars fall on the earth*, will you not be at a loss to place them? . . . A thousand expressions of this kind should show you that it pleased God sometimes to let men speak at will, according to the reigning ideas of such and such an epoch, at other times to hide under apparently simple and occasionally vulgar forms high mysteries not made for all eyes. Now, given these two assumptions, what harm is there in excavating these seams of grace and divine goodness as we mine in the earth for gold or diamonds? More than ever, gentlemen, we should devote ourselves to these broad speculations, for we must hold ourselves ready for a huge event in the divine order, toward which we are moving with an increased speed that cannot fail to strike every observer. Religion no longer holds sway on earth, and humanity cannot remain in this state. Moreover, formidable prophets are foretelling that *the time is here*. . . . There is hardly one truly religious man in Europe (I speak of the educated class) who is not at this time

awaiting some extraordinary event. . . . How can we make light of
this general persuasion? And what right have we to condemn the men
who, warned by this sign from heaven, devote themselves to holy
studies.

Would you like another illustration of what is brewing? Look for
it in the sciences: consider carefully the progress of chemistry and
even of astronomy, and you will see where they are leading us. . . .
Wait until the natural affinity of religion and science manifests itself
in the head of one man of genius. The appearance of such a man cannot be far off, and perhaps he exists even now. He will be a monumental figure and will put an end to the eighteenth century, which
still endures today; for intellectual centuries do not conform to the
calendar like *centuries* properly speaking. Then opinions that seem to
us bizarre or nonsensical today will be axioms impossible to doubt.
Men will talk of the *stupidity* of our times as we talk of the superstition of the Middle Ages. . . . At the moment, European thinkers are
like conspirators or initiates who have made a kind of monopoly of
science and who are absolutely opposed to anyone knowing *more* or
otherwise than they. But this science will be continually execrated by
an *enlightened* posterity, who will justly charge today's adepts with
having been unable to draw from the truths God had confided to them
those conclusions most valuable to man. The whole of science will
then change its face. The spirit, for long dethroned and forgotten, will
take its former position. It will be shown that all the ancient traditions
are true, that the whole of paganism is nothing but a system of tainted
and ill-conceived truths which need only cleaning, so to speak, and
restoring to their place to shine brilliantly. In a word, all ideas will be
changed. . . .

You, my dear Count, who are so severe an apostle of unity and
order, you have no doubt not forgotten all you told us at the beginning
of these conversations about the many extraordinary events of the
times. Everything foretells, and your own observations themselves
demonstrate it, *some kind of great unity toward which we are moving
very rapidly.* Therefore you cannot without contradicting yourself
condemn those who *greet this unity from afar,* as you put it, and who
try according to their abilities to penetrate mysteries no doubt difficult
but nonetheless comforting to us. . . .

THE COUNT: That there are mysteries in the Bible is beyond doubt,
but to tell you the truth it does not matter much. I am very little con-

cerned with knowing what a *coat of skins* is. Do you, who have worked to discover this, know more about it than I? And would we be better men if we did know it? Once more, search as much as you please, but take care, however, not to go too far and not to mislead yourself by giving rein to your imagination. It has been well said, as you recall, *Search the Scriptures,* but how and why? Read the text, *Search the Scriptures and you will see that they testify of me.*[47] Thus it refers to an already certain fact and not to interminable researches into a future which is none of our concern. . . .

[47] John 5:39.

Enlightenment on Sacrifices

CHAPTER I. SACRIFICES IN GENERAL

I by no means accept the blasphemous axiom, *Human fear first invented the gods.*[1]

On the contrary, I am happy to notice that men, by giving God names expressing greatness, power, and goodness, by calling him *Lord, Master, Father,* and so on, show clearly enough that the idea of divinity cannot be born of fear. It can be seen also that music, poetry, dance, in a word all the pleasing arts, have been called on in religious ceremonies and that the idea of rejoicing was always so closely involved in the idea of *festival* that the last became everywhere synonymous with the first.

Far be it from me, moreover, to believe that the idea of God could have started with humanity or, in other words, that humanity can be older than the idea.

It must, however, be confessed, after having made sure that this is orthodox, that history shows man to be convinced at all times of this terrible truth, *that he lives under the hand of an angry power and that this power can be appeased only by sacrifice.*

At first sight, it is not at all easy to reconcile so apparently contradictory ideas, but, if they are studied closely, it can easily be understood how they agree and why the feeling of terror has always existed side by side with that of joy without the one ever having been able to destroy the other.

"The gods are good, and we are indebted to them for all the good things we enjoy: we owe them praise and thanks. But the gods are just and we are guilty. They must be appeased and we must expiate our sins; and, to do this, the most effective means is *sacrifice.*"

Such was the ancient belief and such is still, in different forms, the

---

[1] *Primus in orbe deos fecit timor.* This passage, whose true author is unknown, is to be found amongst the fragments of Petronius. It is quite at home there.

belief of the whole world. Primitive men, from whom the whole of humanity has received its fundamental opinions, believed themselves culpable. All social institutions have been founded on this dogma, so that men of every age have continually admitted original and universal degradation and said like us, if less explicitly, *our Mothers conceived us in sin*; for there is no Christian dogma that is not rooted in man's inner nature and in a tradition as old as humanity.

But the root of this debasement, or this reification of man, resides *in sensibility, in life*, in short *in the soul*, so carefully distinguished by the ancients from *the spirit* or intelligence.

Animals have received only a *soul*; we have been given both *soul and spirit....*

The idea of two distinct powers is very *ancient*, even in the Church. "Those who have adopted it," said Origen, "do not think that the words of the apostle *the flesh lusteth against the spirit* (Galatians 5:17), should be taken to mean *the flesh* literally, but to refer to *that soul* which is really *the soul of the flesh*: for, they say, we have two souls, one good and celestial, the other inferior and terrestrial: it is of the latter that it has been said *its works are manifest* (*ibid.*, 19), and we believe that this soul of the flesh resides in the blood."[2]

For the rest, Origen, who was at once the most daring and the most modest of men in his opinions, did not persist in this problem. *The reader*, he said, *will form his own opinions*. It is, however, obvious that he had no other explanation for two diametrically opposed impulses within a single individual.

Indeed, what is this power that opposes *the man* or, to put it better, his conscience? What is this power which is not *he, or all of him*? Is it material like stone or wood? In this case, it neither thinks nor feels and consequently cannot be capable of disturbing the spirit in its workings. I listen with respect and dread to all the threats made *by the flesh*, but I want to know what it is....

Fundamentally, it appears that on this point Holy Scripture is in complete agreement with ancient and modern philosophy, since it teaches us "that man is double in his ways,[3] and that the word of God is a living sword that pierces to the division of the soul and the spirit and discerns the thoughts of the heart."[4]

[2] Origen, *De Principiis*, Book iii, Chap. iv.
[3] James 1:8.
[4] Hebrews 4:12.

And Saint Augustine, confessing to God the sway that old visions brought back by dreams still had over his soul, cried out with the most pleasing simplicity, "Then, Lord, am I myself?"[5]

No, without doubt, he was not HIMSELF, and no one knew this better than he, who tells us in the same passage, *How much difference there is between* MYSELF *and* MYSELF; he who so well distinguished the two powers in man when he cried out again to God: *Oh, thou mystic bread of my soul, spouse of my intelligence, I could not love you!*[6]

Milton has put some beautiful lines into the mouth of Satan, who howls of his appalling degradation.[7] Man also could suitably and wisely speak them. . . .

I am aware that the doctrine of the *two* souls was condemned in ancient times but I do not know if this was by a competent tribunal: besides, it is enough to understand it. That man is a being resulting from the union of two *souls,* that is to say, of two intelligent constituents of the same nature, one good and the other bad, this is, I believe, the opinion which should have been condemned and which I also wholeheartedly condemn. But that the intelligence is the same as sensation, or that this element, which is also called the *vital principle* and which is *life,* can be something material, completely devoid of understanding and consciousness, is what I will never believe, unless I happen to be warned that I am mistaken by the only power with a legitimate authority over human belief. In this case, I should not hesitate a moment, and whereas now I have only the *certainty* that I am right, then I would have the *faith* that I am wrong. If I were to profess other opinions, I would directly contradict the principles which have dictated the work I am publishing and which are no less sacred to me.

Whatever view is taken about the duality of man, it is on the *animal power,* on *life,* on *the soul* (for all these words meant the same thing in the ancient language), that the malediction acknowledged by the whole world falls. . . .

Man being thus guilty through his *sensuous principle,* through

[5] *Confessions,* X, xxx.
[6] *Ibid.,* I, xiii.
[7] "O foul descent! that I who erst contended
    With gods to sit the highest, am now constrain'd
    Into a beast; and, mix'd with bestial slime,
    This essence to incarnate and imbrute,
    That to the height of deity aspired!"—*Paradise Lost,* ix, 163-167.

his flesh, through *his life*, the curse fell on his blood, for blood was the principle of life, or rather blood was life.[8] And it is a remarkable fact that old Eastern traditions such as these, which had long been forgotten, have been revived in our own day and upheld by the most distinguished physiologists. Let us accept the vitality of blood, or rather the identity of blood and life, as a fact which antiquity never doubted and which has been acknowledged again today; another opinion as old as the world itself was that *heaven grew angry with the flesh*, and *blood could be appeased only by blood*. No nation doubted that there was an expiatory virtue in the spilling of blood. Now neither reason nor folly could have invented this idea, still less get it generally accepted. It is rooted in the furthest depths of human nature, and on this point the whole of history does not show a single dissenting voice. The entire theory rests on the dogma of substitution. It was believed (as was and always will be the case) *that the innocent could pay for the guilty*; from which it was concluded that, life being guilty, *a less precious life could be offered and accepted in place of another*. Thus the blood of animals was offered, and this *soul*, offered for a soul, the ancients called *antipsychon, vicariam animam*, as you might say a *soul for a soul* OR *substitute soul*. . . .

It should be noticed that, in sacrifices properly speaking, carnivorous or nonintelligent or nondomestic animals like deer, snakes, fish, birds of prey, and so on, were not slaughtered. Always, among the animals, the most valuable for their utility, the gentlest, the most innocent, those nearest to man by instinct and habit were chosen. Since in the end man could not be slaughtered to save man, the most *human*, if I can put it like that, in the animal world were chosen as victims; and the victim was always burned wholly or in part, to bear witness that the natural penalty for crime is the stake and that the *substitute flesh* was burned in place of the *guilty flesh*. . . .

The roots of so extraordinary and so general a belief must go very deep. If there was nothing true or enigmatic about it, why should God himself have retained it in the Mosaic law? Where could the ancients have found the idea of a spiritual regeneration through blood? And why, at all times and in all places, have men chosen to honor, supplicate, and placate God by means of a ceremony that reason points out to all and that feeling rejects? It is absolutely necessary to appeal to some hidden and very powerful cause.

[8] Genesis 9:4–5; Leviticus 17:11; Deuteronomy 12:23–24.

CHAPTER II. HUMAN SACRIFICES

The doctrine of substitution being universally accepted, it was thought equally certain that the effectiveness of sacrifices was proportionate to the consequence of the victims; and this double belief, at bottom just but vitiated by the force that vitiates all things, gave birth on all sides to the horrible superstition of human sacrifices. In vain did reason tell men that they had no rights over their fellows and that they even testified to this themselves by offering the blood of animals to atone for that of man; in vain did gentle humanity and natural compassion reinforce the arguments of reason: in face of this compulsive dogma, reason remained as powerless as feeling.

One would like to be able to contradict history when it shows us this abominable custom practiced throughout the world, but, to the shame of humanity, nothing is more incontestable. . . . Once again, where did men take their opinion from? And what truth had they corrupted to reach their frightful error? It is quite clear, I think, that it all results from the dogma of substitution, whose truth is beyond dispute and is ever innate in man (for how could he have acquired it?), but which he has abused in a deplorable manner: for, accurately speaking, man cannot take up an error. He can only be ignorant of or abuse the truth, that is to say, extend it by false induction to a case which is irrelevant to it.

It seems that two false arguments lead men astray; first, the importance of the subjects which are to be freed from anathema. It is said, *To save an army, a town, even a great sovereign, what is one man?* The particular characteristics of the two kinds of human victim already sacrificed under civil law are also considered, and it is said, *What is the life of a criminal or an enemy?*

It is very likely that the first human victims were criminals condemned by the laws, for every nation believed what the Druids believed according to Caesar,[9] *that the punishment of criminals was highly pleasing to the Divinity.* The ancients believed that every capital crime committed in the state *bound* the nation and that the criminal was *sacred* or consecrated to the gods till, by the spilling of his blood, he had *unbound* both himself and the nation. . . .

Unfortunately, once men were possessed with the principle that

[9] *De bello gallico,* vi, 16.

the effectiveness of sacrifices was proportionate to the consequence of the victims, it was only a short step from the criminal to the enemy. Every *enemy* was a *criminal*, and unfortunately again every *foreigner* was an *enemy* when victims were needed. . . .

It seems that this fatal chain of reasoning explains completely the universality of so detestable a practice, that it explains it very well, I insist, in human terms: for I by no means intend to deny (and how could good sense, however slightly informed, deny it?) the effect of evil that had corrupted everything.

Evil would have no effect at all on men if it involved them in an isolated error. This is not even possible, for error is nothing. If every previous idea was left out of account, and a man proposed to slaughter another in order to propitiate the gods, the only response would be to put him to death or lock him up as a madman. Thus it is always necessary to start from a truth to propagate an error. This is especially striking if one thinks about paganism which shines with truths, but all distorted and out of place in such a way that I entirely agree with that contemporary theosophist who said that *idolatry was a putrefaction*. If the subject is examined closely, it can be seen that, among the most foolish, indecent, and atrocious opinions, among the most monstrous practices and those most shameful to mankind, there is not one that we cannot *deliver from evil* (since we have been granted the knowledge now to ask for this favor), to show then the residue of truth, which is divine.

It was thus from the incontestable truths of the degradation of man and his original unity, from the necessity of reparation, from the transferability of merits and the substitution of expiatory sufferings that men were led to the dreadful error of human sufferings. . . .

But we, who blanch with horror at the very idea of human sacrifices and cannibalism, how can we be at the same time so blind and ungrateful as not to recognize that we owe these feelings only to the *law of love* which watched over our cradle? Not long ago a famous nation, which had reached the peak of civilization and refinement, dared formally to suspend this law in a fit of madness of which history gives no other example: what happened?—in a flash, the mores of the Iroquois and the Algonquin; the holy laws of humanity crushed underfoot; innocent blood covering the scaffolds which covered France; men powdering and curling bloodstained heads; the very mouths of women stained with human blood.

Here is the *natural* man! It is not that he does not bear within him the indestructible seeds of truth and virtue: his birthrights are imprescriptible; but without divine nurture these seeds will never germinate or will yield only damaged and unwholesome fruits.

It is time to draw from the most undeniable historical facts a conclusion which is no less undeniable.

From four centuries' experience, we know *that wherever the true God is not known and served by virtue of an explicit revelation, man will slaughter man and often eat him.*

Lucretius, having told us of the sacrifice of Iphigenia (as a true story, that is understood, since he had need of it), exclaimed in a triumphant tone, *How many evils can religion spawn!*

Alas, he saw only the abuses, just like all his successors, who are much less excusable than he. He was unaware that the scourge of human sacrifice, however outrageous it was, was nothing compared to the evils produced by absolute godlessness. He was unaware or he did not wish to see that there is not and even cannot be an entirely false religion, that the religion of all civilized nations, such as it was in the age when he wrote, was no less the cement of the political structure, and that, by undermining it, Epicurean doctrines were about to undermine by the same stroke the old Roman constitution and substitute for it an atrocious and endless tyranny.

For us, happy possessors of the truth, let us not commit the crime of disregarding it. . . .

CHAPTER III. THE CHRISTIAN THEORY OF SACRIFICES

What truth is not to be found in paganism? . . .

How then can we fail to recognize that paganism could not be mistaken about an idea so universal and fundamental as that of sacrifice, that is to say, of *redemption by blood*? Humanity could not guess at the amount of blood it needed. What man, left to himself, could suspect the immensity of the fall and the immensity of the restoring love? Yet every people, by admitting this fall more or less clearly, has admitted also the need and the nature of the remedy.

This has been the constant belief of all men. It has been modified in practice, according to the characteristics of peoples and religions, but the principle always remains the same. In particular, all nations are agreed on the wonderful effectiveness of the voluntary sacrifice of the innocent who dedicates himself to God like a propitiatory victim. Men have always attached a boundless value to the submission of the just to sufferings. . . .

As has been said in the *Dialogues*, the idea of redemption is universal. At all times and in all places, men have believed that the innocent could atone for the guilty, but Christianity has corrected this idea as well as a thousand others which, even in their unreformed state, had in advance borne the clearest witness to it. Under the sway of this divine law, the just man (who never believes himself to be such) still tries to draw near to his model through suffering. . . .

Index